THE
ARCHAEOLOGY
DETECTIVES

THE ARCHAEOLOGY DETECTIVES

CONSULTING EDITOR

Paul Bahn

Reader's Digest

A Reader's Digest Book

Copyright © THE IVY PRESS LIMITED 2001

Reader's Digest Project Staff
Editorial Director: Fred DuBose
Senior Designer: Judith Carmel
Editorial Manager: Christine R. Guido
Contributing Editor: Leslie Gilbert Elman

Reader's Digest Illustrated Reference Books
Editor-in Chief: Christopher Cavanaugh
Art Director: Joan Mazzeo
Director, Trade Publishing: Christopher T. Reggio
Senior Design Director, Trade: Elizabeth L. Tunnicliffe
Editorial Director, Trade: Susan Randol

Library of Congress Cataloging in Publication Data
Bahn, Paul G.
    The archaeology detectives/Paul Bahn.
        p. cm.
    Includes bibliographical references and index.
    ISBN 0-7621-0306-X
        1. Archaeology—Methodology 2. Archaeology—History. 3. Antiquities.
        4. Excavations (Archaeology). 5. Civilization, Ancient. I. Title.

    CC75 .B325 2001
    930.1—dc21   00-045745

This book was conceived, designed, and produced by
THE IVY PRESS LIMITED
The Old Candlemakers, West Street
Lewes, East Sussex, BN7 2NZ, England

Art Director: Peter Bridgewater
Publisher: Sophie Collins
Editorial Director: Steve Luck
Designer: Andrew Milne
Editor: Katherine Seely
Picture Researcher: Vanessa Fletcher

Printed in Singapore by Star Standard Industries (s) plc.

BIOGRAPHIES

General Editor

PAUL BAHN is a leading archaeological writer and lecturer. He was Research Fellow at the University of Liverpool and subsequently J. Paul Getty Postdoctoral Fellow. Among his many edited books are the bestselling *Story of Archaeology* (Phoenix, 1996), the *Collins Dictionary of Archaeology* (Harper Collins, 1992) and the *Cambridge History of Archaeology* (CUP, 1996). He is currently editing a major new archaeological series, atlas, and dictionary. He has lectured frequently in the United States, Australia, China, and Japan, as well as in Western Europe.

Author of site: ALTAMIRA

Contributors

CAROLINE BIRD taught for several years at La Trobe University in Melbourne, Australia, before going on to run the Aboriginal Site Officer Training program at the Victoria Archaeological Survey.

Author of site: THE RAPID

PETER BOGUCKI is Associate Dean for Undergraduate Affairs at the School of Engineering and Applied Science at Princeton University.

Author of sites: THE TALHEIM BURIALS, CORTAILLOD, THE ICEMAN, EGTVED, HALLSTATT, SUTTON HOO, NOVGOROD, ALTAI

PHILIP DUKE teaches at the Department of Anthropology at Fort Lewis College, Durango, Colorado, and is a Fellow of the Society of Antiquaries.

Author of sites: OLSEN-CHUBBUCK, PECOS PUEBLO, L'ANSE AUX MEADOWS

CHRIS EDENS is the Resident Director of the American Institute for Yemeni Studies in Sana'a; he is a Research Associate of the University of Pennsylvania Museum of Archaeology.

Author of sites: ÇATAL HÖYÜK, CITY OF UR, EBLA, JERICHO, SOLOMON'S TEMPLE, BABYLON

DAVID GILL is Sub-Dean for the Faculty of Arts and Social Studies at the University of Swansea in Wales and is a Fellow of the Society of Antiquaries.

Author of sites: CERVETERI, ATHENS, HERCULANEUM, VINDOLANDA, MASADA

GEOFFREY McCAFFERTY teaches in the Department of Archaeology at the University of Calgary, Alberta, Canada.

Author of site: PAKAL'S TOMB

JANE McINTOSH taught at Cambridge University, England, before becoming a full-time freelance writer, covering both archaeological principles and practice.

Author of sites: PEKING MAN, MEHRGARH, MOHENJO DARO, KHOK PHANOM DI, MAWANGDUI, DUNHUANG

LOUISE STEEL is a Lecturer in the Department of Archaeology at the University of Wales, Lampeter.

Author of sites: AKROTIRI, MYCENAE, TROY

ANNE THACKERAY is a research associate of the Department of Archaeology at the University of the Witwatersrand in South Africa.

Author of sites: STERKFONTEIN, SWARTKRANS, OLDUVAI GORGE, KLASIES RIVER MOUTH CAVES, GREAT ZIMBABWE

JOYCE TYLDESLEY is an Honorary Research Fellow at the School of Archaeology and Oriental Studies, Liverpool University, England.

Author of sites: THE AMARNA LETTERS, TUTANKHAMEN, GOLDEN MUMMIES, BOXGROVE, ULU BURUN

KAREN WISE is the Associate Curator of Anthropology at the Los Angeles County Museum of Natural History.

Author of sites: CHINCHORRO, SIPÁN, MACHU PICCHU

MARC ZENDER is a doctoral candidate in the Department of Archaeology at the University of Calgary, Alberta, Canada.

Author of sites: CACAXTLA, COPÁN

CONTENTS

INTRODUCTION

Why is archaeology so fascinating? It is probably safe to say that virtually everyone has some interest in the past, whether of their own family or of all humankind. Archaeology constitutes our only means of learning about the vast majority of that past — and about the really big questions such as the origins of farming, or of settled life, or of humankind itself. What's more, as the authors of this book — all of them archaeologists — would doubtless agree, it can be tremendous fun. The feelings aroused by unearthing something which has not seen the light of day for hundreds or even thousands of years are indescribable. Speaking for myself, I first learned of the joys of archaeology through childhood visits to the medieval abbeys and castles and the Roman ruins of northern England, but also — and perhaps even more vividly — through some of the stories by Hergé about Tintin, the journalist-detective, particularly The Temple of the Sun *and* Cigars of the Pharaohs.

Can the work of archaeologists be equated with that of detectives? Most definitely. Detectives try to reconstruct past actions and events — as well as the motives and consequences of those actions — through the painstaking collection and analysis of all available evidence. Archaeologists do exactly the same. And in both cases, much of the evidence consists of material items marked by time — objects that have distinct marks or patterns, or that show signs of wear and tear. Where possible, detectives also have to question as many people as they can to obtain further information. Here they have a distinct advantage over archaeologists, all of whose informants are long dead. Nevertheless archaeology can sometimes draw on oral or written testimony — for example, in cases where we have ethnography or ethnohistory to help us, such as the writings of the first Europeans to encounter the cultures of places like the New World or the Pacific islands. In other cases, invaluable information can be obtained from people who

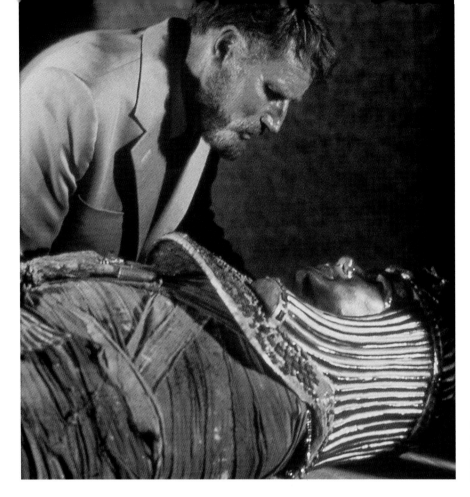

Left: *Charlton Heston in* The Awakening *plays an archaeologist whose newborn daughter is possessed by an ancient and evil Egyptian princess.*

still have certain lifestyles, or who make tools or constructions in traditional materials which feature in the archaeological record. Another way in which archaeologists resemble detectives is that the work of both requires care and patience in the search for and gathering of clues – a great deal of trial and error, and a massive amount of unglamorous work before any possible results can be achieved. As the old cliché has it, their work involves a lot of perspiration and only a little inspiration. So, just as real police work bears little relation to the style of fictional detectives, real archaeology is about as far removed from the world of Indiana Jones as one can get.

EDUCATED GUESSES

Nevertheless, fiction occasionally comes close to the truth. In the 1980 movie "The Awakening," Egyptologist Charlton Heston says "Of course I'm guessing, what do you think we do for a living?" – and to some extent that is true, but archaeologists' guesses need to be educated guesses (hypotheses) based on evidence and logical processes of thought. Otherwise they would just be idle speculations, plucked from thin air, which would be a pretty pointless exercise: one might just as well make everything up. Certainly some modern archaeologists are often sorely tempted to do just that, weaving tales and telling stories to satisfy the media's thirst for simple answers. Today, it is often frowned upon to say "we don't know," let alone "we shall never know," even when these are the

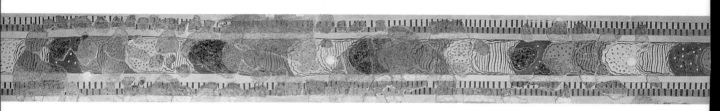

Above: *Part of a border of one of the many decorative friezes at the palace of Knossos in Crete.*

honest answers. The new analytical techniques available to archaeology have led some practitioners to a curious optimism that nothing is now unknowable. It is certainly true that we can now extract far more information from the archaeological record than the early archaeologists could ever have dreamed of, and no doubt this trend will continue – but unless and until a time machine is invented, it is hard to see how most of our deductions about the past will ever be tested, let alone verified.

EXPLAINING THE PROCESS

In this book we have tried to present a sample of the many different ways in which scholars have been able to make deductions and attain insights about the past in a wide variety of areas and with material from every time period. Such a small selection is always difficult to make, but it is hoped that the book will whet the reader's appetite to delve more deeply into some aspects of this supremely rich and fascinating subject. It will be seen that many of the advances have come about through hard work and stubborn searching, as in the case of Howard Carter's dogged pursuit of Tutankhamen's tomb; but luck can also play a major role, through a sudden chance discovery like that of China's Terra-cotta Army or Italy's Iceman. In other cases, progress is made through a flash of inspiration by a remarkable mind, such as Sanz de Sautuola's realization of the significance of the Altamira ceiling, or Ventris's deciphering the meaning of Linear B.

Right: *Painted limestone bust of Queen Nefertiti, discovered by Ludwig Bochardt during excavations at Amarna, Egypt, between 1908 and 1914.*

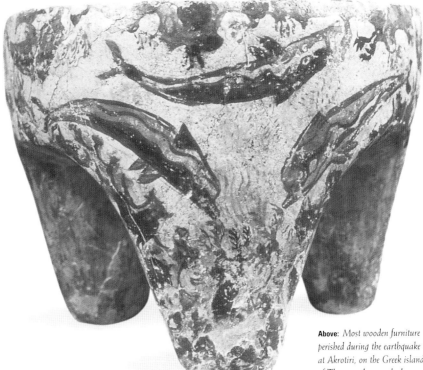

THE INFLUENCE OF TECHNOLOGY

Our research methods have changed significantly over the 150 years of archaeology's existence as a discipline. For example, the advent of aerial photography led to a massive increase in known sites of different kinds, and today we have satellite photos, thermal imagery, and so forth, to aid in the location and study of sites. Other technological advances have led to a revolution in remote sensing, so that we can now "see" what lies beneath the surface before excavation and thus better choose where and what to dig – a most useful advance since the costs of excavation never cease to rise. Excavation is a very expensive exercise, not only in money and manpower, but also in time, since the extremely slow and painstaking digs of today always constitute a major undertaking, often followed by years of analysis of finds and preparation of publications. Microscopy has been a tremendous help to archaeologists, enabling them to study, for example, the pollen grains which help in environmental reconstructions, or the traces of microwear on tools which point to their precise functions. A further technological advance that opened a whole new world to archaeology was the invention of the aqualung, which for the first time made it possible to investigate and excavate ships and other remains in deep water. Most recently, the latest submarines have extended this world even further, leading to discoveries of wrecks of every period in very deep water.

DATING METHODS

Doubtless the biggest scientific impact of all has come in the field of dating, where the invention of radiocarbon dating after the Second World War at last gave archaeologists the "holy grail" of absolute dates for any organic material. Many other dating methods have followed, some more reliable than others. Previously, a great deal of laborious work had to be devoted to determining some kind of chronological sequence for archaeological material. The development of such absolute dating methods made it possible to focus more attention on other aspects of the past. At the same time, methods for accurately analyzing materials of all kinds have enabled us to reconstruct ancient manufacturing processes, as well as to trace numerous kinds of artifacts to their sources, and hence better understand trade routes and the movement of materials. Forensic and medical advances have ensured that we can learn far more from human remains, using everything from endoscopes to CAT-scans to bone chemistry, which reveals a great deal about diet. The relatively new field of genetic analysis is opening up whole new vistas in reconstructing movements and interrelationships of different human populations through space and time. And recently, of course, computers have become ubiquitous in almost every aspect of archaeology, from the storage of data to the rapid manipulation of large quantities of information, and the generation of imagery of every kind, culminating in complex "Virtual Reality" versions of long-vanished sites and buildings.

THE PAST IN THE FUTURE

In short, every branch of the hard sciences has made an enormous contribution to archaeology, and archaeologists are now armed with a tremendous array of techniques that can be brought to bear on the hitherto mute testimony that has come down to us from the past. We have come a long way from the crude, fumbling excavations of the 19th century, which usually employed workmen, armed with pickaxes, to rip objects out of the ground, bereft of the context which tells us so much. This caused the destruction of huge amounts of crucial information, but we need to judge our predecessors in the context of their time. Who, in the 19th century, could have foreseen the slow, careful excavations of today, let alone aerial photography, radiocarbon dating or remote sensing? Doubtless, in another 150 years' time, archaeologists will likewise look back on our efforts as worthy and well-meaning but primitive and unimaginative. Faced with the incredible pace of technological development, we cannot possibly imagine what information the archaeologists of the future will be able to extract from the apparently insignificant material traces of the past. And this is why it is imperative that we leave them plenty of such material to study, by protecting the known sites and by preventing the clandestine robbery and destruction of this precious and irreplaceable heritage. As long as the looters are kept at bay, the prospects for broadening and deepening our understanding of the past will be bright. But as any detective knows, if the evidence is obliterated, the case can never be solved.

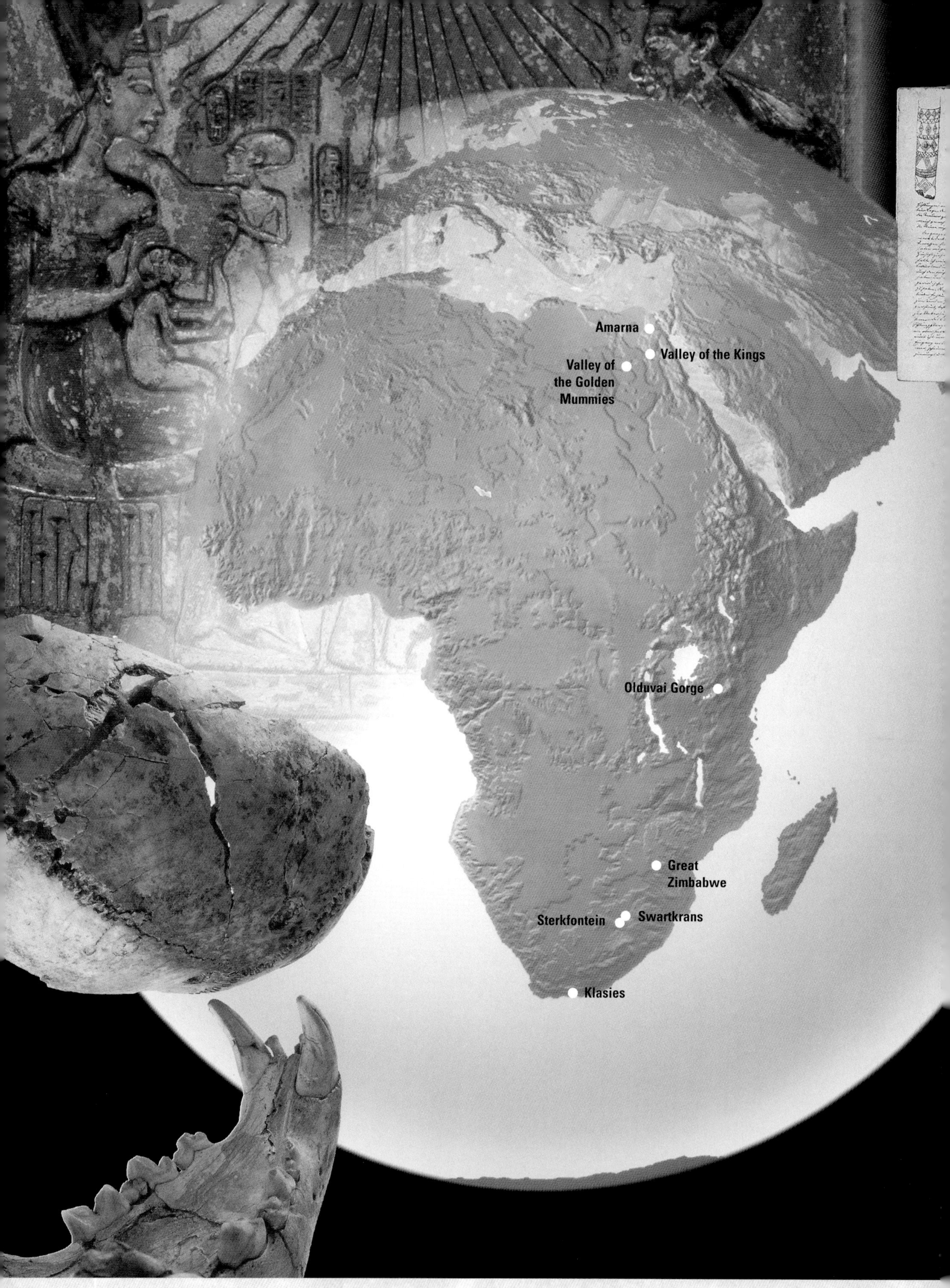

Amarna

Valley of the Kings

Valley of
the Golden
Mummies

Olduvai Gorge

Great
Zimbabwe

Sterkfontein   Swartkrans

Klasies

SECTION ONE
AFRICA

O n present evidence, it is Africa where the human story began, and some of the most difficult problems in archaeological detective work involve these very early sites, with their scraps of fossil hominid remains and their crude stone tools. How close to modern humans were these early hominids? Were they hunters or, more often, prey? Our own species, anatomically modern humans, also seems to have emerged from Africa, so this continent is the scene of important excavations that investigate our immediate ancestors – their way of life, their increasing mastery of their environment, and the first clues to artistic activity.

But Africa is not merely important for these remote periods – it also houses a wealth of archaeological material from later times, such as the stunning rock art of the Sahara and of the southern regions. None evokes more interest or enthusiasm than the remains of Ancient Egypt. The decipherment of this great civilization's writing system by means of the Rosetta Stone stands as one of the classic early episodes in archaeological detective work, while today the meticulous study of mummies, using the latest forensic and scanning techniques, continues this long tradition of problem-solving.

STERKFONTEIN
THE CASE OF LITTLE FOOT

Concealed beneath the high grasslands of Gauteng Province in South Africa, a short drive northwest of the sprawling metropolis of Johannesburg, are the Sterkfontein Caves. Ever since Guglielmo Martinaglia, a lime miner, first blasted into them in 1896, visitors have descended into the underground caverns to gaze in wonder at spectacular cave formations, some resembling folds of curtains and others delicate icicles. But Sterkfontein is also renowned for its fossils, particularly from the period 1.5–3.5 million years ago, when small groups of early hominids, members of the family to which humans and their immediate ancestors belong, roamed parts of eastern and southern Africa.

Above: *One of the entrances to the spectacular collection of subterranean dolomite caves found at Sterkfontein.*

Alun Hughes' dream

The hominids living in the area included australopithecines, now-extinct, ape-like creatures that walked upright and had brains slightly larger than those of the great apes of today. Following Robert Broom's 1936 discovery at Sterkfontein of the first adult australopithecine fossil known, the caves have become a rich source of the fossils of these creatures and of the animals with which they shared their environment.

The odds against the preservation and discovery of australopithecine fossils are huge. The australopithecines were relatively rare and did not bury their dead, so their corpses were quickly destroyed by other animals and natural forces. Almost all their known fossils consist of small fragments of bones or teeth preserved by chance, through being covered over by sediment or volcanic ash before complete destruction. The fossils were later exposed by erosion or excavation by fossil-hunters. Often so little of a fossil is found that it is difficult to be sure to which species it belongs. This leads to lively debate among paleoanthropologists, the scientists who study the fossils of early humans and their immediate ancestors.

Alun Hughes (1916–92), who spent the last 25 years of his life uncovering fossils at Sterkfontein, used to tell his colleague Ron Clarke that he had a

SOUTH AFRICA

Sterkfontein

Biologists group humans in the same biological order as great apes and monkeys, because they share biological features and evolutionary history: about 98.4 percent of the genetic material in modern humans is identical to that of modern chimpanzees. Primates, the biological order that includes great apes, monkeys, and humans, first appeared about 65 million years ago. The hominids, the family to which humans and their immediate ancestors belong, split from the great ape line some 6–8 million years ago. This occurred in Africa, the only place where fossils of the earliest hominids have been found.

The first step on the road to humanity taken by the early hominids was the appearance of creatures that walked on two legs. The oldest known remains of such creatures may belong to a 4.4 million-year-old ape-like creature from Ethiopia known as *Ardipithecus ramidus*.

The first discovery of a very early hominid fossil was made in South Africa in 1924. The 2-million-year-old face and brain case of a very young child was named *Australopithecus africanus* (meaning southern ape of Africa),

thus coining the term australopithecine. These hominids were probably dark-skinned, hairy, ape-like creatures that walked on two legs but possibly also spent some time in trees. This is suggested by scientists who have studied Little Foot and by the 3.7 million-year-old australopithecine footprints preserved in hardened volcanic ash at Laetoli in Tanzania.

The oldest known species of australopithecine is *Australopithecus anamensis*, found in deposits in eastern Africa dating to 3.9–4.3 million years ago. Many different species of australopithecines have been recognized in the period between 1–4 million years ago, but they have been found only in Africa.

About 2.3 million years ago, overlapping in time with the australopithecines, bones of fossils belonging to our own genus, *Homo*, first appeared, and were followed by a series of different species of *Homo*. The most recent of these, our own species, *Homo sapiens*, is the only hominid survivor – all other species of hominids, including the australopithecines, are now extinct.

Above left: *Homage to paleoanthropologist Robert Broom (on the right in the black-and-white photograph), comprising his original notes, press cuttings, and two fossil finds, including a near-complete skull of Australopithecus africanus.*

recurrent dream of stumbling into a sealed cavern and finding a complete skeleton of an australopithecine lying there. Remarkably, it turned out that there was just such a skeleton lying waiting to be discovered in the Sterkfontein deposits, the first ever found.

BOXES OF BONES

In 1978, the director of the excavation program at Sterkfontein, Phillip Tobias of the University of the Witwatersrand in Johannesburg, decided to investigate the Silverberg Grotto, a cave system where some of the oldest deposits at the site are exposed. At the time, the floor of this cavern was covered in a dump of blocks of hardened cave infilling known as breccia, which had been blasted away from the sides of the cavern by lime miners in the 1920s or '30s. Tobias instructed Hughes to move the dump material to the surface. Bones in the breccia, mostly of monkeys, were removed by technicians at Sterkfontein, labeled with the date found and "D20" (Dump 20), then stored at the University of the Witwatersrand. Two boxes of miscellaneous bone fragments were left in the workshed at Sterkfontein.

Almost 20 years later, on September 6, 1994, Clarke was puzzling over a collection of bones from the Silverberg Grotto. He went to check the D20 material in the boxes in the workshed for comparison. To his amazement, among the assortment of bones in the boxes, he spied first an ankle bone, and then three more foot bones, of an early hominid. A world-renowned fossil reconstructor, Clarke pieced the bones together and found they made up the inner arch, or instep, of an australopithecine's left foot. There were also two other possible early hominid foot bones, one badly damaged and the other too fragmentary to identify further. The first four bones, nicknamed "Little Foot" were cataloged with the number StW 573, wrapped in red velvet and placed in a safe at the University of the Witwatersrand.

THE LITTLE FOOT BONES

Now paleoanthropologists were closer to answering a question over which they had long puzzled: were the australopithecines completely adapted for two-legged walking, or did they retain tree-climbing features of their four-footed ancestors, as seen in modern chimpanzees and gorillas? Clarke and Tobias's examination of the Little Foot bones led them to conclude that the big toe was mobile and separated from the other toes by a wide angle, rather than being parallel to them as in modern humans. This meant that the foot could have been used to grasp branches when climbing trees, although it was also adapted for standing, walking, and running on two legs. Little Foot's remains therefore suggested that changes toward humanization in the foot occurred first in the ankle, and only later in the forefoot, and that australopithecines retained ape-like climbing abilities long after they became upright walkers. This was exciting stuff indeed, but Clarke mused that it was highly unusual to find four early hominid foot bones in a row, and suspected that even more startling revelations might soon emerge.

The breakthrough On May 15, 1997, Clarke opened a cupboard in the storeroom at the University of the Witwatersrand to retrieve a fossil, when he noticed a box labeled "D18 cercopithecoids." On opening it, he found it also contained cercopithecoids (monkeys) from D20. Since he was interested in these monkeys from the Silverberg Grotto, he took a closer look. Not only did he find more hominid foot bones that fit the StW 573 bones, but he also found a damaged fragment of a lower leg bone, or

STERKFONTEIN CAVES

The Sterkfontein Caves are famous for their beautiful rock formations. They are also one of the world's richest sources of australopithecine fossils. They have produced several hundred fossils of these creatures, as well as thousands of fossil bones and teeth of animals, over 300 fragments of fossil wood, and more than 9,000 early stone tools. Sterkfontein was declared a World Heritage Site by UNESCO in 1999.

Above: *Dr. Alun Hughes perched amid the Sterkfontein excavations that he directed in the 1970s. This was the second opening of the caves. Robert Broom had been first on the scene in the 1930s.*

tibia. Noting that the damage could have been caused by blasting, he took another look in the two boxes of D20 material in the workshed at Sterkfontein and, on May 27, in a bag labeled "bovid tibiae" found a left hominid tibia which fit the ankle bone of StW 573. The damaged tibia fragment was a mirror image of it and clearly belonged to the right leg of the same individual.

Further searching brought more fragments to light and indicated that the badly damaged bone found in 1994 was part of the right foot of the individual. Clarke now had 12 foot and lower leg bones of the same australopithecine and was convinced that the rest of the skeleton must still be entombed in the Silverberg Grotto. The clincher was the fact that the bones showed no signs of chewing damage from carnivores, which usually begin their meal with the hands and feet. He believed that if the feet were intact, chances were that a carnivore had not eaten from the skeleton, and that the rest of the bones still existed.

THE NEEDLE IN THE HAYSTACK

Clarke made a copy of the right tibia and asked two fossil specialists, Nkwane Molefe and Stephen Motsumi, to comb the dark surfaces of the huge Silverberg Grotto for an exposed cross-section of bone that would fit it exactly. Molefe and Motsumi searched with a brush and hand-held lamps for two days, looking in the blackness for a piece the size of a coin. Their patience finally paid off and they found the match on July 3, 1997. The fit was perfect, despite the passage of decades since the bone was blasted apart by miners. Now the breccia is being carefully chiseled away and so far the lower legs, left arm and hand, and the skull of Little Foot's skeleton have been exposed. When all the bones have been located, they will be removed so that the final cleaning can be done with the aid of a microscope in a laboratory.

LITTLE FOOT'S STORY

It will be many years before Little Foot is completely cleaned, reassembled and studied, and it is not yet known to which species of australopithecine it belongs. Yet it is already yielding a wealth of information about the anatomy and locomotion of these creatures. The indications that Little Foot was arboreal (lived in, or among, trees), inferred from the initial find of the four foot bones, are confirmed by the hand bones and elbow joint. Clarke suggests that our human ancestors, like Little Foot, probably spent the nights nesting in the trees as protection from big cats and hunting hyenas, whose bones are also found at Sterkfontein, and could also have spent parts of the day feeding in trees.

Little Foot probably fell into the cave through a narrow shaft, and was either killed in the fall, or was unable to climb out and eventually died there. Dating of the layers above and below the skeleton indicate the sad event occurred about 3.3 million years ago. Without the curiosity, intuition, determination and skill of Clarke, Tobias, Molefe, and Motsumi, Little Foot's story would have remained buried with its bones in a subterranean cave.

Below: *Juvenile skull, lower jaw and endocast (petrified sediment) of the right side of the brain of* Australopithecus africanus, *discovered near Taung, South Africa, in 1924 by Professor Raymond Dart. His reconstruction of the complete skull, finished in 1925, can be seen in the background.*

SWARTKRANS

WHO KILLED THE AUSTRALOPITHECINES?

*The remains of at least 100 individuals of a genus of now-extinct hominid called
Australopithecus robustus have been unearthed from the oldest layers of the
Swartkrans Caves in South Africa. These heavily-built, ape-like creatures,
with massive jaws and thick-enameled teeth, lived in eastern and southern
Africa between 1 and 1.8 million years ago. Bob Brain of the
Traansval Museum decided to investigate their deaths.*

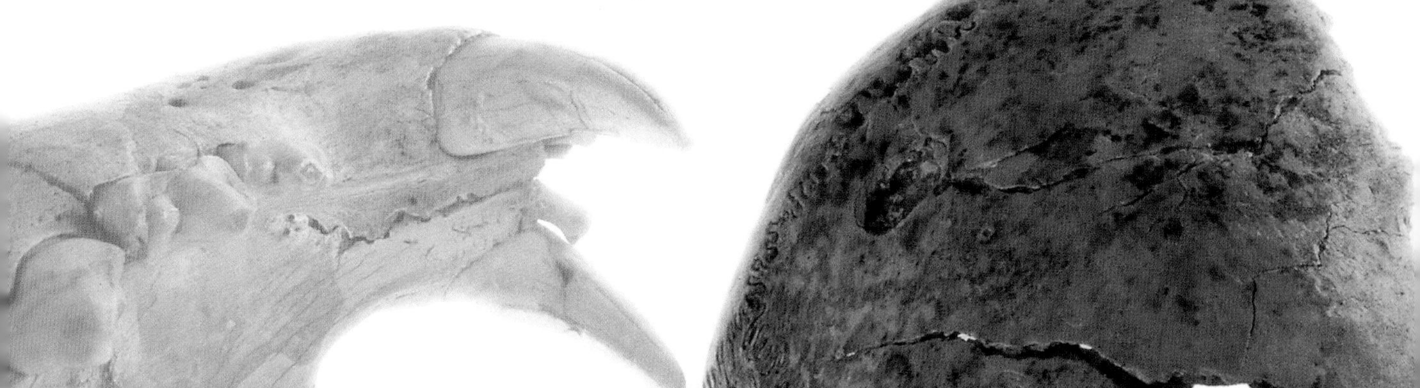

SOUTH AFRICA

Swartkrans

Left: *Paleoanthropologist C.K. "Bob" Brain at Swartkrans site, where he spent 27 years investigating fossils. He attempted to establish why the australopithecines had gone into the caves, and how they had died there.*

A new approach

Australopithecines were ape-like human ancestors that lived in eastern and southern Africa from about 4 million until 1 million years ago. However, the remains found in the Swartkrans caves between 1948 and 1992 were from the species *A. robustus*, which is not considered to have been on the evolutionary line that eventually led directly to modern humans. The Swartkrans australopithecines died between 1 and 1.8 million years ago. Paleontologist Bob Brain of the Transvaal Museum in Pretoria, South Africa, who excavated at Swartkrans from 1965 until 1992, noted that their remains were fragmentary, that only certain body parts tended to be preserved, and that several of the bones bore suspicious carnivore tooth marks. He suspected that the australopithecines did not go voluntarily to the caves to die, and decided to use the bones of other animals found in the caves to assist him with his enquiries.

Brain had no textbook to guide him in the interpretation of bony clues more than a million years old, so he had to compile his own. To find out what parts of skeletons tended to be preserved, and what collections of bones were accumulated by different carnivores, he studied the remains of carnivore kills and bones found in carnivore lairs. He also examined bones assembled by other animal bone collectors like porcupines and owls. His work has become a standard reference for all archaeology detectives seeking to understand why certain bones end up in archaeological sites. This specialized study forms part of the discipline of taphonomy, a term coined in 1940 by the Russian paleontologist J.A. Efremov from the Greek words meaning "the law of burial."

THE SUSPECTS

Tell-tale tooth and chewing marks on the Swartkrans australopithecine bones, as well as the absence of certain body parts, indicated to Brain that carnivores were implicated in the australopithecine deaths. But which carnivores? A remarkable range of carnivores, some now extinct, is represented at Swartkrans, including the leopard, the true saber-toothed cat, the false saber-toothed cat, and brown and spotted hyenas, as well as the hunting hyena. Smaller carnivores, including the aardwolf, jackals, and mongooses, were also present, but Brain believed that they probably did not prey on relatively large creatures like australopithecines, and were more likely to have been the prey of the larger carnivores instead.

BAGS AND BONE TOOLS?

Seventy-seven bones from Swartkrans layers dating between 1 and 1.8 million years ago show evidence of possible use as tools. Microscopic examination shows wear, scratching and polish that could have resulted from use as digging tools, as well as fine lines and glassy polish that could indicate rubbing against a soft substance like leather, possibly the result of being carried around in some kind of bag.

It has been suggested that these bones might have been used to dig up tubers or extract termites from their mounds. But since both australopithecine and early *Homo* remains were also found in these layers, which of them made and used the simple stone and bone tools found?

Far left: *Twin puncture holes in the skull of a young* A. robustus *found at Swartkrans exactly fit the lethal canine teeth of a leopard found in the same archaeological layer.*

EARLY *HOMO* AT SWARTKRANS

The detective skills which brought Ron Clarke acclaim as the discoverer of Little Foot at Sterkfontein (see page 18) were honed on the fossil material from Swartkrans.

Nearly 20 years before he pieced Little Foot together, while examining australopithecine collections in the Transvaal Museum in Pretoria, Clarke not only noticed that several isolated bits of face and skull bone fit together and came from the same individual, but also that bones previously assigned to another species belonged with them, and that they were the remains of a partial cranium of an early *Homo* rather than an australopithecine.

This creature, now cataloged as Sk 847, lived some 1.5 million years ago, which shows that at least two kinds of early hominid were present at Swartkrans.

Below: *Fragmentary remains of a skull known as Sk 847, found by Ron Clarke, the discoverer of Sterkfontein's Little Foot. Recent research indicates that the remains are hominid, not australopithecine. It is the only hominid so far found on the site.*

The leopard hypothesis

Bob Brain observed that leopards often have to carry their prey into an inaccessible place such as a tree if they do not want to lose their meal to spotted hyenas. The Swartkrans environment 1–2 million years ago was probably quite similar to that of today, which comprises grassland in which large trees are scarce. However, in the relatively damp and protected shaftlike cave openings, large stinkwood and fig trees flourish. This means that the trees available to leopards would probably have been those overshadowing the shafts leading to subterranean caves. Fragments of carcass that fell down, and were not consumed by the hopeful hyenas waiting below, could have fallen through the entrance shaft into the underground caverns and eventually ended up as fossils in cave infills.

Possible evidence for leopard involvement in australopithecine deaths at Swartkrans is the spacing of two holes in the skull of an australopithecine child, known by its catalog number Sk 54, which exactly match the spacing of the lower canine teeth of a leopard fossil, Sk 349, found in the same layer as the skull. The damage is consistent with a leopard killing the child and then picking it up by the head to drag it to a secure feeding spot.

However, it is possible that the holes could have been made by a young carnivore larger than a leopard. Indeed, many of the animals represented in the Swartkrans collections are too large to have been leopard prey. Also, Brain noted that there was an unusually high number of bones of baboons in the fossil collections and studies of modern leopard behavior show that such primates form only a small part of leopard diet.

The Swartkrans baboons and australopithecines would have been difficult prey for a carnivore because they lived in groups that would retaliate against any attack. However, a stealthy predator, hunting at night or focusing on a lone straggler, with powerful forelimbs to hold the victim down and penetrating canine teeth to kill quickly, could have been a successful hunter of these creatures. Animals that fit this bill include the true saber-toothed cat, (although its exceptional slicing teeth probably would not have caused the extensive damage seen on the australopithecine bones), the false saber-toothed cat, and hunting hyenas. Because these animals are extinct their behavior cannot be observed today, but it is possible that they went out to hunt and that their prey included australopithecines which they brought back to their cave lairs.

Brain's observations of modern baboons living near Swartkrans showed that they use caves as sleeping places and shelters during cold winter nights. On one occasion, Brain even hid in a cave and made his presence known only after the baboons had entered just before sunset. Although the baboons were greatly disturbed, they would not leave the cave in the dark. Brain considers it possible that, like modern baboons, australopithecines used the dimly lit areas near the cave shaft entrances as sleeping places, while big cats and hyenas might have had lairs much deeper within the cave. The australopithecines would then have provided easy pickings for the predators. If baboons in Swartkrans times also used cave overhangs as sleeping places, such a scenario would additionally account for the high numbers of baboon bones in the fossil collections.

THE HUNTERS AND THE HUNTED

Brain's comparisons between the patterns in the Swartkrans bones and his observations of modern carnivore and baboon behavior showed that, while leopards could have hunted the australopithecines, it is likely that our distant cousins were mainly victims of big cats and hunting hyenas. While some hunting in open country could have occurred, the quantities of baboon bones suggest that carnivores using the caves as lairs regarded sheltering baboons, and australopithecines who could well have sheltered there too, as fast food. This conclusion depicts the heavily built Swartkrans australopithecines as powerless hunted creatures, which, indeed, eventually became extinct. On the other hand, the descendants of their more lightly built australopithecine relatives survived to become the hunters rather than the hunted, and are now the most powerful inhabitants of Earth.

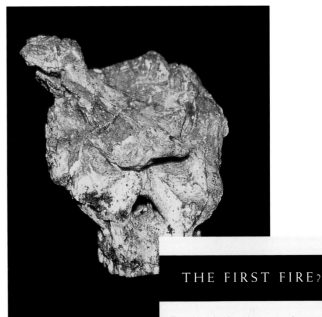

Above: *The crushed skull of an australopithecine, a genus of ape-like human ancestors.*

THE FIRST FIRE?

Two hundred and seventy burnt bones found at Swartkrans in a layer dating between 1 and 1.5 million years ago, may be early evidence for the use of controlled fire by hominids. The bones were mainly from antelope, but also included examples of zebra, warthog, baboon, and even australopithecines.

Brain conducted experiments to find out what effect different kinds of fires and temperatures had on bones, and compared the Swartkrans burnt bones with his results. He and his colleagues found that color and structural changes on the fossil bones suggested they had been burnt at temperatures consistent with a campfire rather than a veldt fire.

However tantalizing this may be, it is not conclusive evidence for the mastery of fire by early hominids over a million years ago. The bones originated outside the cave and the fire could have been natural. Also, even if hominids made or gathered and controlled fire, its use is not known, nor is it certain which of the hominids present, australopithecines or early *Homo*, used the fire.

OLDUVAI GORGE

THE DISCOVERY OF NUTCRACKER MAN

The 19th-century scientist Charles Darwin wrote in The Descent of Man*: "It is . . . probable that Africa was formerly inhabited by extinct apes closely allied to the gorilla and chimpanzee; and as these two apes are now man's nearest allies, it is somewhat more probable that our early progenitors lived on the African continent than elsewhere." At the time, Darwin's idea had few supporters because exciting discoveries of early human fossils were being made in Asia. However, the second half of the 20th century saw Africa firmly established as the cradle of humankind, in which the efforts of Louis and Mary Leakey played a pivotal role.*

A passion for Africa Louis Leakey was born in Kenya in 1903 to English missionary parents and spent his formative years developing a passion for everything African, including the African past. He was determined to prove that the first humans lived in Africa. After studying at the University of Cambridge, he undertook a number of archaeological expeditions to East Africa, hoping to find a place near an ancient lake where game would have been plentiful in early human times, and where fossils could be found.

AN AFRICAN ARCHIVE

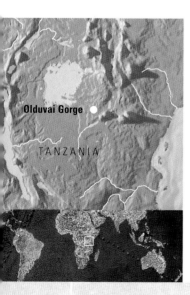

Olduvai Gorge

TANZANIA

Such a place was Olduvai Gorge on the Serengeti Plains of northern Tanzania, a spectacular canyon some 25 miles (40 km) long and up to 330 feet (100 m) deep. The first foreigner to see it was German entomologist Wilhelm Kattwinkel, who, in 1911, led a medical expedition to what was then German East Africa to find

Olduvai Gorge was carved out of a layer-cake of ancient lake and volcanic sediments by an occasionally flowing river to expose a sequence of sediments containing fossils and artifacts dating from some 1.9 million to less than 10,000 years ago. This is the longest known record in a single locality of the remains of past humans and their relatives, their activities, the environments in which they lived, and the animals with which they shared the landscape.

the insects responsible for sleeping sickness. He took a collection of fossils, including some of an extinct three-toed horse, from the gorge back to Germany. There they attracted the attention of paleontologist Hans Reck. In 1913, Reck discovered a complete fossil human skeleton in the gorge, and was convinced that the skeleton was as old as the extinct animals found nearby, but he was met with skepticism. He was prevented from returning to Olduvai by World War I, after which the territory became the British colony of Tanganyika. In 1925, while on a visit to Germany, Leakey met Reck who told him about the skeleton. The two developed a friendship and, in 1931, undertook the long, bumpy ride over dirt tracks from Nairobi, Kenya, to Olduvai together. Leakey "nearly went mad with delight" when he won a £10 bet with Reck by discovering handaxes, then thought to be the earliest stone tools, within 24 hours of arriving at the site.

In the decades that followed, whenever finances and time permitted, Leakey and his second wife and colleague, Mary, undertook the difficult journey to Olduvai from their home in Nairobi, where Leakey was a museum curator. They found impressive collections of fossil animals and simple early stone tools which they called Oldowan after the gorge. These were the oldest known stone tools

Above: *Observed by her dalmatians, Mary Leakey investigates the gully where she found "Nutcracker Man."*

Many animals use and even make tools. For example, wild chimpanzees have been observed stripping leaves off twigs to make spoons with which to extract termites from their nests. However, they do not deliberately and consistently shape stones for use as tools; only humans are known to do this. The earliest known stone tools, found in Ethiopia, were simple sharp-edged flakes chipped off a stone, and date back 2.5 million years. Large collections of such tools attracted Louis Leakey to Olduvai Gorge, because he assumed that where there were tools, the bones of the toolmakers would be found.

Olduvai has in fact given its name to the first known stone tool technology, which is called Oldowan. Microscopically visible damage and polish on Oldowan stone tools shows that they were used on a wide range of materials, including meat, bone, skin, and plants. It is thought that the sharp-edged flakes were used mainly for cutting and slicing. The patterns seen in animal bone collections of this period suggest that early humans were more likely to have been scavengers than hunters of meat.

Rare examples of worked bone show that Oldowan toolmakers also used this material for tools. Much later and more refined stone tools, mainly handaxes, are also abundant at Olduvai.

Below: *Layers of stone tools, including cleavers and handaxes, found at Olduvai. They can be dated to about 700,000 years ago, during the time of Homo erectus.*

at the time. Although even earlier stone tools have since been found at other African sites, dating back as far as 2.5 million years, the term Oldowan is still used for the first stone technology.

Excavations at Olduvai involved hard work under the blazing African sun with meager resources. On one occasion, the team was reduced to eating rice mixed with sardines, maize meal and apricot jam, which Mary eventually found "quite revolting," and drinking muddy water from a pool in which wild animals bathed. Yet the Leakeys pressed on, and Louis was convinced that they would one day find the bones of the maker of the early stone tools and "make the world believe" that humans originated in Africa.

Luck at last

The fateful day dawned on July 17, 1959. The Leakeys were waiting for the arrival of a film crew before continuing excavation. Louis was ill and stayed in camp, while Mary took her dalmatian dogs Sally and Victoria out to search the gorge as she had done countless times before. She decided to examine a site not far from the camp, called FLK, or Frida Leakey Korongo (gully), which had been discovered by Louis' first wife.

Mary scrambled over the slope, checking the stone tools and fragments of animal bone that littered the surface. The sun rose higher in the sky, the glare beginning to make it difficult to distinguish artifacts from stones, and she began to think about returning to camp. Just then, a scrap of bone sticking out from the slope caught her eye. She carefully brushed away a little of the soil, saw two large teeth of an early hominid set in a jawbone and realized that more of the skull was present. With the dogs in tow, she raced into camp shouting "I've got him!" Louis later recalled that he "became magically well within moments" and immediately went down into the gorge to confirm Mary's discovery. He wrote "we almost cried with sheer joy, each seized by that terrific emotion that comes rarely in life. After all our hoping and hardship and sacrifice . . . we had discovered the world's earliest-known human."

Above: *Louis Leakey, at work on the skull found by his wife. Although it was an exciting find, the skull was to prove something of an evolutionary dead end.*

However, this was not to be. The skull was not of an early human or member of the genus *Homo*, but an ape-like human ancestor called an australopithecine. Called "Dear Boy" or the "Nutcracker Man" because of its huge molar teeth, the fossil was assigned to a new genus and species by Louis, *Zinjanthropus boisei*. Today this 1.8 million-year-old creature is generally ascribed to *Australopithecus* or *Paranthropus boisei*, and is considered to belong to a side branch of the human family that became an evolutionary dead end.

Despite Louis' disappointment, it was a remarkable and important discovery. The arrival of the film crew meant that the excavation was captured on film for the world to see, which created tremendous public interest. This in turn resulted in the Leakeys receiving funding on a scale "beyond [their] wildest dreams," and sparked a gold rush of intensive early hominid research in East Africa, on which much of our knowledge of human evolution has been based.

TWISTS IN THE TALE

Ironically, the film crew had been invited to Olduvai in order to film the excavation of a site where one of Louis' field assistants, Heslon Mukiri, had found a hominid tooth embedded in a jaw fragment shortly before the discovery of the Nutcracker Man. This was forgotten in the excitement of the discovery of the spectacular skull, but later turned out to belong to the early human that Louis had hoped to find!

In 1960, the Leakeys' oldest son, Jonathan, discovered the remains of the skull and hand bones of a child dating roughly the same as the Nutcracker Man, but far less massive and with a larger brain. In 1964, it was announced that these bones belonged to an early kind of human, or member of the genus *Homo*, which lived some 1.75 million years ago and had a brain slightly bigger than that of its australopithecine contemporaries. It was called *Homo habilis*, or "Handy Man," the first remains of the earliest member of our genus then known. Louis believed he had at last found the remains of the Oldowan tool-maker. Mukiri's find was also assigned to *H. habilis*. Louis' early human had been under their noses all the time!

Above: *A reconstruction of the skull of* Homo habilis, *together with the original fragments. The crushed and broken original next to it was found in 1968 by Mary Leakey.*

A COMPLEX ANCESTRY

H. habilis was, for many years, recognized as the oldest-known species of *Homo*, and regarded as the evolutionary link between australopithecines and the human line. However, recent discoveries suggest that the evolution of early *Homo* is a more complex story. Some specimens attributed to *Homo* are thought to date from before 2 million years ago, and include at least two other species, *H. rudolfensis* and *H. ergaster*, which are roughly contemporary with *H. habilis*. Because the fossils are so fragmentary, it is difficult to assign them to species, and there is ongoing debate about the classification of early *Homo* and australopithecine remains. In fact, it has even been recently suggested that *H. habilis* and *H. rudolfensis* are actually australopithecines.

Just as a team of detectives gets its man by refusing to give up and by return-ing to the clues time and time again, the Leakeys got their fossils. The belief of Louis Leakey, and of Charles Darwin before him, that humans evolved in Africa was vindicated. The early human fossils from Africa are considerably older than those found anywhere else in the world. However, many chapters in the story are still untold, so the file remains open.

POTASSIUM-ARGON DATING

The fossils and artifacts at Olduvai Gorge are found in layers that include volcanic materials. Crystals in such deposits can be dated by an ingenious method known as potassium-argon dating, which was developed in the 1950s. When material is spewed out of volcanoes, the heat drives off existing argon-40. But potassium-40 is present and undergoes radioactive decay to argon-40 at a known rate.

Measurement of the proportions of the two thus provides an age for the rock. One of the first fossils dated by the potassium-argon method was the Nutcracker Man, found at Olduvai Gorge by Mary Leakey.

KLASIES RIVER MOUTH CAVES

THE SEARCH FOR MODERN HUMANS

There is no doubt that our human ancestors evolved in Africa. Decades of research show that the earliest known Homo *fossils from Africa are older than those found anywhere else in the world. However, the most recent event in human evolution – the emergence of modern humans – remains poorly understood. Until the late 1960s, discoveries suggested that modern humans replaced archaic-looking Neanderthals in Europe and in Africa about 35,000 years ago. Then new finds and new dating techniques suggested that at least "near-modern" humans were present in Africa and the Near East a staggering 100,000 years ago. One of the places that has yielded the most vital evidence for this claim is the mouth of the Klasies River in South Africa.*

Coastal caves in southernmost Africa Around 25 miles (40 km) west of Cape St. Francis on the southern coast of the Eastern Cape Province of South Africa, a small stream known as the Klasies River gurgles noisily over a series of waterfalls and eventually empties into the sea. At the mouth of the river, huge breaking waves crash against high sea cliffs, as they did long ago when they carved a series of caves and shelters. Archaeologists know these as the Klasies River Mouth Caves 1–5.

Some 125,000 years ago, as a result of global climatic changes, the sea level was 20–26 feet (6–8 m) higher than it is today, and the sea would have washed into and cleaned out the lower caves. Shortly after, however, the sea level gradually dropped and the caves were used for shelter by the people living in the area. Material began to accumulate on the cave floors, until eventually there was a huge pile, up to 65 feet (20 m) thick, of layers containing the artifacts, food refuse and the bones of the people who camped there.

SOUTH AFRICA

Klasies

The complex of caves and rock shelters at the Klasies River Mouth has provided one of the most complete and detailed sequences of stone artifacts and animal remains dating from about 60,000 to 125,000 years ago.

Of particular interest are some of the oldest known remains of anatomically modern humans and early evidence for the eating of shellfish by humans. Caves 1, 1C and 2, and Shelters 1A and 1B are located adjacent to each other at the Main Site. The 65 feet (20 m) or so of deposits that built up here look like a layer-cake of clearly distinguishable levels. Cave 5, some 1¼ miles (2 km) east, contains material dating to the last 5,000 years, including burials with rich collections of shell beads and painted stones.

Left: *The cave complex at the mouth of Klasies River.*

The caves were brought to the attention of archaeologists by a member of a nearby mountaineering club. At the time, knowledge of South African prehistory of the last 125,000 years – the late Pleistocene period – was very vague. There was particular interest in finding out about Middle Stone Age toolmakers, whose remains were known to date to the late Pleistocene, and who made stone tools by knocking flakes off specially prepared cobbles. This "prepared core" technique enabled them to chip off pieces of a predetermined size and shape.

Below: *The remains of a "modern human" skull, possibly 100,000 years old, found in Border Cave, a cavern on the Swaziland/South African border.*

Examination of the exposed layers in the caves at Klasies showed that rich accumulations of Middle Stone Age stone artifacts were indeed present. The presence of calcitic formations, stalagmites, and stalactites in the caves indicated that conditions were conducive for the preservation of bones. The presence of animal bones suggested that human remains might also be found there. The proximity of the sea allowed comparisons with dated sea level changes, and importantly the deposits were essentially undisturbed.

With all these conditions in their favor, pioneering excavations at the site were conducted by Ronald

Singer and John Wymer from 1966 to 1968, and have been continued since 1984 by H.J. Deacon. The archaeologists divided the caves into convenient areas for investigation. They removed layers one at a time by working with small trowels and brushes, then passed the material through sieves to catch what escaped their eyes as they dug, carefully recording what was found.

THE DISCOVERY OF HUMAN BONES

In the course of the painstaking excavations, several fragments of human bone, including jawbones, pieces of skull, teeth, and, rarely, other pieces from the rest of the skeleton, were discovered lying in the soil from the lowest and oldest of the layers upward. These human bones had apparently been discarded in the same manner as the animal bones found with them.

Measurements and anatomical comparisons show that they are physically similar to those of modern humans (*Homo sapiens sapiens*). The face does not protrude forward as it does in more archaic populations but is positioned well under the braincase. The brow ridges are very slight, and there is evidence of a well-developed chin. Interestingly, some specimens are very slender, while others are quite robust. Some scholars suggest this may reflect differences between genders, or is perhaps evidence of an ancient lifestyle in which heavy chewing and strenuous activities were the norm.

Strangely, some of the human bones found in the caves were charred and damaged. One piece of skull bone even had cut marks and evidence that the bone had been torn while still fresh, as if the victim had been scalped before the braincase was ripped open to extract the contents. Some specialists suggest that such breakage patterns and damage are similar to those found on human bones in the American Southwest, which have been used as controversial evidence for cannibalism. The Klasies bones offer further provocative evidence to suggest that the practice of cannibalism, whether for ritual or dietary reasons, may have been an occasional part of early modern human behavior.

Kindred spirits or not-so-great hunters?

The Klasies Middle Stone Age cave-dwellers may have looked physically modern, but did they behave like modern hunter-gatherers? Or was their way of life an extinct form of behavior for which no modern equivalent exists?

Some archaeologists believe that the presence of small stone blades, as well as hearths surrounded by plant food debris, suggests that they behaved like Later Stone Age people. The presence of red ocher in the deposits is also seen by some as evidence for the existence of ritual and symbolism in Middle Stone Age times, but there is little, if any, indisputable evidence for art and few examples of artifacts made from bone and shell in the Middle Stone Age period. Also, the stone artifacts found at Klasies are only vaguely patterned, making it difficult to identify discrete types in collections. Studies of the distribution of Middle Stone Age artifacts suggest that there is no evidence for discrete activity areas as seen in later material. Moreover none of the late Pleistocene human remains at Klasies had been deliberately buried.

The early modern humans at Klasies ate tortoise and shellfish – indeed the site provides some of the oldest known evidence for humans collecting and eating seafood – but did not exploit them as heavily as later people did. This could be a reflection of low population density, but there are other indications that the Klasies folk did not exploit their environment intensively. For example, they appear not to have had any fishing equipment like fish hooks, nor nets for catching fish or flying seabirds. They also preferred to hunt relatively docile animals like eland, rather than more ferocious creatures like bushpig and Cape buffalo.

Accordingly, some archaeologists consider that modern behavior developed only toward the end of the Middle Stone Age, in the period between 50,000 and 40,000 years ago, perhaps as a result of changes in the structure and organization of the brain. These changes may be impossible to detect in fossil bone, but the consequences can be seen in the explosion of art, ritual and symbolism in the archaeological record of the last 40,000 years. The jury is still out on this issue.

Klasies River Mouth contains some of the oldest known evidence for the systematic collection and eating of shellfish by humans. These creatures are not only tasty, but are also helpful for archaeologists seeking dates for their sites. Marine organisms like the delicious alikreukel, which lives under submerged rocks, take in oxygen from sea water. Oxygen occurs in three different forms, each with a different mass, and the ratio between these forms in sea water changes over time as a result of global climatic changes.

Records have been made of the sequence of changes in these ratios over time from sea creatures preserved in cores of sediment collected from the ocean floor and dated by various radioactive dating methods. By comparing the oxygen from ratios measured in alikreukel shells from Klasies with the dated deep sea record, archaeologists could determine that the shells in the oldest layers are likely to have grown during the conditions that prevailed 125,000 years ago.

Below: *The study of rock layers can reveal a great deal of information to archaeologists.*

THE AMARNA LETTERS

DECODING THE ROYAL COURT

Akhenaten, Egypt's so-called Heretic Pharaoh who ruled at the end of the 18th Dynasty, abandoned Thebes and its traditional state gods and created his own capital city, Amarna, dedicated to one supreme deity, the Aten. A fascinating archive of official letters, discovered accidentally among the ruins, has given Egyptologists an unprecedented insight into this royal court.

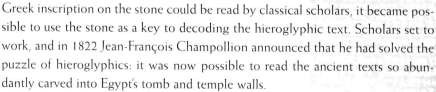

The breakthrough

For centuries the written evidence of Egypt's glorious past was unreadable, its language and the meaning of strange hieroglyphic symbols forgotten with the passing of time. Then, in 1798, Napoleon's invasion of Egypt led to the recovery of the Rosetta stone, a black basalt slab inscribed with text in three different languages: Greek, Egyptian hieroglyphics, and Demotic. The Rosetta stone was transported to London and housed in the British Museum, where it remains to this day. Since the Greek inscription on the stone could be read by classical scholars, it became possible to use the stone as a key to decoding the hieroglyphic text. Scholars set to work, and in 1822 Jean-François Champollion announced that he had solved the puzzle of hieroglyphics: it was now possible to read the ancient texts so abundantly carved into Egypt's tomb and temple walls.

The deciphering of the inscriptions found on Egypt's mighty monuments allowed scholars access to the formal, impersonal texts left by Egypt's kings and queens and wealthy elite. While these texts are of great interest, the inscriptions

Amarna
EGYPT

Left: *The Rosetta stone, found by Napoleon's troops in the town of Rashid. Its conveniently comparative scripts enabled scholars to begin decoding the hieroglyphic secrets of Ancient Egypt.*

Above: *Pharaoh Akhenaten, Queen Nefertiti, and three of their six daughters bathe in the beneficent rays of the Aten, the deified solar disc.*

found on the tomb and temple walls can largely be classed as propaganda texts, designed to impress both the reader and the gods. Still missing were the more informal, personal written records which would allow modern readers an invaluable insight into the daily lives of the Pharaoh, his queen and their court.

ACCIDENTAL DISCOVERY

In 1887 a peasant woman started to dig for *sebbakh* in the ruins of the ancient city of Amarna. *Sebbakh* is the nutrient-rich remains of ancient mud bricks that is used by peasants as a cheap form of fertilizer. Digging for *sebbakh*, although highly profitable, was illegal because it threatened to destroy unexcavated archaeological sites. This may explain why, when her illicit excavation uncovered hundreds of clay tablets inscribed with a wedge-shaped script, the woman did not immediately report her discovery to the authorities. Instead, she sold her finds on the antiquities black market and the tablets slowly began to appear in private collections. The "experts" declared the tablets to be fakes, so no steps were taken to confiscate them, or to conduct an official excavation of the site where they were found. By the time the tablets were recognized as genuine antiquities, the collection had been irretrievably dispersed. Today, the whereabouts of fewer than 400 tablets and fragments are known. These are now principally housed in national museums, with Berlin, Cairo, and London holding major collections.

The tablets are now recognized to be the remains of the royal correspondence stored in the archive of the Amarna royal court in the mid-14th century BC. The puzzling, wedge-shaped writing is cuneiform, and the texts themselves are written in the language of ancient Babylon, the diplomatic language of the ancient world. Most of the letters are addressed to the king of Egypt, but a few are copies of replies sent from Amarna to neighboring states. Even though the surviving collection is incomplete and presents many difficulties of dating and translation, these letters allow scholars a behind-the-scenes glimpse of everyday life at the Egyptian royal court, and of diplomacy within the Bronze Age Mediterranean.

The letters' contents

We might have expected the Amarna letters to reveal a world of gracious phrases and elegant compliments. Instead, they show mighty kings squabbling like children over the merits of gifts given and received. Tushratta, King of Mitanni, for example, believed his brother monarch Amenhotep III (Akhenaten's father) to be fabulously wealthy, and could see no reason why some of this wealth should not be diverted toward himself. He wrote to Egypt imperiously demanding that Amenhotep send him gold, noting "in your country gold is as plentiful as dirt." This blunt demand was softened by a magnificent gift including teams of horses, chariots, and 30 men and women. Many of the letters concern the acceptance of women into the royal harem. Most rulers wanted to form a close alliance with Egypt, the world's dominant state, and Amenhotep III was happy to accept brides from Mitanni, Syria, and Babylon even though he was not prepared to send an Egyptian princess to marry abroad.

Above: *Cuneiform "letter" from Tushratta, king of Mitanni (now the border country between Syria and Turkey) to Akhenaten's father, Amenhotep III. Such letters were written in Babylonian, the diplomatic language of the Near East, and most of them requested military back-up or financial aid.*

The letters sent to and by Akhenaten at Amarna reveal a Pharaoh absorbed in his own life in the royal court, and indifferent to the concerns of his neighbors. For example, Akhenaten was not interested in military matters. Isolated at Amarna, and perhaps ignorant of the terrible upheavals that were threatening international stability at the time, he was quite prepared to abandon his "brother" Tushratta of Mitanni as he faced the mighty Hittite army. Similarly, Akhenaten ignored the desperate requests for military help sent to him by his weak vassals. The letters reveal Akhenaten was even happy to make distinguished foreign ambassadors stand for hours before him in the baking heat of the Egyptian sun. The letters confirm, too, that the military action Akhenaten did eventually sanction was both too little and too late. Not surprisingly, the Amarna Period ended with a rapid contraction of Egypt's once-mighty empire and sphere of influence within the Near East.

THE ROYAL COURT

Amarna was built both quickly and cheaply using small-scale stone blocks and a great many mud bricks. Here, between 1550 and 1307 BC, Akhenaten lived with Queen Nefertiti and their six daughters. Here, too, the sculptor Tuthmosis worked on the world-famous bust of Nefertiti which now resides at the Berlin Museum, and the civil service ran Egypt on the Pharaoh's behalf. However, the cult of the Aten was not destined to last. Within 10 years of Akhenaten's death, Amarna was abandoned and the royal court moved back to Thebes, where Amen once again became the king of Egypt's many gods. The once-mighty capital slowly collapsed into ruin, its precious stone stolen for use at other sites, and its mud-brick architecture disintegrating into mounds of fertile soil, or *sebbakh*.

Left: *Painted limestone bust of Queen Nefertiti, discovered by Ludwig Bochardt during excavations between 1908 and 1914.*

TUTANKHAMEN
THE QUEST FOR THE LOST PHARAOH

Most of the opulent tombs in Egypt's Valley of the Kings were stripped of their riches, first by grave robbers and then by the necropolis priests who guarded them. However, a fortunate combination of circumstances allowed one Pharaoh, Tutankhamen, to lie forgotten for over 3,000 years. Years of painstaking work by British archaeologist Howard Carter eventually led to the spectacular discovery of the missing king in 1922.

EGYPT

Valley of the Kings

Secret tombs The Pharaohs of the Old Kingdom intended their tombs to form a bridge between the earth and the sky. Conspicuous and uncompromising, the enormous pyramid tombs they built symbolized the unassailable might of Egypt's ruling families. Unfortunately they also acted as signposts to the riches buried alongside the dead kings. By the dawn of the New Kingdom, all the pyramids had been thoroughly ransacked and the precious royal mummies lost forever. Since the Egyptians believed that the survival of the body was essential for the survival of the soul after death, this was a disaster.

The New Kingdom saw a break with tradition. The pyramid tomb was abandoned and the royal tomb itself was split in two; the mortuary temple would be erected on the desert fringes where it could serve as an obvious cult center, while the mummy and its paraphernalia would be buried in a hidden, rock-cut grave. The Biban el Muluk, or Valley of the Kings, is a desolate valley on the West Bank of the Nile opposite Thebes. Here the royal architect Ineni was the first to build a tomb with "no one seeing, and no one hearing."

Through the implementation of stringent control measures, the Valley of the Kings remained relatively secure for hundreds of years. However, the end of the New Kingdom saw an outbreak of lawlessness in Egypt. The royal graves were looted and the fragile mummies, targeted because of the jewelry beneath their bandages, were reduced to mere tatters. The necropolis priests acted to safeguard their dead. The tombs were re-opened, their contents seized, and their mummies re-wrapped, labeled, and stored in caches throughout the necropolis. Here they lay forgotten for centuries.

THE SEARCH BEGINS

The Egyptologists who first explored the Valley of the Kings sought an intact royal burial, but in vain. Every tomb they found had been opened and emptied; there was a strange absence of mummies. It was not

Left: *Decked in his royal regalia, the golden face of Tutankhamen stares at us after his 3000-year sleep in the Valley of the Kings.*

Above, far left: *The discovery of Tutankhamen's tomb in 1922.*
Below, far left: *Soul food for Pharaoh on his way through the underworld.*

The real treasure of the tomb is undoubtedly the body of Tutankhamen himself. Unfortunately Carter was of the generation of Egyptologists who, working before the development of CAT scans and DNA analysis, believed that mummies were curiosities of relatively little interest. He therefore paid little attention to the conservation of the king. Today, with scientific mummy analysis firmly established as a valuable branch of Egyptology, Carter's haste in unwrapping and partially dismembering Tutankhamen is only to be regretted. The acquisition of a fully authenticated named member of the late 18th Dynasty royal family opens up the possibility of comparative work on the mummies recovered from the royal caches.

Right: *Howard Carter examining the mummy case in which the king was found.*

until 1871 that the riddle of the missing Pharaohs was solved with the discovery of a collection of royal mummies housed in a single tomb. Here, in the Deir el-Bahari cache, rested many of Egypt's monarchs including Tuthmosis I–III, Seti I, and Rameses II. In 1898 a second cache discovered in the tomb of Amenhotep II supplied more of the royal mummies. By the turn of the 20th century, when the English archaeologist Howard Carter teamed up with his patron Lord Carnarvon, it seemed that the necropolis had yielded all its secrets.

Carter, however, was certain that one king remained in the Valley. In 1917 he started to search for the tomb of Tutankhamen, a short-lived Pharaoh who had ruled Egypt at the end of the Amarna Period, dying in approximately 1323 BC. Tutankhamen had not been identified in either mummy cache, so Carter suspected that his body still lay in his tomb. Without the benefit of modern scientific survey techniques, Carter relied on simple manpower to clear thousands

of tons of sand and rubble from the Valley floor. He then embarked on a sweeping survey, systematically excavating the Valley down to the bedrock. Lord Carnarvon was less certain that Tutankhamen remained to be found, and after four expensive, disappointing years he decreed that there should be one final season of work.

On November 4, 1922, Carter's men discovered steps descending to a mysterious doorway. The doorway was sealed with the name of Tutankhamen. They had found the tomb at last. Careful examination of the door indicated that the tomb had been sealed, illegally opened, restored, and re-closed in antiquity. Soon after the final sealing of the tomb, tons of rubble, dumped during the excavation of the nearby tomb of Rameses VI, had completely hidden the entrance, protecting it from all subsequent invaders, including the necropolis priests. Now, cleared of all debris, the doorway opened into a short, sloping passageway leading to a second re-sealed entrance. Had the dynastic thieves stripped the tomb or were the riches still there? Carter, making a small hole in the door of the inner tomb, peered into the gloom to see "wonderful things, a mass of golden objects with two statues of the dead Tutankhamen guarding the sealed entrance to the burial chamber."

Golden treasures

The discovery of the tomb caused enormous public interest. Carter's determination to empty the tomb in a methodical manner, cataloguing and conserving as he went along, was a great disappointment to the journalists who recorded his every move. It took many months of careful work to clear the antechamber and at last enter Tutankhamen's burial chamber. It was not until February 12, 1924 that the lid of the king's magnificent granite sarcophagus was finally lifted. Carter, seeing the outermost of the three nested golden coffins, finally knew for sure that he had found his missing king.

Tutankhamen had died young, before his regal tomb could be prepared. His is a hurried, atypical royal burial with the minimum of grave goods stuffed into an inadequate private tomb. Nevertheless, the sheer quantity of precious material buried alongside the king gives modern observers pause for thought – if a relatively insignificant monarch such as Tutankhamen was buried in such style with such a cache of wonderful treasures, what would the burial of a wealthy and long-lived king such as Amenhotep III or Rameses II have been like?

While the public marveled at Tutankhamen's golden treasures, scholars were disappointed that there was very little written material in the tomb; no personal letters or even official proclamations which would expand our knowledge of the 18th Dynasty royal family. However, the artifacts recovered from the tomb, now housed in the Cairo Museum, are still the subject of detailed scholarly study.

Left: *Alabaster lid of one of the canopic jars found in the tomb, made in the shape of a bust of Tutankhamen.*

Below: *A miniature gilded coffin, designed to hold the viscera of the young king, extracted in the mummification process.*

GOLDEN MUMMIES

THE SECRET INVESTIGATION

The accidental discovery of an extensive, substantially undisturbed Greco-Roman cemetery in Egypt's Western Desert was for three years a closely guarded secret. Ongoing excavations in the Valley of the Golden Mummies, also known as the Oasis of the Dead, suggest that the necropolis may eventually yield as many as 10,000 burials, casting a new light on life and death in Egypt 2,000–2,500 years ago.

Mummification

For 3,000 years Egyptians believed that it was possible for a person's spirit to cheat death and live forever. For the spirit to survive, they thought it was essential that the body, too, should defy death and corruption. Thus started the centuries-long quest for the perfect means of preserving a decaying corpse with bandages and techniques of desiccation and evisceration. Mummification, initially reserved for Egypt's ruling elite, eventually became available to all who could afford it. By the end of the dynastic age, hundreds of thousands of mummies had been produced and the undertakers' workshops flourished.

The quality of these mummies varied enormously. Earlier experimental mummies were prone to decay and are mostly lost to us. The mortician's art peaked during the New Kingdom (around 1550–1070 BC; Dynasties 18–20), and the beautifully preserved heads of Kings Seti I and Rameses II show just what a

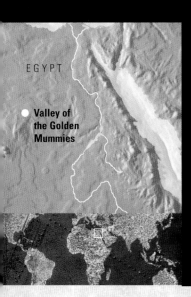

EGYPT

Valley of
the Golden
Mummies

skilled embalmer could achieve. Then came a rapid decline in standards. Today we can use modern x-ray analysis to glimpse below the neat bandages of the later dynastic mummies and inspect the hastily prepared, bitumen-coated muddle of bones that are revealed beneath.

Alexander the Great's conquest of Egypt saw the end of the dynastic age and the start of a period of Greco-Roman rule (332 BC–AD 400). Greeks and Romans settled in Egypt in increasing numbers, bringing with them their own cultural traditions. However, the more ancient traditions of Egypt filtered into these new communities. Although mummification was a practical Egyptian response to a purely Egyptian theological problem, it was soon adopted by the new arrivals who started to mummify their dead. As if to compensate for their often inadequate embalming methods, Greco-Roman mummies are usually beautifully wrapped, their bandages forming intricate criss-cross patterns decorated with golden studs. Many exhibit hybrid Egyptian-Classical decoration with characteristic features belonging to each artistic tradition, so that mummies with lifelike, non-Egyptian style portrait heads are also beautifully decorated with Egyptian religious motifs.

Above: *Together for eternity; a collection of mummies from a family tomb. The mummies vary greatly in style, depending not only on the significance of the person, but also when they were buried. Not all had beautifully painted, gilded masks like those above.*

Above left: *Two more mummies are uncovered. The site of the Valley of the Golden Mummies may contain thousands of burials—207 mummies have been discovered so far.*

SECRET WORK

Work in the cemetery was initially classified as top secret. Tomb robbers are an age-old problem in Egypt, and strict security was considered essential to guard against looting, especially as the number of substantially intact burials grew.

The site was not revealed to the general public until mid-1999. Excavation of the cemetery is still in progress, and it is estimated that it will take at least a decade for the multi-disciplinary team of archaeologists, conservationists, drafters, and artists to fully explore and publish the site. It is hoped that, as the work progresses, the site will furnish important information about many aspects of life and death in Egypt some 2,000 years ago, with scientific analysis of some of the hundreds of mummies providing information about health, diet, and disease.

Below: *Archaeologists at work on the seven newly uncovered tombs in May 2000. It will take at least a decade to explore fully all the new material uncovered at the cemetery.*

Beneath the sand

Bahariya Oasis lies in the Western Desert, 230 miles (368 km) to the southwest of the ancient pyramids of Giza. Here a ruined settlement site, near the modern city of Bawiti, is recognized as home to a sizeable Greco-Roman community, and the nearby temple of Alexander the Great has already been the subject of archaeological investigation. Finds from this region had, however, been unexceptional until, in May 1996, a donkey ridden by a guard at the Temple of Alexander tripped in a mysterious, sand-filled hole. Peering into the gloom, the guard realized that his donkey had stumbled across the entrance to a rock-cut tomb filled with gilt-covered mummies. News of the find was immediately conveyed to Zahi Hawass, Undersecretary of State for the Giza Monuments. Under his direction, Egyptologists began to clear the tomb. It soon became apparent that the tomb was merely one of many, part of a graveyard of between two and four square miles (3.2–6.4 km²) with multichambered tombs each housing as many as 100 Greco-Roman mummies. The tombs, undisturbed by the robbers who emptied the dynastic graveyards and unaffected by later construction which destroyed many unexcavated sites, still smelled of the sweet resin used to embalm their long-dead residents.

THE DISCOVERIES

With only four rock-cut tombs excavated and 207 mummies discovered, differences in burial style have already been identified. While some coffinless individuals were simply wrapped in linen bandages and then ignominiously stacked in alcoves cut into the tomb walls, other burials show a more sophisticated approach and are equipped with pottery coffins, painted mummy-covers, and gilded portrait masks. It is tempting to correlate these differences in burial style with differences in wealth and social status. Yet differences in age may also prove to be important since the cemetery must have been in use for many centuries. The mummies once again show religious themes crossing the cultural divide. Perhaps the best example of this is provided by the burial of a woman whose obviously Roman hairstyle and coronet contrast with the figures of the Egyptian goddesses Isis and Nephthys that adorn the tomb.

Many of the mummies were buried with personal property; the jewelry so far recovered includes earrings, necklaces, and amulets, while included among the coins is one that shows the image of Queen Cleopatra VII. Tomb 4, a series of interlinked rooms, has yielded statues of mourning women and an array of pottery vessels including wine jars. The Bahariya region was famous for its wine production during the Greco-Roman era, and it seems that this thriving industry produced great wealth for its population, allowing them to enjoy lavish burials.

One tomb has been identified as that of a man already well known to archae- ologists, Djedkhonsuefankh, a local governor during the reign of Pharaoh Apries (589–570 BC). Eyuf had portrayed himself as the Pharaoh's equal, appearing in the style of a king on the walls of a temple that he had built in his honor. The burial complex of nobles who had served him was discovered in the 1940s. Djedkhonsuefankh's own remains have now been uncovered, laid to rest inside two 12-ton sarcophagi, one fitted inside the other.

Below: *The decoration on the chests of many of the mummies is classic ancient Egyptian religious imagery. This image shows how the level of preservation can vary enormously from one mummy to the next.*

GREAT ZIMBABWE

A POWERFUL EMPIRE

Near the town of Masvingo in the southeast of Zimbabwe lies a complex of awe-inspiring, stone-walled enclosures built on a hill and in the valley below. This is the site known as Great Zimbabwe. The nation of Zimbabwe took its name when it became an independent state in 1980. This fascinating site has inspired more myths, romantic interpretations, and political passions than perhaps any other archaeological locality in the world.

A myth is born The site first became known to the Western world in the early 16th century, after the Portuguese established a fort at Sofala on the coast of present-day Mozambique. The outpost was intended to control the gold trade in southeast Africa. Reports from Muslim Swahili merchants at Sofala about the existence of stone buildings deep in the interior were recounted by Portuguese chroniclers like João de Barros. In 1552, he wrote of stories about ancient mines in a land "in the midst of which there is a square fortress . . . built of stones of marvelous size, and there appears to be no mortar joining them. . . . The wall is more than twenty-five spans in width. . . . This edifice is almost surrounded by hills, upon which are others resembling it in the fashioning of stone and the absence of mortar, and one of them is a tower more than twelve fathoms high. . . . The natives of the country call all these edifices Symbaoe."

In 1609, João dos Santos, a missionary who worked in southeast Africa, wrote about stone ruins in another part of Zimbabwe: "Some aged Moors assert that they have a tradition from their ancestors that these houses were anciently a factory of the queen of Sheba. . . . Others say that these are the ruins of the factory of Solomon . . . whence gold was brought to Jerusalem." The Queen of Sheba and King Solomon were well-known figures in Muslim folklore. Swahili merchants probably named them as the stone builders partly because they had no better information about the builders. Perhaps they also thought it would

ZIMBABWE

Great
Zimbabwe

Left: *Carl Mauch, the German explorer and archaeologist who was the first European to investigate the ruins of Great Zimbabwe. He was convinced that the ruins were a copy of the Queen of Sheba's palace.*

Right: *A spread from Mauch's diary, in which he noted and sketched his discoveries. On these pages he has recorded a carved column, a soapstone dish, a chevron pattern on the great wall, and a form of gong.*

legitimize their link with the country in their struggle with the Portuguese for control over the gold trade. The idea that the source of the wealth of biblical rulers could be found at stone ruins in the unexplored heart of Africa was so exciting that the shakiness of the premise on which it rested became irrelevant. By the 19th century, many educated Europeans firmly believed that, in the hinterland of southeast Africa, there were stone-walled ruins of gold mines that had been built at the time of King Solomon.

EXOTIC INTERPRETATIONS

Inspired by such stories, a young German geologist, Carl Mauch, set off in 1871 to find the "most mysterious part of Africa" and became the first European to explore and publicize the Great Zimbabwe ruins. Searching for some means of determining the age of the structures, he compared wood from a doorway with that of his pencil. He concluded that the similarity of the two indicated that it

A MIGHTY CITY

Great Zimbabwe is perhaps the most famous and impressive ruined town in sub-Saharan Africa. Some archaeologists suggest that it was laid out to reflect the structure of the society of the Shona people. According to their traditions, leaders were compared with height and mountains. At Great Zimbabwe, the king, his family and important officials lived in stone-walled enclosures located on top of a large hill of granite boulders. Places of ritual and religious importance were also located here. The houses of noblemen were located on the lower slopes of the hill. The royal wives lived in a central area in the valley below, near a huge enclosure known as the Great Enclosure, the outer wall of which is estimated to contain some 900,000 stone blocks. The ordinary folk lived in the valley.

Great Zimbabwe was built by the ancestors of the modern-day Shona people of Zimbabwe. It was the capital of an empire that reached beyond the borders of modern Zimbabwe to adjacent areas of Botswana, South Africa and Mozambique, at its height from about AD 1270–1450. Social organization was based on class distinction between a ruling class and commoners, in contrast to other southern African Iron Age societies at that time. "Zimbabwe" refers to the court or house of a chief, which traditionally consists of stone-walled enclosures on a hill. There are many Zimbabwes, but Great Zimbabwe is the most impressive.

Left: *The Great Enclosure, the largest of the structures at Great Zimbabwe. It contained a huge, conical tower, thought to represent a grain silo, a symbol of kingship.*

"can be taken as a fact that the wood we obtained actually is cedar-wood and from this that it cannot come from anywhere else but from the Libanon [sic]. Furthermore only the Phoenicians could have brought it here." Mauch was not to know that the wood from the doorway was actually a local hardwood (*Spirostachys africana*). His 1872 romantic account of overgrown ruins claimed to have been built by the Queen of Sheba became very popular in Europe and gave credence to the centuries-old tall tales that some still believe.

After the region around Great Zimbabwe was occupied in 1890 by the British South Africa Company of Cecil Rhodes, a mining magnate and politician, the site became regularly visited by European settlers and travelers. They were convinced that Africans they perceived as "backward" could not have built the impressive walling. Like some early investigators, Rhodes himself was sure that the ruins were of Phoenician origin and viewed them as a symbol of the need for a superior external colonizing power to move in and uplift the people of "darkest Africa." Others believed that apparent similarities with ruins in southern Arabia indicated Arabians were responsible, while still others favored ancient Egyptians as the site's builders. Even today, accounts claiming an exotic origin for Great Zimbabwe are still occasionally published.

THE "ESSENTIALLY AFRICAN" INTERPRETATION

The first professionally trained archaeologist to investigate the ruins was David MacIver, who was sent by the British Association for the Advancement of Science to conduct research in 1905. He found that the artifacts were indistinguishable from those of local Africans and noted the presence of two imported objects originally made in the Near East and China between the 14th and 16th centuries AD. These finds led him to conclude that the site dated to medieval times and had been built by Africans.

The emotions and politics involved in the exotic interpretations of Great Zimbabwe ensured that MacIver's archaeological-based inquiry ignited fierce

debate. To resolve the issue, the British Association asked Gertrude Caton-Thompson, whose work in Egypt and the Near East had earned her a formidable reputation as an archaeologist, to investigate the ruins in 1929. Her extensive excavations, detailed descriptions of all artifacts, and meticulous studies of the stratigraphic relationships of the structures, led her to conclude there was "not one single item . . . not in accordance with the claim of [local African] origin and medieval date." People wanted to believe that the findings dated back to earlier times. Her conclusions were greeted with such scorn and outrage in some quarters that Caton-Thompson decided never to work in southern Africa again, declaring that she preferred "passionless archaeology."

The radiocarbon revolution

Radiocarbon dating, a method for determining the age of carbon-containing materials, was pioneered by American chemist Willard F. Libby in the late 1940s. Two wooden lintels from Great Zimbabwe, analyzed by Libby himself, provided some of the earliest known radiocarbon dates in the 1950s. Unfortunately, the dates were determined at a time when the technique was still under development. The dates turned out to be surprisingly early, and incompatible with the datable imported material found at the site by MacIver and Caton-Thompson. These radiocarbon dates fueled support for an early, and therefore exotic, origin of the site. However, subsequent radiocarbon re-dating of the beams indicates that they were cut in the 14th century AD.

In 1958, extensive excavations were undertaken by Roger Summers, Keith Robinson and Anthony Whitty. These provided a detailed account of the pottery and architectural sequence at the site, as well as a series of radiocarbon dates, which have been supplemented and further refined by more recent studies. The finds and dates consistently showed that the site was first occupied by African Early Iron Age farmers in the 5th century AD, but that the main occupation associated with the impressive stone walls occurred in a 200-year period between the mid-13th and mid-15th centuries AD, and is associated with the African Late Iron Age Zimbabwe culture. Thereafter, other sites became more economically and politically important, although people still lived at Great Zimbabwe at the time of the Portuguese accounts.

Far left: *The Great Enclosure, also known as the Elliptical Building, was protected by a huge stone wall containing over 900,000 bricks, a major feat of dry-stone engineering.*

Novgorod

Vindolanda

Egtved

Sutton Hoo

Boxgrove

Talheim   Cortaillod
Ötztal glacier   Hallstatt
(Iceman)

Altamira

Cerveteri
Herculaneum

Athens
Mycenae
Akrotiri
Knossos

SECTION TWO
EUROPE

O f all the continents, Europe displays the greatest variety of archaeological detective work, partly because this is where archaeology, as a discipline, has been practiced the longest. Europe also offers a tremendous range of material on which to work, from the earliest Stone Age (as at Boxgrove) and the wealth of Ice Age art to the first Mediterranean civilizations, the rise and fall of Greece and Rome, the Vikings, and the Medieval world.

From a frozen corpse in the Alps to cities preserved by volcanic ash, from ship-burials to saltmines, from letters on birchbark to great monuments of standing stones, Europe presents the archaeologist with innumerable tantalizing puzzles. The early antiquarians and collectors, in the 16th and 17th centuries, were polymaths whose curiosity about the past rapidly developed into a more systematic approach, as it was realized that information could be teased from these ancient relics in different ways. The enthusiastic but crude excavations carried out in the 18th and 19th centuries eventually gave way to the more rigorous methods of the 20th century, when the full weight of science and technology was applied to archaeology.

BOXGROVE

BRITAIN'S FIRST HUMANS

A warm climatic intermission during the Ice Age saw hunter-gatherer groups living in West Sussex, England. The traces of their occupation — discarded stone tools, animal bones, teeth, and even a hominid leg bone — were discovered during what had started as a routine excavation in a gravel pit at Boxgrove. Boxgrove Man, some 500,000 years old, is now recognized as Britain's oldest inhabitant.

Hard evidence Half a million years ago, a hunter-gatherer made a stone tool. Selecting a suitably sized nodule of flint he roughed out a preliminary blank using a pebble-stone hammer. He then used a softer hammer of bone or antler to detach a series of long, delicate flakes, whittling the core down to the required ovate shape. The resulting biface, or handaxe, was a hand-sized, multi-purpose implement with a continuous razor-sharp edge useful for cutting, chopping, or animal butchery. Satisfied, he moved on, taking the biface and leaving behind a heap of discarded flint flakes.

The gravel pits which dig deep into the landscape of West Sussex allow archaeologists and geologists access to the ancient land surfaces which lie hidden beneath our modern ground. Prehistoric tools had first been recognized at Boxgrove during the early 1970s, and preliminary survey work by Andrew Woodcock had indicated that Boxgrove, West Sussex, might be of considerable archaeological interest. His discovery of large numbers of artifacts and their debris suggested that the pit had once housed a temporary camp on the banks of

GREAT BRITAIN

Boxgrove

Above: *The gravel pits at Boxgrove, where Boxgrove Man was found, along with thousands of well-preserved flint artifacts.*

a stream. In 1982, with the site threatened by ongoing commercial quarrying, Mark Roberts, then an undergraduate student of the Institute of Archaeology at London University, conducted a small-scale survey. He was able to confirm that an undisturbed biface manufacturing site lay on a preserved land surface trapped between the commercially valuable layers of sand and gravel. This led to the establishment of the Boxgrove Lower Paleolithic Project, a program dedicated to the survey and excavation of the pit. Careful excavation yielded hundreds of well-preserved flint artifacts associated with a wide range of animal remains, including a rhinoceros tooth that indicated a date for the living floor of about 500,000 years ago, some 300,000 years earlier than most experts expected judging from the tools that were found there.

Above left: *Artist's reconstruction of what daily life might have been like for the oldest known inhabitants of England. The focus is on flint tool-making techniques.*

Given the poor survival rates of organic material, the understanding of stone tools and stone tool manufacturing is essential to the study of European prehistory. The pioneers who first dared to challenge the assumption that these ancient artifacts were natural "elf-bolts" or "thunder-stones" understood this point, and spent their lives amassing large collections of bifaces, plus the characteristic debris of their manufacture. Stone tools are, however, notoriously difficult to assess when taken out of their archaeological context. Until relatively recently, prehistorians have relied heavily on typology when analyzing their finds. The assumption has been that tools become more sophisticated over time, with the earliest artifacts being crude forebears of the delicate implements made by Neanderthals and by early modern man.

Advances in scientific analysis have forced a change in this approach, and it is now possible to extract a great deal of information from one tool. Some 500,000 years ago the Boxgrove hunter paused to "knap" a handaxe, by breaking off flakes of stone. Scrupulous excavation has made it possible to gather the discarded flakes and fit them back together, reassembling the original flint nodule around a biface-shaped space. Later, careful replication of the knapping technique brought to light the sophisticated use of the soft and hard hammers, while the analysis of ancient and modern knapping debris indicated that at least one of the Boxgrove flint-knappers had been left-handed. High-powered microscopic examination of the many Boxgrove bifaces has suggested that they were primarily used to butcher game.

Right: *The flint nodule (above), which was used to create the biface (below), has been recreated from discarded flint shards.*

HOMINID REMAINS

In 1993, after all quarrying had stopped and the main phase of excavation had ended, Mark Roberts returned to Boxgrove to conduct a small-scale exploratory dig that, he hoped, would assist in interpreting his earlier work on the geology of the site. On Friday November 13, Roger Pederson, working in Trench 5, discovered a large, broken bone, soft and delicate, conserved by the chalky water that filtered through the archaeological layers. It was extracted from the trench in a protective block of dirt, then carefully excavated back at the laboratory. From the silt emerged a long, thick bone, snapped in half and with the ends missing. This proved to be the shin of a hominid, an ancestor of, or precursor to, both Neanderthal man (*Homo sapiens neanderthalensis*) and modern man (*Homo sapiens sapiens*). This hominid is usually called *Homo heidelbergensis*, named for a jaw discovered near Heidelberg, Germany, in 1907. The 500,000 year dating of the site makes Boxgrove Man the earliest hominid recovered from Britain.

The size and thickness of the bone astonished the experts. The hominid, most probably a male at least twenty years of age, had stood almost 6 feet (1.8 m) tall with very well developed leg muscles indicating an athletic lifestyle involving much walking or running. The finding of the leg bone caused intense scientific and popular interest, and excavation started once again at Boxgrove. This led to the discovery of two hominid teeth close to the place where the leg bone had been discovered. With the use of dental analysis they found that the teeth came from the same jaw.

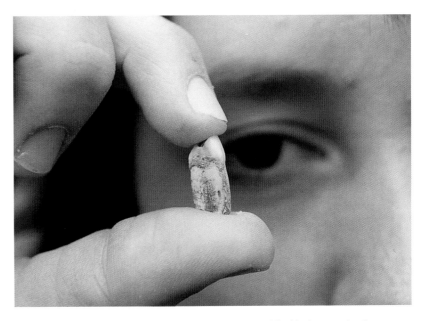

Above: *The oldest human tooth so far found in Britain.*

The evidence from Boxgrove allows us to reconstruct with a fair degree of accuracy the lives of Britain's first hominids. Living during a period of warm weather within the Ice Age, they inhabited a fertile grassy plain at the base of a cliff, fed by a stream that flows into a lake. On top of the cliff flourished a dense, mixed forest. The open plain was populated by large herbivores as well as less welcome animals, including lions, bears and hyenas. Here, for over a century, the hominid group foraged for food, and here they hunted, possibly using wooden spears. Their prey, which included giant deer, rhinoceros, and horse, was butchered using bifaces that were manufactured around the carcass and then discarded. These tools were sophisticated and varied in design, suggesting a well developed manual dexterity and a correspondingly well developed brain capable of speech, planning, and social interaction. The dated, stratified evidence from Boxgrove has caused prehistorians to rethink their entire hypothesis regarding the early occupation of Britain.

Below: *Archaeologists at work at Boxgrove. The site was only discovered in 1982 after the threat of commercial quarrying prompted an emergency excavation. Human remains were found a decade later. Today, Boxgrove is one of the most important sites in Britain.*

ALTAMIRA

THE DISCOVERY OF ICE-AGE ROCK ART

By the second half of the 19th century, it was generally accepted that there had been a "prehistoric" period during which humans had co-existed with now-extinct animals such as mammoths. The clinching evidence came in the early 1860s when items of carved and engraved Ice Age art were found together with early stone and bone tools. These pieces of art often depicted such animals – most notably the image of a mammoth engraved on a piece of mammoth tusk found in the rock-shelter of La Madeleine in the Dordogne region of France. After this discovery, digging in caves and shelters to find the tools and art objects became a popular pastime for amateur archaeologists.

Art on the walls

One or two of the scholars who visited these sites in southern France in the 1860s and 1870s noticed paintings and engravings on some of the walls, but they either ignored them or merely wondered about their possible significance. The concept of prehistoric images drawn on, and surviving on, the walls of caves had not yet arisen, so there was no reason to suspect that these pictures were of great antiquity or of any importance.

ALTAMIRA

The crucial mental leap was made by a landowner in northern Spain, Don Marcelino Sanz de Sautuola, whose lands contained a cave known as Altamira, discovered in 1868 by a local hunter. He had explored the cave and noticed some black geometric drawings at the back, but thought little of them. In 1878, however, Sanz de Sautuola visited the Universal Exhibition in Paris and became fascinated by the specimens of Ice Age portable art on display there – carvings in

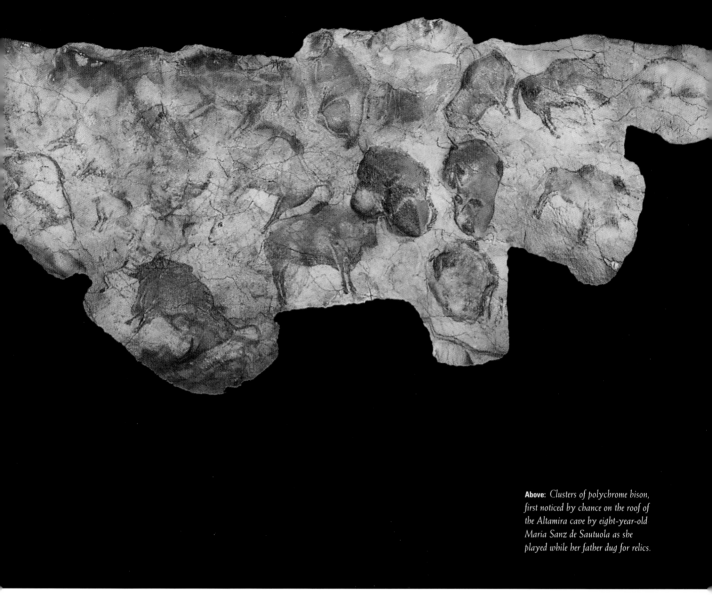

antler, engravings on stone and so forth. On returning home he decided to explore Altamira's sediments. In November 1879, while he was digging in the floor near the cave's entrance, unearthing tools and animal bones from what proved to be Ice Age occupation layers, his eight-year-old daughter Maria, who was playing in the cave, looked up and saw animals painted on the low ceiling. She cried "Look, Papa, oxen!" Her father was amazed and then intrigued. He saw that these images – the now-famous polychrome bison of Altamira – had been made with a fatty paste, and he recognized their similarity in style to some of the Ice Age art objects he had seen in Paris. In 1880 he published a pamphlet about his excavations, in which he presented a drawing of the ceiling and suggested tentatively that its paintings might be ancient.

SKEPTICAL "EXPERTS"

Unfortunately the great majority of established prehistorians of the day rejected his claim completely, driving him to an early death, under suspicion of fraud and

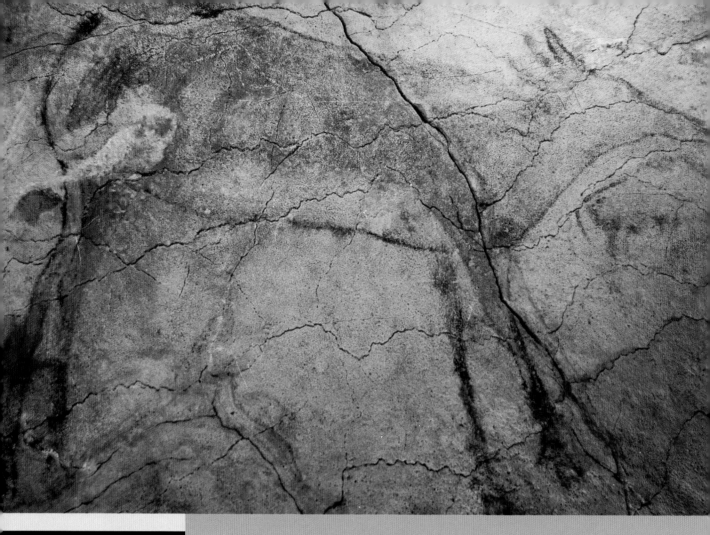

We currently know of about 300 decorated caves and rock shelters in Eurasia with imagery that is thought to date to the Ice Age, spanning a period from over 30,000 to about 10,000 years ago. Discoveries continue even today, with one or two examples turning up every year, mostly in France and Spain.

Above: *Polychrome deer from the walls of Altamira. Deer, horses, and bison are the most frequent subjects for European cave art, but rhinoceroses and big cats have also been found.*

naiveté. The most fundamental reason for their refusal to accept his ideas was that nothing similar had ever been found before. Also, it was hard to believe that "primitive savages" could have produced such sophisticated paintings – despite the remarkable quality of Ice Age art objects that had already been found. They also found it difficult to believe that paint could have survived on a damp ceiling for so long (Altamira's art dates back 13,000–16,000 years). Their other problem was that no soot had been found on the ceiling of the cave to indicate that Ice Age lighting had been used there. However, experiments have subsequently shown that animal-fat lamps of the type used in the Ice Age leave no soot traces.

As a result of all these doubts, Sanz de Sautuola's pioneering piece of archaeological detective work was rejected for 20 years, until other decorated caves were discovered – in France this time – which simply could not be denied. Most notable was the cave of La Mouthe in the Dordogne region, where engraved figures were found on the walls of a gallery whose entrance had been totally blocked by Ice Age occupation layers, putting their authenticity beyond question.

LASCAUX AND BEYOND

Once the phenomenon of cave art was finally accepted and authenticated in the beginning of the 20th century, a phase of exploration and discovery began.

Numerous caves were examined for imagery, and many important examples were found. However, the biggest discovery of all came in 1940 when four French schoolboys stumbled upon a hole in a hillside which led them to the cave of Lascaux, the greatest artistic treasure that has come down to us from the Ice Age. In recent years, major caves like Cosquer and Chauvet in southeastern France, and La Garma in northern Spain, have also come to light.

Attempts to analyze and interpret the imagery come and go, but in the last 20 years a new aspect of the phenomenon has been discovered: Ice Age rock art in the open air. It was generally assumed that the cave artists must also have worked in the open – after all, much of their work was located in cave mouths and rock-shelters in full daylight. It was also thought that Ice Age painting and artwork left in the open could not possibly have survived to the present day. But since 1980 it has become apparent that, in mild climates and in exceptional circumstances of preservation, pecked and engraved images on rocks from the period have indeed survived. Currently they are known at seven sites in Portugal, Spain, and France. Some of these sites comprise only single figures or panels, but at Foz Côa, in northeastern Portugal, hundreds of images are scattered over 10.5 miles (17 km) of a river valley.

Below: Detail from the bison ceiling at Altamira. The paints used were primarily red (iron oxide) and black (manganese dioxide and charcoal).

How have specialists deduced that these undated images in the open air are attributable to the Ice Age? Primarily from their style and content. They comprise mostly horses, aurochs (wild cattle), ibex, and deer, the very creatures whose bones are recovered from occupation sites of the period in this part of the world. Comparison of the style of the figures with those in some caves, and especially on the well-dated and abundant portable imagery from the Ice Age, leaves little room for doubt – the figures are identical. Most are adult animals in profile, with no ground-lines, no landscapes, no scenes, and virtually no humans.

Left: Not all artwork was in caves; there are a surprising number of examples of outdoor art from the same period, including this incised rock art from Foz Côa, Portugal.

THE TALHEIM BURIALS

MYSTERIOUS MASS GRAVES

The first farmers in the forests of central Europe spread west and north from the Hungarian Plain between 5500 and 5000 BC. They settled in the fertile river valleys, living a peaceful life harvesting their crops and tending their herds, building houses and making pottery. This peaceful image of early farming life was contradicted, however, by a discovery made in 1983 at Talheim, in the Neckar valley of southwestern Germany.

Linear Pottery culture

As early farmers colonized the valleys of rivers like the Danube, Rhine, Elbe, Oder and Vistula, they settled in the valleys of small tributary streams. The pottery of these people is similar from one end of central Europe to the other, and its characteristic incised lines have led archaeologists to call these communities the "Linear Pottery culture." Timber longhouses are another distinctive feature of the Linear Pottery farmers, who occupied such dwellings on their farmsteads. Cattle, sheep, goats, and pigs, along with wheat and barley, formed the major part of their

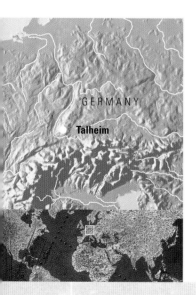

GERMANY

Talheim

diet. Only rarely did they hunt wild animals. From time to time they came into contact with the hunter-gatherers who had lived in this area before the farmers arrived. When the Linear Pottery farmers died, they were buried lying on their sides in a crouched position in cemeteries set away from the settlements. Often some small pottery vessels, stone axes, and bracelets made from the shells of an Aegean mussel, *Spondylus*, are found in the graves. The overall impression, which is reflected in artistic reconstructions of Linear Pottery life, is of peaceful farming families growing crops, raising animals, building houses, and making their distinctive pottery.

THE DISCOVERY

While digging in his garden in 1983, a homeowner in Talheim discovered a number of human bones and quickly alerted the local authorities. A small, week-long excavation was immediately organized, and revealed the bones of several bodies lying in a normal anatomical orientation. The following year, two weeks of formal excavations took place to expose the concentration of bones and also to recover any associated finds.

The skeletons at Talheim formed a densely packed concentration of bones about 8 feet (2.5 m) long, 5 feet (1.5 m) wide, and 10 inches (25 cm) thick. A first glance at the photographs and drawings of the excavations show what appears to be a chaotic jumble of bones, but upon closer examination the outlines of complete skeletons start to emerge. Rather than being in the standard crouched position of Linear Pottery burials, some skeletons are lying face down with their arms and legs splayed out, while others are on their sides or backs. The Talheim bones were not broken and are well-preserved, indicating that they were buried very quickly in a pit and not exposed to wind, sun, water or scavenging animals. Lying among the bones were small fragments of Linear Pottery ceramics, and the radiocarbon dating of the bones directly confirmed that they were about 7,000 years old.

Once the bones were brought to a laboratory for analysis, it was determined that this pit contained

Above: *The damage done to this skull was most likely caused by a violent blow from a neolithic stone axe.*

Left: *The fertile river valleys of modern southern Germany provided early farmers with ideal conditions for growing crops, such as wheat and barley, and tending livestock including cattle, pigs, sheep, and goats.*

the remains of at least 34 individuals, including 16 children, 11 men, and 7 women. Infants were not found. Most of the adults were fairly young, in their twenties, although a few were over fifty and one was over sixty. The average height of the Talheim men was 5 feet 6 inches (1.69 m) and the women 5 feet 2 inches (1.56 m). The individuals were generally in very good health, although some of the bones showed signs of healed fractures, typical of the grueling life of the early farmers.

Right: *An example of Linear Pottery, after which a whole culture is named. The pottery was used primarily for storage or carrying water.*

The myth shattered

The most shocking discovery was that the 34 individuals at Talheim died a violent death. Twenty of them, including some of the children, had received brutal blows to the head. Many of these blows were so hard that they penetrated the skull and were probably lethal. Others were made with blunter objects that caused depressions and deformations of the skulls, which probably injured the brain severely. Two of the adults, including the sixty-year-old, had been struck in the head by flint arrowheads or spears. The individuals whose skulls do not show evidence of a traumatic blow probably also died a violent death.

Who did it? What possible reason could there be to kill not only the farmers, but the women and children? Did rogue hunter-gatherers living in the woods nearby emerge to slaughter the members of this peaceful community? Sadly, all of the evidence points to other Linear Pottery farmers as the culprits. Many of the holes and depressions in the skulls are oval and correspond to the cross-section of the kind of polished stone axe used by the Linear Pottery culture. The killing appears to have taken place all at once, since the bodies were thrown into the pit not long after death. We can only imagine the scene of men, women, and children being indiscriminately slaughtered by axe-wielding marauders. It does not seem to have been part of any ritual, because the bodies were piled into the

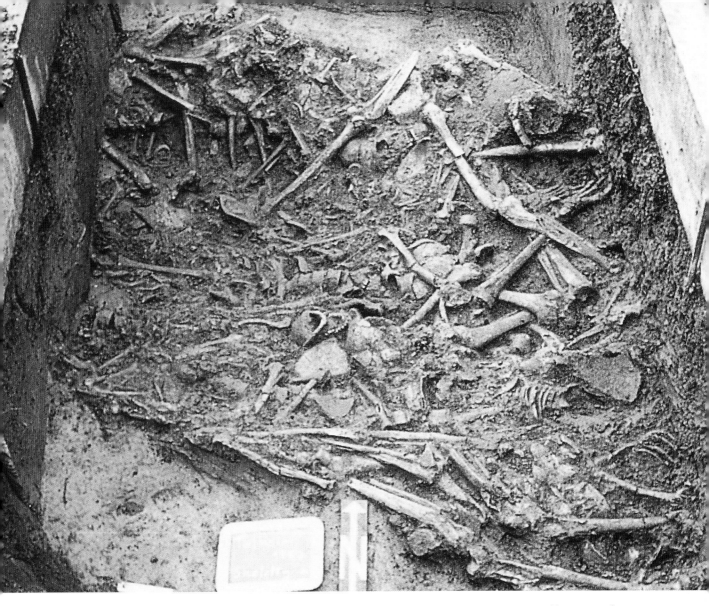

pit without any grave goods and without any effort to arrange them. We can only speculate about what provoked this violence. Was this the result of a dispute between different settlements? Was it a dispute over territory? Was it a punishment of some sort? Or was it simply an effort by one group of farmers to terrorize another?

There are signs that Linear Pottery society at this time was becoming generally unsettled and violent. In recent years, fortifications in the form of defensive ditches and palisades have been found at sites like Darion, Oleye, and Longchamps in Belgium and at Vaihingen/Enz in Germany not far from Talheim. Some specialists, like Lawrence Keeley of the University of Illinois at Chicago, have suggested that the purpose of these fortifications was to protect Linear Pottery farmers against the indigenous foragers who had been pushed out of their hunting grounds by the farmers. Talheim, however, suggests that the farmers also had to fear attacks from other Linear Pottery communities. All was not peaceful in central Europe 7,000 years ago.

CORTAILLOD
A ROMANTIC INTERPRETATION

The winter of 1853-54 was cold and dry, and the water levels of many lakes near Zürich, Switzerland, dropped by up to 12 inches (30 cm). At Meilen, the local residents noticed that the receding water revealed a layer of black organic sediment, 12–30 inches (30–75 cm) thick, unlike the typical yellow lake-bottom mud. Sticking out of this layer were the stumps of wooden posts, split stems of oak, beech, birch, and fir, arranged in rows. The dark sediment also contained a large quantity of animal bones and antler pieces, as well as pottery and tools made from wood, bone, antler, and flint.

Prehistoric settlements

As was often the case in 19th-century Europe, the local schoolteacher collected antiquities and was the nearest authority on ancient finds. The inhabitants of Meilen notified the teacher, Johannes Aeppli, who in turn contacted Dr. Ferdinand Keller, president of the Antiquarian Society of Zürich. Keller recognized that the posts were the remains of structures and the artifacts were the objects discarded or lost by their inhabitants. It was clear that these were prehistoric sites and that the extraordinary preservation of the artifacts, especially those of wood and other organic materials such as hide and textiles, provided a remarkable glimpse into the lives of the people who had lived there.

Keller's imagination was seized by the possibilities, and from his first newspaper report of 1854, which ascribed these settlements to "Celts," these finds also aroused the fascination of the public. Not only were the finds remarkably well preserved but their lakeside locations, and the upright posts that were the most prominent architectural elements, triggered speculation about the type of settlement.

KELLER'S THEORY

Within a short time, Keller had proposed two different theories about Meilen and other settlements like it that were being discovered in the 1850s. The first was that the post dwellings were built on the lake shores, on terra firma which was covered by water during a subsequent rise in water level. The

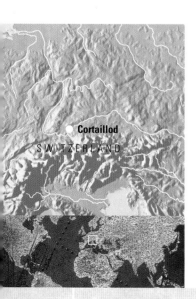

Cortaillod
SWITZERLAND

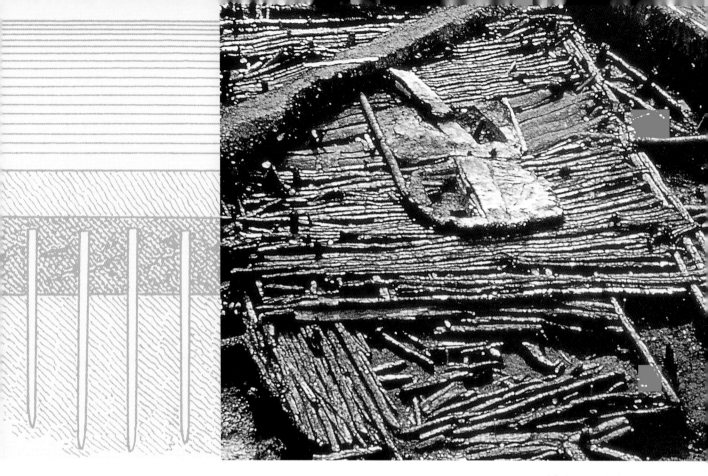

alternative idea was that the houses were actually built on platforms over the lake, supported by posts over shallow water and connected to the shore by gang-planks. In this conception, the posts that were sticking out of the mud were not structural members of the houses but the piles that supported the platforms on which the houses were built. Keller embraced this second hypothesis, illustrating the "wooden islands," and referring to these settlements as pile dwellings whose inhabitants dropped their rubbish into the surrounding water. Thus the German word *Pfahlbauten*, or "pile building," came to characterize these settlements and is still used in the archaeological literature today.

It is unclear what inspired Keller to come up with this idea, but there are a number of sources that were available to him. Since he had originally ascribed these structures to the "Celts," perhaps he was thinking of the lake crannogs of Ireland that were built during the first millennium AD and are mentioned in Irish annals, although these artificial islands were constructed very differently from Keller's concept. He

Above: *The houses were built in quite a complex way. This shows the construction of the floor, and the central fireplace.*

Below: *Usually it is only the stone part of the axes that are preserved, but the conditions at Cortaillod were perfect for preserving organic artifacts, such as these axe handles.*

THE WEALTH OF ARTIFACTS

The quantity and variety of artifacts from these sites was staggering. Wooden artifacts included picks, hoes, sickles, ladles, stirrers, axe-handles, arrows, wheels, and yokes. The gentle water-logging had preserved objects made from plant and animal fibers such as fish nets, baskets, ropes, and pieces of textile. The most distinctive antler artifacts were the sockets which were used to anchor stone axe blades into their wooden handles and provide a degree of shock absorption.

Animal bones provided the first glimpse of the Neolithic diet. Although domestic animals such as cattle, sheep, and goats were present, many of the bones came from wild species such as red deer, beaver, and boar. The variety of plant remains was also astonishing, including wheat and barley, wild fruits and nuts (crabapples, sloes, acorns, beech nuts and hazelnuts), vegetables (peas, beans, and lentils), weeds, and marsh plants.

may also have been familiar with the writings of the ancient Greek historian Herodotus, who described a pile dwelling in the 5th century BC on Lake Prasias in Macedonia. Another possible source for Keller's interpretation lies in accounts by travelers of pile dwellings in Malaya and the East Indies.

Keller's romantic interpretation of the lake sites was embraced by the public and by archaeologists alike. Paintings and models made during this period propagated the notion of wooden islands, with each reconstruction growing ever more fanciful and romantic. Meanwhile, the artifacts from these sites were determined to be those of an early farming society, predating the Celts by some time. We now know that these sites were occupied between about 4000 and 2000 BC. In the late 19th century, they provided the definitive view of the material culture of early European farmers, the benchmark to which the finds from other sites that lacked such good preservation were compared. Dozens of lakeside pile sites were discovered in Switzerland, France,

Italy, Austria, and southern Germany. Modern techniques for excavating in water-logged sediments had not been developed, so as new sites were discovered they were simply mined for their artifacts, many of which were sold and dispersed to museums in Europe and North America.

A reappraisal Although the notion of people living on wooden islands became established in the romantic imagination of the public, professional excavations in the first half of the 20th century led to a reappraisal of Keller's idea. In particular, advances in geosciences made it possible to trace the pattern of rising and falling lake waters over the centuries, and the remains of floors and hearths could be identified among the posts. By the early 1950s, the weight of new evidence finally overwhelmed the concept of wooden islands, and most archaeologists came to accept the view that the settlements were built on the lake shores, not actually on the lake itself. The new interpretation is that the houses were built on the soft soils along the lakes, and the pilings were not only upright structural elements to support the walls and the roofs, but also footings to keep the structures from sinking. As lake levels rose, the settlements were abandoned, then covered over by lake silt which preserved the layer of discarded rubbish as well as the bottoms of the posts that were later discovered by the inhabitants of Meilen.

Despite the fact that archaeologists today have now abandoned the idea of the existence of ancient, over-water dwellings, the significance of these late Neolithic sites has not diminished. Modern techniques of excavation and analysis of the superbly preserved remains continue to yield important information about the lives of these early European farmers.

Above: *Keller mistakenly pictured the pile dwellings at Cortaillod to be built above the water. This is the way he believed the settlement would have looked.*

Far left, top: *Amazingly, these pieces of charred apple have survived for thousands of years.*

Far left, bottom: *This fragment of a wooden yoke provides archaeologists with a glimpse of the agricultural life of the early peoples of Cortaillod.*

THE ICEMAN

A WINDOW ON THE PAST

On September 19, 1991, Helmut and Erika Simon hiked along a ridge in the Tyrolean Alps. From there, they could look south into Italy and north into the Ötztal range in Austria. The landscape was rugged. Melting glacial ice had exposed boulders and rock ledges, and the German couple had to walk carefully. When they reached a trench in the rock, they came upon the macabre sight of a male human torso protruding from the ice and slush. Back at a nearby mountain lodge, they reported their discovery. Thus began one of the most remarkable investigations in European prehistory.

The ultimate mystery

At first, the corpse was thought to be that of some unfortunate modern-day tourist who had died from exposure and whose body had been swallowed by the glacier. Since it was unclear which country had jurisdiction over the location where the body was found, both Austrian and Italian authorities were notified. It was decided that the Austrian gendarmes would take charge of the case, although the Italian carabinieri believed that the man's body was on their side of the border, and therefore under their jurisdiction.

The following day, recovery of the corpse began, using hand tools and a small jackhammer to free the body from the surrounding ice. It was slow going. Prying the corpse from the ice took almost four days. The remains were treated rather roughly; at that stage the goal was simply to retrieve them and identify them, perhaps to solve a missing-person case from recent memory. As the removal proceeded, investigators noticed a large quantity of wood, leather, and grass objects – materials and items which did not naturally occur at this high altitude and must have been brought there. A small metal axe found next to the body was the first hint that this might not be an ordinary hiker.

Within a few days, suspicions increased that the corpse may be at least several centuries old. The wooden and other organic artifacts found in the trench had a decidedly old-fashioned feel to them. Word of the find soon spread to archaeologists. A remarkable window was about to be opened on the past.

AUSTRIA

Ötztal glacier
(Iceman)

ITALY

THE CRUCIAL CLUE

On Tuesday, September 24, 1991, Konrad Spindler of the University of Innsbruck arrived at the office of the medical examiner and recognized the significance of the find. The metal axe was the central clue to the antiquity of the corpse. Spindler and his colleagues believed it was made of bronze, an alloy of copper and tin. It was similar in shape to those used at the beginning of the Bronze Age in central Europe, about 4,000 years ago. A small dagger found with the corpse was clearly made from flint, which was used during the early part of the Bronze Age before it was supplanted by metal for making tools. Since organic materials are typically not preserved on most archaeological sites, the archaeologists had never before seen artifacts like those made from wood, leather, and grass that were found alongside the body.

Above: *The body of Iceman, or Ötzi, is gradually revealed as he is dug out of the ice which has preserved him for the last 5,300 years. Initial excavation was rather crude as it was not at first realized how old the body was or what immense significance it would have.*

Many more organic artifacts had been left on the mountain where the body had been found, and the archaeologists set out to find them. The crude recovery of the body had damaged many artifacts, but some were pieced together. Conservation experts from central Europe were called in to restore the finds. Samples of grass were sent for radiocarbon dating to Paris and Uppsala, Sweden. Meanwhile the corpse lay in a freezer in Innsbruck at 20° F (-6° C) and 98 percent humidity.

Below: *The deerskin quiver found beside the body, together with a yew-wood long bow.*

In early October 1991, it was determined that the site lay 300 feet (93 m) inside Italy. This posed a delicate political problem. Would the corpse and finds be repatriated to Rome? Luckily, the find occurred in the autonomous Italian province of Alto Adige in the South Tyrol. The people of Alto Aldige speak German and have cultural and ethnic ties to Austria. Italian authorities were sensitive to the local pride of Alto Adige, so it was agreed that the study of the corpse could continue in Innsbruck, after which it would be moved to Alto Adige.

Above: *The iceman on display in controlled conditions at the Museum of Bolzano, in Italy.*

Ötzi the iceman

By December, results of the radiocarbon dating of the grass samples were available, and they contained a surprise. Rather than dating the find to the early Bronze Age, about 2000 BC, the dating placed the finds at 3300 BC. Closer examination of the axe revealed that it was made from almost pure copper, the earliest metal to be smelted. This was a revelation. It indicated that the axe form was in use earlier than believed, and more importantly it showed that this find was from the so-called Copper Age, a fascinating but lesser-known period in this part of Europe. The Iceman, or Ötzi as the press had taken to calling him (after the Ötztal glacier), had taken on even greater significance for European prehistory.

Over the next year, forensic examination of Ötzi's corpse and the study of his equipment proceeded. It was established that he was in his forties and and stood just 5 feet 2 inches (1.57m) tall. He had lived a hard life. His toes showed signs of repeated frostbite and several of his ribs had been fractured; some had healed and

Above: *Ötzi's 24-inch (60-cm) axe had a copper head fixed to a yew-wood handle with leather thongs.*

others were in the process of healing when he died. Ötzi's arteries were hardened and smoke from fires had blackened his lungs. His teeth were worn, suggesting that he ate coarsely ground grain. Traces of arsenic in his hair suggested that Ötzi had been exposed to copper smelting. Mysterious tattoos adorned his back and legs.

ÖTZI'S ARTIFACTS

Where did Ötzi come from? Where was he going? Why was he high in the Alps? How did he die? At what time of year? Perhaps the artifacts found with him could provide answers. He was not traveling lightly – in addition to the axe and knife, he was carrying a yew bow, a leather quiver with 14 arrows (only two of which were finished with flint points), two containers made from birch bark, a backpack with a hazel and larch frame, and a variety of other bone, wood, plant, and flint objects. The flint came from the southern side of the Alps, suggesting that Ötzi's trip had started from that direction. The varieties of wood from which the artifacts were made would all have been found in the warmer valleys on the Italian

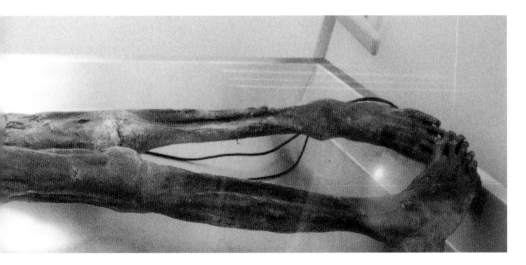

side of the Alps. It seems unlikely that he was a shepherd, since he was found too high for that activity. Perhaps he was hunting or seeking metal ores, or perhaps he was part of a larger party traveling across the Alps.

Pollen from the hop hornbeam found in Ötzi's stomach indicates that he died not in early autumn, as had been previously assumed, but in late spring or early summer. Before going up the mountain, he ate a meal of bread, vegetables, and meat. The evidence of his final moments is difficult to interpret. A likely scenario is that Ötzi died from a fall. His body tumbled into the depression, where it was preserved for 5,300 years by being dried out and covered by snow and ice.

But the story of Ötzi is still being told, as new analyses are completed. Returned with his equipment and clothing to Bolzano, the capital of Alto Adige, in 1998, he now resides in the South Tyrol Museum of Archaeology. This remarkable discovery fired the imaginations of both prehistorians and the public and focused attention on many unanswered questions about Copper Age life.

Ötzi's clothing would have represented the best Neolithic gear for Alpine travel. He was wearing leather shoes and leggings that attached to a leather belt, which also supported a loincloth. The shoes had been stuffed with grass for insulation and had been repaired many times. Over this was a fur wrap, or coat, of some sort. Much of the matted grass turned out to be the remains of a cape that had reached down to Ötzi's knees and was apparently worn as an outer garment. On his head, Ötzi wore a bearskin cap. The striking feature of Ötzi's garments is that none of them is made from woven fibers such as wool or flax.

Below: *How the Iceman may have looked in his grass, leather, and fur traveling clothes.*

AKROTIRI
A QUESTION OF TIME

The sudden disappearance of the brilliant Minoan civilization (c. 3000–1100 BC) in violent conflagrations has long excited controversy, but when Greek archaeologist Spyridon Marinatos argued that the cause of the catastrophe was the eruption of the Theran volcano, it was met with considerable skepticism. Marinatos' quest for evidence led to the discovery of a magnificent ancient city which, although it contributed much to our understanding of the Bronze Age Aegean, completely undermined his theory.

The hidden city In 1967, Spyridon Marinatos began excavations on the Greek island of Thera (Santorini) near the village of Akrotiri to search for evidence to support his theory of the end of the Minoan civilization. Here, beneath volcanic ash and pumice, he uncovered the remains of an ancient city. Ironically, what he found demonstrated that there could be no link between the destruction of the Minoan centers on Crete and the Theran eruption. The pottery found there indicates the abandonment of Akrotiri, and hence the eruption, some 20–30 years before the collapse of the Minoan civilization. However, the city was to yield a wealth of art and artifacts that have fascinated scholars ever since.

Excavations at Akrotiri posed problems for Marinatos, not least because of its excellent state of preservation, with many houses of more than one story. Removal of the thick layer of ash and pumice that had for so long protected the settlement's architecture would in fact involve the removal of the very structure that supported the ancient walls. The timber wall reinforcements and door and window frames had long since perished, leaving only an impression within the surrounding ash. This meant the buildings had no internal structural support. To prevent them from collapsing during excavations, Marinatos poured concrete into the voids that the timbers had left.

EXCAVATION TECHNIQUES

Initially Marinatos had intended to excavate the settlement by tunneling through the layers of pumice and ash, hoping to enter the buildings through their doorways, but keeping them buried underground. Not surprisingly Marinatos soon

Akrotiri

CRETE

Above: *The remains of staircases led to the discovery that many of the houses had been two or even three stories tall. They were built of brick and rubble supported by timber beams and posts.*

abandoned such a plan. Not only was this idea impractical and potentially dangerous, but the technique itself was scientifically unsound, as it would not allow archaeologists to map out the different historical layers of the site and their relative positions. Once he had discovered this, Marinatos began excavations using a more conventional method.

Marinatos' excavations revealed a prosperous late Bronze Age town which displayed close cultural and commercial links with Minoan Crete. For example, texts written in the ancient Cretan script known as Linear A, and lead weights using the Minoan metric system, have been found at the site. And many of the houses incorporate typical Minoan architectural elements.

The houses of ancient Akrotiri were built of rubble and mud-brick. Most had an upper story and in some cases were preserved to a height of three stories, allowing archaeologists a glimpse of how domestic life must have been led. The ground floor served as a work and storage area, where foodstuffs were kept in large ceramic jars, or *pithoi*. The residential and reception rooms were located on the upper stories and tended to be large, well lit and airy. Many houses had internal bathrooms and one of them, known by archaeologists as the West House, contained a clay bathtub and a bronze vase.

The evidence of the wooden furniture used in the houses, unique to the Bronze Age Aegean, is of special interest at Akrotiri. Being a perishable, organic material, wood tends not to survive unless the conditions are particularly dry or waterlogged. However, although the furniture at Akrotiri had long since vanished, it had left an impression within the ash. Plaster casts taken from these hollows illustrate a variety of finely carved items including beds, tables, chairs, and stools.

Above: *Most wooden furniture perished during the earthquake and can only be resurrected in the form of a cast. This dolphin-decorated table was rebuilt from the impression left by its original. It was probably used for religious offerings.*

A town abandoned

Although there were many artifacts found *in situ* in the buildings, there were few valuables and no hoards. Together with the absence of human skeletons inside the settlement, this would suggest that the town's inhabitants had plenty of warning of the coming catastrophe and were able to escape with their most valued belongings before Akrotiri was destroyed in the eruption.

The wealth of material found at Akrotiri is remarkable, in particular the ceramics used as storage containers, cooking utensils, and dining sets. Most of the pottery was made locally, but there are also imports from Minoan Crete which are of considerable importance in establishing the date of the town's destruction in relation to the Cretan chronological sequence.

ELEGANT MURALS

Akrotiri is perhaps best known for the elegant wall paintings which adorned the walls of many of the houses. The first wall paintings appeared in 1968: the head of an African, the head of a blue monkey, and some large flying birds. These were all very fragmentary, but by 1970 a remarkably well-preserved painting was uncovered still adhering to the walls – the so-called Spring Fresco. Subsequently a vast range of wall paintings have been found, revealing unique and tantalizing details of life in the town of Akrotiri, including scenes of a ship procession, everyday pastoral scenes, fishermen, a group of warriors, numerous well-attired females indicating ancient hairstyles and fashions, and intriguing glimpses into the religious beliefs of the town's inhabitants. To excavate the fragile wall paintings, Marinatos brought in a team of specialist conservators who had great experience working on the rich Greek heritage of Byzantine icons and frescoes.

Right: *Excavations yielded an immense number of pots and jars, used to store food, oil, and wine. Many of them were locally made, but some were imports from neighboring Crete.*

The chronology debate

Akrotiri is of considerable importance for its contribution to the debate on the absolute time scale of the Aegean Bronze Age. Traditionally, Minoan and Mycenaean archaeologists have worked within a relative chronological framework based on the types of ceramics common in different periods through time. The absolute dates have been derived from comparisons with the Egyptian chronology. However, there are a number of problems involved in this cross-dating method and it had been hoped that the advent of radiocarbon dating would resolve these problems and provide a reliable, independent dating tool. The Theran eruption took place around the time when ceramics of the Late Minoan IA period were being used. The radiocarbon date of 1630–20 BC that was reached for this period is controversial, since it is more than a century earlier than most archaeologists had supposed. Although the matter is still under debate, the radiocarbon dates are gradually gaining ground among archaeologists.

MYCENAE

THE FACE OF AGAMEMNON?

The legend of "Mycenae rich in gold," that derives from Homer's epic poem, the
Odyssey, has reverberated down the centuries, but it was only in the latter years of
the 19th century that legend became reality. In 1876 the German entrepreneur and
archaeologist, Heinrich Schliemann, began excavations at Mycenae to try to discover
the lost city of King Agamemnon. During his work there he literally struck gold.

Schliemann's early work Schliemann had long been interested
in unearthing the remains of the
civilization described in Homer's epic poems. In 1868 he visited Corfu, which he
identified as Phaeacia in the *Odyssey*, and Ithaca, home of Odysseus. Yet he soon
turned his attentions away from Greece, to western Turkey and the site of Troy,
which was to occupy his resources for several years. However, ensuing his
discovery and appropriation of the gold of Troy in 1872 and the following scan-
dal (see pages 142–45), Schliemann decided to turn his attentions back to
Greece, specifically to the site of Mycenae.

EXCAVATIONS AT MYCENAE

In 1876, when Schliemann began his exploration of Mycenae in earnest, very
little was known about the pre-classical civilization of Greece, although many of
the Bronze Age remains at Mycenae were still standing, most notably the fortification walls, the Lion Gate and several of the *tholos* tombs (beehive-shaped stone
chambers). However, these remains were as yet without cultural and chronological context. Indeed, Schliemann's excavations at Mycenae were fundamental in
mapping the chronology of the Greek Bronze Age. Schliemann decided first to
excavate within the still extant citadel walls, inside the Lion Gate. Almost immediately he uncovered Bronze Age remains – a series of buildings and a large number
of terra-cotta female figurines. Most important was Schliemann's discovery of a
circular enclosure lined by a double row of stone slabs. Horizontal slabs laid
across these gave the enclosure the appearance of a meeting place. However, the
enclosure was soon revealed to be an important burial ground, within which a
number of stelae were uncovered, the grave markers of Mycenae's earliest rulers.

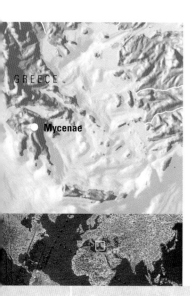

GREECE

Mycenae

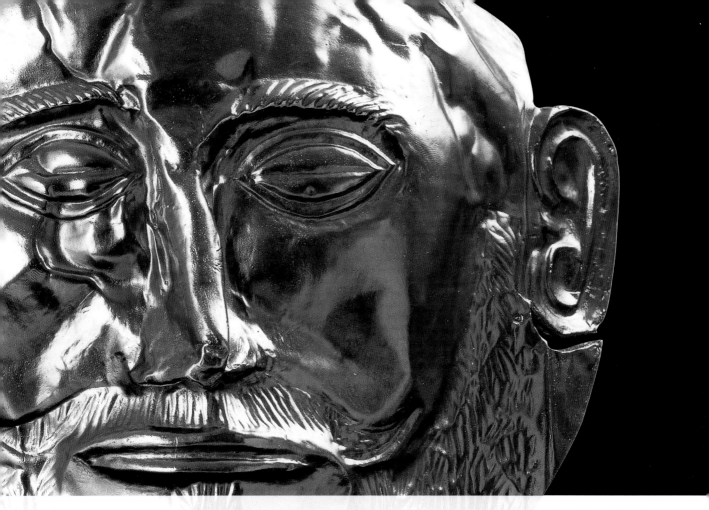

Mycenaean gold uncovered

Schliemann excavated five graves within the circular enclosure, and a sixth was subsequently uncovered. The graves comprise substantial rectangular shafts sunk deep into the ground and lined with a rubble wall which supported a roof of wooden beams and wattle. The shaft graves each housed three or more bodies, interred successively in the tomb rather than being buried on a single occasion. The human remains were surrounded by fabulous grave goods, many of them made of precious metals. In total 19 burials were identified in the graves: 17 adults and two children, the latter identified by their sheet gold coverings. The grave goods were dominated by large quantities of gold dress ornaments (discs decorated with bees, cuttlefish and spirals, and gold plaques), gold crowns, gold signet rings (symbols of office), gold, silver and bronze vessels, elaborate ceremonial weapons (such as the famous inlaid daggers) and, perhaps most famously, a series of breathtaking gold death masks.

These graves have since been found to date to the 16th century BC and mark the earliest appearance of the Mycenaean civilization typical of the late Bronze Age on the Greek mainland. They predate the remains of the citadel, fortifications and *tholos* tombs by two or three centuries, but without the benefit of an established relative chronology, Schliemann mistakenly assumed that the shaft graves were later than the fortifications.

Above: *The most famous of the gold funerary masks found by Heinrich Schliemann in the shaft graves of Mycenae. He mistakenly believed it to be that of Agamemnon himself.*

Below: *Investigation into Mycenae continued long after Schliemann's original discoveries. Here an archaeologist can be seen at work in the early 1950s.*

THE GREEK AUTHORITIES

The Greek authorities attached a number of conditions to Schliemann's permit to excavate Mycenae, marking a move away from early treasure-seeking to the more orderly discipline of archaeology. All finds were to remain on Greek soil, as property of the Greek government. The extent of the excavations was to be strictly controlled, as was the number of workmen. In addition, a local representative of the Greek archaeological society was appointed to supervise the progress of the excavations.

THE SECOND CIRCLE

Excavation of a second grave circle (Grave Circle B) just beyond the citadel walls in 1951 has refined our knowledge of the burials and the funerary ritual. Slightly earlier than the first grave circle (Grave Circle A), some structures in Grave Circle B are simple pits or stone-lined coffins very much in the middle Bronze Age tradition. The majority of the graves, however, are of the same type as the large shaft graves excavated by Schliemann.

Although their grave goods do not match the wealth of those found in Schliemann's graves, they are not far behind. The graves in both circles were family tombs re-used for several burials. After burial, the lower shaft was roofed and the upper part of the shaft was filled with soil and raised into a mound into which the funerary marker (a stone stela) was set. An important element of each burial was a banquet laid out alongside the grave; the debris of animal bones, shells and drinking vessels, broken ritually after use, was thrown into the fill of the shaft.

Schliemann was primarily interested in material, rather than skeletal, remains. His excavation techniques, combined with a poor degree of preservation, have made it difficult subsequently to study the occupants of Grave Circle A in any detail. However, analysis of the occupants of Grave Circle B has revealed a great deal about the ancient population. The men were powerfully built, and varied in height from 5 feet 3 inches to 5 feet 9 inches (1.61 m–1.76 m). The women ranged in height from 5 feet 2 inches to 5 feet 3 inches (1.58 m–1.61 m). Although the individuals were well nourished and exhibited good dental hygiene, the average life expectancy was only thirty-eight years.

Above: *Decorated wooden box from Grave Circle A, within the citadel of Mycenae. The rich, thick gold decoration is an obvious indication of great wealth and power.*

Above: *In contrast to the dazzling extravagance of the treasure from the shaft graves, this plain bronze bowl from a 13th-century BC chamber tomb is elegantly austere.*

The mighty rulers of Mycenae

The enormous metallic wealth deposited in the graves is probably the most striking aspect of Circle A, especially when seen in contrast to the poverty of the time. The source of the wealth has been attributed variously to piracy, trade with the east or central Mediterranean, and loot from mercenary activities in Egypt. Certainly, the vast quantities of gold on display in Myceanae underline the pre-eminence of a new and powerful elite group. In this respect the relationship between Circles A and B is problematic. Although there is a slight degree of overlap, it seems that Circle B is the earlier of the two. When the walled area of the citadel was expanded in the 14th and 13th centuries BC, Circle B was encroached upon, whereas Circle A was left undisturbed. This might indicate that the occupants of Circle A continued to be venerated by later inhabitants of Mycenae. This evidence, together with the greater wealth and slightly later date of Circle A, suggests that the people buried within it were members of a powerful new ruling class which supplanted the earlier rulers of Mycenae buried in Circle B.

Although Schliemann did not discover the burial ground of Agamemnon and his followers, he did uncover evidence of a previously unknown pre-Classical civilization. Continuing analyses of his finds in Grave Circle A, and more recent finds of comparable date elsewhere in the Peloponnese, are still shedding light on the formative stages of this important Bronze Age civilization.

EGTVED

A BRONZE AGE DISCOVERY

The landscape of southern Scandinavia is dotted with burial mounds from many different prehistoric periods; those that are found on the higher points of the terrain tend to date to the early Bronze Age, between 1400 and 1100 BC. In a few of the mounds the bodies have been sealed in massive oak coffins, which has led to exceptional preservation of their contents. These coffins are like time capsules, shedding light on the daily lives of the people buried inside.

Perfect preservation The practice of interring the dead in mighty oak coffins continues an earlier tradition of placing skeletons in stone chambers called cists. This method of burial was used particularly for those from families or clans that enjoyed high status. An enormous section of oak tree trunk was chosen for each coffin, usually 6 feet (2 m) or more long. This was then split lengthwise, and each part was hollowed out to hold the body and associated grave goods. When put back together, the split halves of the oak trunk formed an airtight seal that prevented the decay of the organic materials inside. Textiles, hides, and often human hair, skin, and nails, have been preserved under these airtight conditions. This is only part of the story, however, for it is still likely that the coffins themselves would decay over the following 3,000 years. Luckily, in a number of cases, the coffins had been kept from decay by the layers of turf that covered them under the mound and kept the wood water-logged.

Some of the Danish coffin burials were robbed in antiquity. Investigators at Guldhøj in 1891 found one coffin that contained only a hooked stick used by thieves to pull out the contents through a small hole in one end. Others, such as

DENMARK
Egtved

Left: *Archaeologists uncover the
first of the three oak coffins found at
Borum Eshøj in 1871. The coffins
and their contents are now displayed
in the National Museum of Denmark.*

ON DISPLAY

Over the last century, the National Museum of Denmark has actively studied the Bronze Age coffin burials. Today, the museum displays coffins from Muldbjerg, Borum Eshøj, and Egtved in a darkened room where the low light prevents damage to the fragile textiles and hides. Neighboring rooms house an array of artifacts that provide a detailed view of everyday life in Bronze Age Denmark.

Below: *An oak coffin from Guldhøj,
split apart to reveal how the body was
preserved within an airtight seal.*

In the Bronze Age society reflected in the coffin burials there were marked differences in status, power, and wealth. Hamlets consisted of several farmsteads made up of longhouses which sheltered both people and animals. These houses were about 80–100 feet (25–30 m) long and 26 feet (8 m) wide with two rows of interior posts. Livestock, especially cattle and sheep, generated immense wealth, which was converted into prestige objects made from bronze and other materials. Since there are no tin sources in Scandinavia and local copper was not exploited at this time, the bronze was obtained by trade from elsewhere in Europe. Local specialists used the bronze to produce goods of local design.

Marshes and bogs were important ritual locations and have yielded many spectacular finds that were placed in them as offerings. Illustrations of boats in rock carvings and in engravings on bronze objects reflect the importance of maritime transport to these people.

Right: *Bronze dagger found in the grave of the young woman from Egtved. Such treasure attracted tomb robbers, who used long hooked sticks to extract booty from the treetrunk coffins.*

the Triundhøj mound, were damaged by clumsy excavation before archaeologists arrived on the scene. Until 1937 there was no law in Denmark to protect burial mounds from destruction, although many did survive. Once the importance of these tombs was realized, systematic investigations in the early 20th century unearthed astonishing finds, which revealed the lives of the Bronze Age elite.

BORUM ESHØJ

Borum Eshøj, near Århus in central Jutland, is one of the largest Bronze Age mounds in Denmark, with a diameter of about 364 feet (111 m) and a height of 30 feet (9 m). Archaeologists excavating the mound found it contained three oak coffins, set among arrangements of stones. The first coffin to be opened contained the body of a woman in her fifties wearing a short woolen tunic and a long skirt, with her hair held in place by a hair net. She was covered by a heavy woolen rug, on top of which was a cowhide with its hairs still intact. Decorative bronze objects, including a dagger, belt disc, and rings, adorned her body.

Unearthed from the center of the mound, the second coffin contained a man in his fifties or sixties. He was lying on top of a cowhide which had been removed from the carcass only a short time before the man's burial, as indicated by the maggots found on it. The man wore a woolen hat, kilt and cape. The third coffin in the mound held the body of a younger man and had been placed into the mound later than the first two.

The Egtved burial

But perhaps the most famous of the Danish coffin burials is that of a young woman found at Egtved, near Vejle in southern Jutland. The oak coffin from the the Egtved Mound was opened in 1921 by archaeologists from the National Museum of Denmark. The coffin was lined with cowhide which covered its valuable contents. Beneath the hide, a woolen blanket covered the body of a woman about twenty years old. Her clothing provided a rare and fascinating insight into Bronze Age fashion. It consisted of a short-sleeved woolen tunic and a short skirt made from woolen fringe rather than cloth. The young woman's shoulder-length hair was held back by a headband, also made from wool. Lying on her abdomen was a bronze spiked belt disc about 6 inches (15 cm) in diameter, which was decorated with concentric bands of spirals. Also in the coffin were the cremated remains of a young girl, whose relationship to the woman remains unclear.

DETECTIVE WORK

Clever detective work permitted the discovery of some unusual details about the Egtved burial. First, the blossom of a yarrow flower was found preserved between the hide and the blanket, which enabled archaeologists to establish that the young woman had been buried sometime during the summer. A birch bark container in the grave contained the residue of a drink with three major ingredients: honey (indicated by pollen from linden, bog-myrtle, and clover); fruits and leaves used for flavoring (including cranberries); and grains of emmer wheat. This drink was probably fermented, like a cross between beer, wine, and mead — and was the last item placed in the coffin before burial.

KNOSSOS
DECIPHERING
LINEAR B

Arthur Evans' fascination for early writing systems and his excavations at Knossos on Crete led to the discovery of a luxurious palace belonging to a previously unknown civilization, the magnificent Minoan empire. The palace's archives contained a wealth of clay tablets bearing three mystery scripts. The final deciphering of one of the scripts, Linear B, over half a century after its discovery, led archaeologists to completely review their understanding of ancient Greece.

The Mycenaean mystery

By the last decade of the 19th century, archaeologists had revealed the existence of a wealthy palatial civilization, the Mycenaean empire, which had flourished on the Greek mainland during the late second millennium BC. But the Mycenaeans were apparently illiterate, since no texts had been found, and it was doubtful that they were indeed Greek speakers. This meant there were no known predecessors for the Hellenic civilization of Classical Greece, a fact that mystified the scholars of the time.

Arthur Evans, curator of the Ashmolean Museum in Oxford from 1884, was particularly interested in early writing scripts and systems. He avidly studied engraved stone seals (sealstones) brought back from Crete by his friend and colleague, John Myres, and in 1894 traveled to Crete himself, where he purchased a number of sealstones. Evans published a work on these stones, *Cretan Pictographs and Prae-Phoenician Scripts* (1895), which was his first foray into Minoan archaeology.

In 1900 he began excavations at Knossos on the northern coast of Crete, near the modern town of Herakleion. Almost immediately he uncovered the remains of a huge complex of buildings – apparently a palace, but much earlier than the Mycenaean palaces known from the Greek mainland, and more luxurious in its architecture. The palace at Knossos was the first indication of a previously unknown Aegean Bronze Age civilization, which Evans christened Minoan after the legendary ruler of Crete, King Minos.

Knossos
CRETE

The relationship between the Minoan and Mycenaean civilizations now moved to the forefront of archaeological debate. Later Greek literary sources, together with the immense wealth of Knossos and other Minoan sites, suggested to Evans that Crete rather than the Greek mainland had been pre-eminent during the Bronze Age. He proposed that a Minoan empire had flourished in Greece in the second millennium BC.

THE PALACE AT KNOSSOS

Perhaps the most important discovery within the palace complex at Knossos, certainly for Evans, was the archive of clay tablets marked with signs in an unknown linear script. These were made of the local clay and had been left unfired in antiquity. Indeed the clay tablets only survived because they were unintentionally baked in a number of different fires which destroyed the palace. The tablets had been intended originally as a short-term archive; possibly the data would later be transferred onto some other medium such as papyrus. Evans was able to identify three separate scripts on the tablets: pictographic (or hieroglyphics), Linear A, and Linear B, which corresponded to

Above: *The portico to the northern entrance of the magnificent palace at Knossos. A fresco of a bull, which was a central cult symbol of the Minoan civilization, can be seen behind the pillars.*

the three major periods during which the palace was inhabited. In 1902 an important cache of Linear B tablets was found north of the so-called Royal Road to the northwest of the palace. These listed chariot parts and arrows, and they were found together with two stashes of arrows which had been stored in sealed boxes, secured by string with clay sealings.

The archives at Knossos were not unique on the island of Crete. Evans was able to compare his Linear A tablets with examples found at Gournia, and excavations at Phaistos have uncovered extensive hieroglyphic archives. Evans concluded that the Linear B script was roughly contemporary with the more widespread Linear A script, but that it was used only at Knossos. Subsequent excavations, however, have demonstrated that Linear B was used in the final palace at Knossos after the destruction and disappearance of the other major Minoan palaces on Crete.

Evans remarked on the similarity between the Cretan linear scripts and the syllabary (set of symbols) used on Cyprus during the first millennium BC to write Greek. Ironically, even though Evans noted that when he applied the values of these signs to the Linear B of the Knossos tablets the word *po-lo* was found to occur next to the ideogram of a horse, recalling the ancient Greek *polos* (horse), he assumed this was a coincidence. He dismissed out of hand the possibility that Linear B might have been used to write an early form of Greek. Instead Evans assumed that the tablets recorded an unknown pre-Greek language. The story of Linear B might have remained thus, an obscure undeciphered script used to write an uncertain language, if it had not been for Blegen's discoveries at Pylos just before World War II.

New discoveries at Pylos

In the spring of 1939, Carl Blegen, a professor at the University of Cincinnati, began excavations at the site of ancient Pylos in the Peloponnese on mainland Greece. Like Evans at Knossos, he was rewarded with almost immediate success, discovering the well-preserved remains of an elegant Mycenaean palace. By the time of Blegen's excavations the chronology of Mycenaean ceramics had been well established, allowing the date of the destruction of Pylos to be fixed at around 1200 BC. In the very first trial trench Blegen found five Linear B tablets – the first to be found on the Greek mainland, demonstrating that the Mycenaean culture had after all been literate. Blegen went on to discover a small archive room. As at Knossos, the Pylos archives were written on clay tablets which had been preserved by a fire that destroyed the palace.

UNLOCKING THE CLUES

The final deciphering of the Linear B script was achieved by an architect, Michael Ventris. His imagination had been fired when still a schoolboy after hearing Sir Arthur Evans lecture on the Minoan world. Fascinated by the tablets, he resolved one day to decipher the script. Following the publication of the Pylos archives in 1951, Ventris finally had a sufficient sample size to attempt to decrypt

Above: *The red-walled Throne Room at Knossos, decorated with frescoes of griffins and plants, was not intended for the king. It is one of a row of small cult shrines that run along the eastern side of the central court, and the throne was probably mean for a priest or priestess.*

the tablets. After detailed analysis he was able to devise a grid in which he placed the signs that appeared to share consonantal or vowel values. Recurrent groups of signs had already been identified on the Knossos tablets by the American scholar Alice Kober. Ventris, noting that these signs did not appear on the Pylos tablets, deduced that they represented the names of places on Crete. Applying values to the Linear B signs from the Cypriot syllabary, Ventris was able to read these groups: *ko-no-so*, he suggested, was Knossos and *a-mi-ni-so* the name of its port, Amnisos. Following on from this, Ventris applied values to other words and was surprised that these bore a remarkable resemblance to an archaic form of Greek. Finally, in 1952, he was able to announce that he had deciphered Linear B. Initially scholars were skeptical that the archives were indeed written in Greek. However, Blegen, who had returned to Pylos, tested the decipherment on an

EVANS' CONTRIBUTION

Although Evans had intended full publication of reproductions of the scripts from Knossos, the vast quantity of material that he uncovered proved beyond him and he published only 100 of approximately 3,000 tablets. However, he made a number of useful contributions to the decipherment of the Linear B script: he distinguished it from Linear A, identified both Linear A and B as syllabic writing systems, identified the script's numbering system, and noted that Linear B appeared to be used to write an inflected language (in which a noun's endings change according to their case).

Background: One of over 4000 clay tablets written in Linear B script, found at Knossos by Sir Arthur Evans.

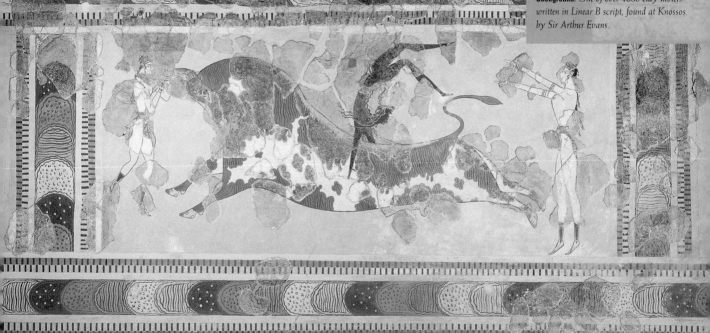

unpublished tablet that had been found the previous summer. Proof came with the reading of *ti-ri-po-de* (Greek *tripodes*, meaning tripod) accompanied with an ideogram of a three-legged cauldron.

Although the Linear B tablets have been deciphered and shown to be an early form of Greek, the other scripts found at Knossos – Linear A and the hieroglyphic script – have remained intractable. Nonetheless, the discoveries at Knossos and Pylos have opened up the Aegean Bronze Age for modern scholars, allowing a fascinating glimpse into the social, economic, and religious life of the palaces.

Above: *One of the many decorative friezes at Knossos shows a young athlete "bull leaping." In myth, bull leapers were young men and women sent in tribute to the legendary King Minos. They leapt with the bulls and then vanished into his palace. It was thought they were fed to the Minotaur, a fearsome creature, half man and half bull, who was locked away at the heart of the labyrinth.*

HALLSTATT

PRESERVED IN SALT

The modern town of Hallstatt, reached by winding roads through the Austrian Alps, lies on the edge of a deep lake surrounded by steep mountain walls. High over the town a narrow valley leads further up into the mountains. This valley, known as the Salzbergtal, is the location of some remarkable prehistoric salt mines and an early Iron Age cemetery, used from 700–500 BC. These sites have made Hallstatt one of the most important places for the study of European prehistory.

Mining through history

Salt has been mined continuously at Hallstatt from AD 1311 to the present day, but the medieval miners soon discovered that they were not the first ones to have done so. As they tunneled into the rock they encountered many traces of prehistoric activity deep within the mountain. Most of these prehistoric mine shafts have long since disappeared, however, closed by the weight of the overlying mountain of salt and stone. But the objects left behind by the prehistoric miners remained preserved in the salty matrix to be found by their successors in recent centuries. By tracing the distribution of the objects in the mountain, as well as examining rare instances where the prehistoric tunnels have been found still open, archaeologists have been able to reconstruct the techniques and methods used by the Iron Age miners.

The salt deposits under the mountain at Hallstatt consist of veins of nearly pure rock salt about 16 feet (5 m) thick, which run through a mixture of clay and salt. Iron Age miners followed these salt veins deep into the mountainside by sinking shafts that angled downward from the surface, as deep as 1,080 feet (330 m). They then excavated side tunnels that branched out from these main shafts. Their principal tools included long, pointed bronze picks mounted on wooden handles. Using these bronze picks, they would cut a deep groove into the salt face, then two curving grooves to the right and left of the first to form a circular or heart-shaped pattern in the salt. When all three of the grooves were deep enough, the two large lobes of salt formed by this cutting pattern were broken off from the face of the rock and transported up to the surface.

Above and left: *Modern Hallstatt has changed hardly at all since Isidor Engl, documenter of the graves, made an engraving of the town in the mid-19th century.*

VISITING THE PAST

A visitor to Hallstatt today can tour the modern mines and also take a special prehistoric tour, which revisits the location where an Iron Age miner was found in 1734. The path up the Salzbergtal crosses the location of the cemetery, where a small exhibit depicts some of the graves. Most of the finds from both the mine and the cemetery can be seen on display in the Natural History Museum in Vienna.

IRON AGE ARTIFACTS

Loose salt was scooped up and shoveled into leather backpacks for transport out of the mine. These backpacks, examples of which are now displayed with other Hallstatt finds at the Natural History Museum in Vienna, are some of the most remarkable artifacts to have been preserved in the salt. They were made from cowhide on a wooden frame. A single strap supported the pack on one shoulder, and a stick was attached to the other side of the bag. When the carrier reached the destination where the salt was to be dumped out, he simply pulled the stick over his shoulder while bending over. This tipped the bag forward and allowed the contents to tumble out.

The prehistoric tunnels were dark and cold, so among the most common traces of human activity encountered inside the mountain are burnt pieces of wood. Bundles of fir and spruce splints provided torches for light, while larger fires helped keep the miners warm. Some of the most interesting finds consist of

the miners' clothing, including articles of wool and linen along with leather shoes and hats. A conical miner's hat, on display in Vienna, has the hairy side of the hide on the inside to insulate the miner's head more comfortably.

Cave-ins were a constant concern for the Iron Age miners, so they took measures to prevent them with shoring and buttresses. Yet for some, work in the mines was lethal. On April 1, 1734, the preserved corpse of a man was found encased in salt, probably the victim of a cave-in. The body was so perfectly intact that it seemed like he had died only a few days before, although the circumstances of the find make it clear that he was an Iron Age miner. Accounts of this discovery show that his clothes and shoes had also survived. The 18th-century miners who found this corpse decided that the man had probably not been a Christian, so a few days later the corpse was reburied in unconsecrated ground reserved for heathens and suicides, next to the local cemetery. Here, sadly, the body decayed quickly. The mountain is presumed to hold other such corpses in its depths.

THE PEOPLE

We do not know where these miners lived, for no settlement has yet been found at Hallstatt. Analysis of the graves at Hallstatt and contemporaneous sites suggests that it was a normal Iron Age community comprising family households, rather than a specialized mining settlement with a disproportionate number of men. It had ties to other communities that also engaged in metallurgy and trade to accumulate wealth.

Below: *Salt miners used cone-shaped leather backpacks to carry their tools into the mine, and to transport salt from the seamface to the collection point.*

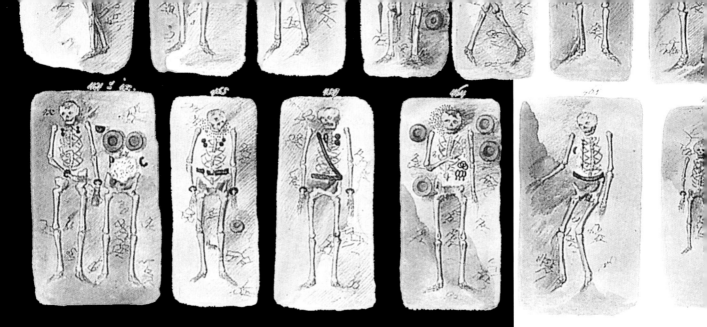

The cemeteries

Salt mining generated tremendous wealth for the Hallstatt community. Salt was the primary means of preserving meat and fish for the Iron Age peoples of Europe and, in the interior of the continent far from the sea, it would have been in great demand. The riches derived from salt are reflected in the Iron Age burials found near the mines in the Salzbergtal. Johann Georg Ramsauer, manager of the salt mines, undertook the first systematic excavations of the Hallstatt burials in 1846–63. During these investigations, Ramsauer found 980 burials, which his assistants recorded meticulously in watercolor sketches. Over the following decades, additional excavations raised the number of recorded graves at Hallstatt to over 1,100, while many more have probably been destroyed over the last several centuries by mining operations.

Both cremation and skeleton burials dating to the 7th and 6th centuries BC are known from the Hallstatt cemetery, one of the largest and richest of its time in Europe. These burials have been found to contain weapons made from bronze and iron, including swords and daggers, along with bronze bowls, cauldrons, helmets, and decorative objects made from metal, amber, and glass. The trading network in which the people at Hallstatt participated reached north to the Baltic and south as far as the Mediterranean. Baltic amber and luxury goods made in Italy attest to this long-distance trade. A sword handle from Grave 573, for example, is made of ivory with amber inlay.

Above: *The occupants and contents of all 980 Hallstatt graves were carefully recorded in watercolor sketches by illustrator Isidor Engl. Contents were also listed in writing. This meticulous documentation can be seen on display today in Hallstatt, although it had been lost after the death of Johann-Georg Ramsauer, the manager of the salt mines, in 1876 and not rediscovered until 1932, when it was found by chance in a used book store in Vienna.*

Left: *The ivory and amber sword handle found in tomb 573 testifies to the wealth and trading connections enjoyed in 7th-century Hallstatt.*

Far left: *The outstanding craftsmanship of Hallstatt culture is clearly in evidence in this 6th-century golden drinking horn (with brass core) and collection of jewelry.*

CERVETERI

THE ETRUSCAN WAY OF DEATH

The Etruscans, an ancient race from central and northern Italy, have long been shrouded in mystery. Archaeologists are fascinated by their extensive and fantastic cemeteries. The decorative tombs are literally cut into the volcanic tufa rock and are found near their former towns in Tuscany, such as Tarquinia, Vulci, and Cerveteri. Antiquarian diggers, looking for exotic trophies for their collections, used to talk of the land of Tuscany yielding antiquities "like truffles."

Early finds The Roman colony at Cerveteri (ancient Caere) in southern Etruria was the subject of minor archaeological explorations during the 18th century. These excavations uncovered the remains of the theater and the temple of the imperial cult. One of the first really "scientific" excavations in Etruria, however, took place in 1836 at Cerveteri. Father Regolini, a local priest, together with General Galassi excavated one of the tombs – now known to archaeologists as the Regolini-Galassi tomb. In this tomb, the two men were rewarded with a number of exotic finds.

The chamber of the tomb, which was covered by an earth grave mound, or tumulus, contained three burials with abundant grave goods. Some of the silver vessels accompanying the dead were inscribed with the female name Larthia, presumably the name of one of the people buried in the tomb. Another of those buried in the tomb seems to have been a warrior since he was accompanied by eight bronze shields. Archaeologists also uncovered four magnificent silver bowls that were decorated in gold with fine scenes showing lion hunts and an Egyptian-like Horus falcon. Similar silver bowls have been found in Etruria at Vulci and Populonia, and in Campania at Pontecagnano. Scholars tend to assign these tombs to the early 7th century BC. The bowls themselves are thought to have been made by Phoenician craftsmen who mixed Egyptian and other Near Eastern motifs, and it may have been the Phoenicians who brought such exotic items – even decorated ostrich eggs – to Etruria in exchange for metals such as iron.

ITALY
Cerveteri

The painstaking excavation of the cemeteries of Etruria has always been the main focus for archaeological work in the region. The burials at Cerveteri are thought to date back to the pre-Etruscan Villanovan period. Three main burial areas have been identified on the outskirts of the ancient city: the Banditaccia, the Monte Abatone, and the Sorbo cemeteries. The organized arrangements and plans of these cemeteries have reminded some archaeologists of the carefully laid-out orthogonal plans of Greek colonies in southern Italy and Sicily.

DECORATIVE FEATURES

The Etruscan cemeteries were used well into the 3rd century BC when Cerveteri's territory was annexed by the developing city of Rome. The rock-cut tombs, such as the Tomb of the Capitals, feature roof beams, designed to evoke the interiors of Etruscan houses for which only basic foundations have ever been recovered. Some tombs were decorated with painted terra-cotta panels, including the series of 6th-century BC Boccanera plaques now in the British Museum. These plaques show the mythological scene of the Judgment of Paris.

One of the most famous of the later Etruscan burials is known as the Tomb of the Reliefs, dating back to the mid-4th century BC. The dead were placed on "couches" cut from the living volcanic rock, complete with pillows for support. The effect was as if the dead had been laid out like guests at a banquet. Even the walls of the tomb were decorated with drinking cups and pieces of armor. All of

Above left: *Etruscan tombs were cut into volcanic rock and buried under earth mounds. The contents remained a mystery until the 19th century.*

Far left and above: *These figures, which represent a soldier and a shepherd, were depicted on the back of a silver Etruscan mirror.*

these decorations were relief sculptures cut out of the rock, and all were highly painted. Though this level of elaborate decoration in a tomb is unusual, many of the Etruscan tombs contained banqueting ware, such as imported black-figured and red-figured pottery from Athens. Indeed, so common were Athenian black-figured and red-figured pots in the tombs of Etruria that Josiah Wedgwood, the 18th-century British ceramicist, named one of his workshops in the English Midlands "Etruria." It was then thought that the pots were Etruscan rather than, as we now know, Athenian.

The Etruscan language

The Etruscan language has long defied scholars' understanding, partly due to the limited number of substantial texts that have been found; many short inscriptions are known from tombs and artifacts, but few longer ones. One of the longest texts discovered, a list of offerings to the gods (such as Nethuns, the Etruscan equivalent of the Roman Neptune), is written on linen and consists of some 1,200 words. It has only survived because it was used as a wrapping for an Egyptian female mummy which had been acquired for a Croatian collection in Zagreb in the 19th century. Other substantial books or texts such as this one are

Etruscan discoveries continue to this day. Our understanding of the Etruscan language has been enormously helped by the discovery of a bronze tablet in the area of Cortona in eastern Etruria some time around 1992. Though the actual discovery site of the tablet was not recorded, it certainly comes from the vicinity of Cortona, as it contains a reference to Lake Trasimene which lies to the south of the region. The tablet, which relates to the acquisition of land including a vineyard (*vina*), appears to have been written in the late 3rd or early 2nd century BC, and at some point in antiquity was cut into eight pieces. One of the pieces is now, sadly, missing.

Right: *A Victorian representation of the back of an Etruscan mirror. Etruscan design was perceived as highly classical and aesthetic.*

Below: *This painted terra-cotta sarcophagus of a couple reclining dates back to the 6th century BC.*

rarely found, but a representation of such a book appears to have been placed in the Tomb of the Reliefs at Cerveteri.

In 1964 during the excavation of Pyrgi, the harbor district of Cerveteri, three gold plaques were found; two were written in Etruscan, but the third was in Phoenician, which can be easily translated by scholars. These parallel texts thus provided, like the Rosetta stone from Egypt, a way of understanding the Etruscan language, though in this case the Phoenician does not appear to have been a precise translation.

A fourth bronze tablet with an Etruscan text was also discovered at Pyrgi. These texts seem to relate to a dedication at the end of the 6th century BC by Thefarie Velianas, the ruler of Cerveteri (known in Etruscan as Cisra), to the Etruscan goddess Uni (Astarte in the Phoenician text), whose temple was located at Pyrgi. The temple itself seems to have been decorated with terra-cotta plaques, a type of decoration rather similar to the stone pedimental sculptures which were being incorporated into Greek temples at this time. This Phoenician association at Pyrgi relates to the historical sources which record a Carthaginian (western Phoenician)-Cerveteri alliance against the Greek colonists of Phokaia who were seeking to gain a foothold in the western Mediterranean at the time.

THE GRAND TOUR

The ancient Etruscans caught the public imagination in Britain through the travels and writings of George Dennis, who made his first tour of the cities of Tarquinia, Viterbo, and Orvieto in the early summer of 1842. Along with Samuel Ainsley, the artist, he visited Cerveteri in the late spring and early summer of 1843, making copious notes about the cemeteries. His accounts of these travels were to appear as *The Cities and Cemeteries of Etruria* in 1848.

Left: *The Tomb of the Reliefs, from the 3rd century BC, was designed to be as home-like and comfortable as possible for its dead inmates. Beams and pillars imitate the decoration in an Etruscan house, and couches cut into the walls offer seating for the dead while they banquet.*

ATHENS

SEARCH FOR THE
BIRTH OF DEMOCRACY

The layout of the ancient city of Athens was well documented in ancient literature. In particular, the travel writer Pausanias, advising Roman tourists in the mid-2nd century AD, described many of its key monuments, including the agora, home of the Athenian democracy. Modern scholars searching for the site of the agora had agreed it was to the north of the Athenian acropolis, west of the visible remains of the Roman market area, and east of the hill on which stood the Hephaisteion, a 5th-century BC temple popularly known as the Theseion. So this was where the search began.

Right: *A reconstruction of the Athenian agora as it might have looked in the 6th century BC.*

GREECE

Athens

Acquiring the land

After the war with Turkey in the early 1920s the Greek population living in Asia Minor began to return to Greece. Land in Athens was at a premium, making it difficult for Greek archaeologists to acquire the land around the agora for excavation. First an unsuccessful political attempt was made to acquire the land from private owners in 1924. When this failed, the area was allocated to the American School of Classical Studies at Athens. In return the school agreed to build private housing in the area. John D. Rockefeller, Jr. came to the rescue and put forward the money; he was eventually to give more than $1 million toward the excavations. Work was commenced in late May 1931 by Theodore Leslie Shear, and has continued, except for a break during World War II, ever since.

Shear's initial work confirmed the layout of the area known from Pausanias's description of the agora. The first buildings to be identified were those nestling at the foot of the hill on the west side of the site, the Royal Stoa (colonnade) and the Stoa of Zeus Eleutherios. The Royal Stoa was known from Pausanias and other

Below: *The excavated site of the public square of the agora. The public space, open to all citizens, marked out by stones called* horoi, *was conceived as a physical representation of the new political doctrine of democracy.*

ancient political texts to be the place where one of the senior magistrates of the city of Athens, the Archon Basileus, could be consulted. Indeed, further work has shown that copies of the laws given by Solon, the early 6th-century BC lawgiver, were put on display in this building, but probably in later extensions which projected forward from the main colonnade.

One of the most cherished features of the Athenian democracy was its law, and the access for all its citizens to the legal system.

Excavations in the northeast corner of the agora revealed the remains of a square building. At one of the entrances was a box which contained a number of pot shards (ballots) used by the jurors.

The Athenians were eager to protect their democracy. One of the safeguards known from political texts was the institution of ostracism, the means by which the citizens could cast votes against any individual who was perceived as a threat. These votes were called *ostraka*. If enough votes were cast against any one individual, that person was sent into exile.

During the excavations in the agora and elsewhere in the city, a number of broken pot shards, apparently used as *ostraka*, came to light inscribed with the names of famous Athenian politicians such as Themistocles (who brought about the defeat of the Persians in 480 and 479 BC).

A study of the handwriting reveals that some of these *ostraka* were cut by the same hand. This suggests that these ostracisms may have been manipulated by skillful politicians who issued the shards to illiterate voters.

Right: *A painted terra-cotta ostrakon (pottery shard) inscribed with the name of the politician and naval strategist Themistocles.*

Excavating democracy As excavations continued along the eastern edge of the hill, archaeologists uncovered a series of buildings. One of the most unusual was a circular structure, with an inner radius of 30 feet (8.45m), built in about 460 BC. This they believed to be the Tholos where the presiding tribe of the Athenian democracy was based during their period of office. One ancient political document, known as *The Constitution of the Athenians*, noted that the Tholos could be used as a communal dining room for those on duty. Perhaps most interestingly, however, this was the building to which Socrates was called before the Thirty Tyrants, who had seized power in Athens in 403 BC after the Peloponnesian War with the rival city states of Sparta, Corinth, and their allies.

Next to the Tholos was a square building where the Athenian *boule* or council of 500 met. This might have been constructed after the expulsion of the Peisistratid tyranny at the end of the 6th century BC. Cleisthenes had then reformed the Athenian constitution, creating 10 tribes (replacing the traditional four), at the instigation of the Delphic oracle. Fifty men from each tribe had then formed the *boule*. Outside the building, archaeologists discovered a long base which, from Pausanias's description, they believed to be the long, raised plinth that displayed statues representing the 10 Athenian heroes for whom the 10 tribes had been named. This sculptural group was used as a place to display notices – such as deployment orders for troops – relating to each of the tribes.

The agora was also a place where public achievements were celebrated. On the north side, open to the square, was a colonnaded building known as the

Painted Stoa. This was decorated by famous Athenian artists around 460 BC. Inside were scenes which included the famous battle of Marathon of 490 BC, when an Athenian force defeated the Persians who invaded eastern Attica to punish Athens for siding with the Greek cities of Asia Minor. Inside this stoa were trophies from victorious campaigns. One of these was a mighty bronze shield with the Greek inscription, "The Athenians from the Lakedaimonians [the Spartans] at Pylos." This had clearly been captured during the Athenian victory of 424 BC at Pylos in the early phase of the Peloponnesian War.

CLUES TO LIFESTYLE

Some of the most important statues celebrated the Tyrant-slayers who had killed the brother of the tyrant of Athens in the late 6th century BC, thereby bringing about the return of democracy. This potent symbol was looted by the Persians when they took the city of Athens in 480 BC, but it was replaced by the Athenians a few years later. Although the statues have not survived, a number of images of them are known. Most famous of these is a plaster cast of one of the heads found in a Roman workshop at Baiae in the Bay of Naples, where lifesized bronze replicas of original Greek statues were being created.

As well as being the birthplace of democracy, the agora was also home to more humble trades. To the south-west of the agora, the excavators found a house, thought to date to the late 5th century BC, which contained a number of iron hob-nails. Among the other finds from the house was a fragmentary pottery drinking cup bearing the name of Simon. Some scholars are trying to link this man with the shoemaker who was known to the philosopher Socrates.

HERCULANEUM
A TOWN FROZEN IN TIME

On August 24, in the year AD 79, the volcanic dome of Vesuvius erupted, engulfing the Roman cities of Pompeii and Herculaneum in ash and mud. These cities, lying on the Bay of Naples in Italy, completely disappeared from view. Pompeii was covered with a layer of pumice and Herculaneum with a layer of volcanic mud up to 65 feet (20 m) deep. Archaeologists estimate that a cubic mile (4 cubic km) of ash was ejected, sending a plume some 20 miles (32 km) into the sky. The buried towns were not, however, forgotten thanks to vivid accounts of the disaster by Pliny the Younger, whose uncle, Pliny the Elder, died in the eruption while commanding the Roman fleet at Misenum.

Early investigation

From time to time, evidence of the two cities buried by the eruption started to appear. The first building to be identified at Herculaneum was the theater, following an exploration in 1709. During this excavation a number of statues were removed from the site and some of the headless bronze riders found there were sadly melted down, as one contemporary account put it, "to make two great medallions . . . with the Pourtraits [sic] of the King and Queen of Naples." The first serious excavations at Herculaneum began in 1738, at the prompting of the mother of Ferdinand I, King of the Two Sicilies. The excavations soon attracted visitors making the Grand Tour of Italy. Lady Mary Wortley Montagu visited "the remains of the ancient city of Hercolana" in December 1740, where she was told "there was a Theatre entire with all the Scenes and ancient Decorations."

The method used to excavate the remains at Herculaneum, where the volcanic ash and mud had hardened to make widespread exploration very

ITALY

Herculaneum

Background: *The House of the Deer at the buried city of Herculaneum.*

PRESERVING ORGANIC MATERIALS

One of the most exciting features of the excavations at Herculaneum was that organic finds were preserved by the hot mud which enveloped the city. Thus, as archaeologists cut through the solid mud, they found carbonized remains – even including bread. In one bakery, the pastry cook, Patuleius Felix, had stamped his monogram onto the food. It could still be read in the carbonized remains.

Of particular interest at Herculaneum were the wooden fittings from houses, including doors and furniture, such as in the aptly named "House of the Carbonized Furniture." Wooden doors were discovered preserved in the "House of the Wooden Partition." Another house contained a wooden shrine (*sacellum*). This had been used to hold the household gods (*lares*).

Traces have been found of a wooden cross, set into the wall of one of the upstairs rooms in the "House of the Bicentenary." Some have wondered if this indicates that there was a Christian chapel at Herculaneum, though the decorative use of the cross at such an early date might be unexpected.

Such remains were in contrast to Pompeii, where organic materials, including human bodies, decayed, leaving air pockets in the mass of pumice and ash. These remains were restored by filling the holes with plaster, thus obtaining a cast of what had originally rested within.

Below: *Most of the bodies in Pompeii decayed in their shroud of pumice, leaving holes which could be filled with plaster to make eerily life-like casts. Such exhibits were particularly fascinating to Victorian travelers.*

Above: *Volcanic mud preserved many wooden structures in Herculaneum, even though they had been partially burned or scorched by the wave of hot air that hit the town once Vesuvius had erupted. This is a door in what was once the public baths.*

HUMAN REMAINS

Only a few bodies have been recovered in the excavations at Herculaneum. Two men, for example, were found at the baths. It is possible they worked there and had stayed at their posts while the patrons fled. It had been believed that the occupants of Herculaneum had plenty of time to evacuate their town in the face of the oncoming mud. However, 48 bodies have recently been discovered and have brought about another view.

Anthropologists from Naples University have concluded that these people died instantaneously when the heat-wave of some 750°F (400°C) from the eruption in effect swept through the town. The lack of bodies in the town may be due to evacuation at the first signs of the impending eruption, but this unfortunate group of 48, found sheltering near the shore, had stayed behind for some reason.

Above: *An archaeologist excavates a skeleton from the Herculaneum mud in 1982.*

difficult, was for tunnelers (who were known locally as *cavamonti*) to dig until they found the remains of a building. They then excavated trenches alongside the newly revealed walls. When the English traveler, Robert Adam, visited the town in April 1755 he recorded, "We traversed an amphitheatre with the light of torches and pursued the tracks of palaces, their porticoes and different doors, division walls and mosaic pavements." The antiquities that were recovered from these underground structures were taken in processions to the newly established museum in Naples. Unfortunately once exploration of each building ceased, the tunnels collapsed. The falling rock damaged the architectural remains and made further investigation unsafe in most cases.

MORE RECENT FINDS

From then on, archaeological exploration around the Bay of Naples seems to have focused, at least for the Roman remains, on the town of Pompeii. Further archaeological work does not seem to have resumed at Herculaneum until 1828, when one of the original 18th-century tunnels was rediscovered. Plans to resume large-scale excavations at Herculaneum started in the early 20th century and, as a result, one section of the town has now been uncovered. This consists essentially of a series of blocks dissected by two north–south roads, and three east–west streets (which originally extended to the sea).

A number of the major public facilities of this small town have been uncovered in this area. The main urban baths, filling part of one of the city blocks, consisted of cold, warm, and hot areas, an exercise yard (*palaestra*), as well as separate areas for men and women. Another set of baths, "the Suburban Baths," were at the southwest corner of the excavations, near the ancient shoreline.

Some of the explorations at Herculaneum have revealed highly significant details. The wealthy, seaside flavor of the ancient town is reflected in some of the houses on its western edge. For example, the "House of the Deer," named after its garden sculptures of deer being hunted by dogs, originally had terraces facing the sea. Another of the luxurious villas, now known as the "Villa of the Papyri," was discovered by tunneling in 1750. Its name comes from the library of several thousand philosophical works that it housed. In particular there was an emphasis in the collection on works by Philodemos of Gadara, who was said to have had Lucius Calpurnius Piso, the

father-in-law of Julius Caesar, as his patron. As a result some scholars have linked the house with this family. The charred documents unearthed from the Villa of the Papyri were so fragile that they had to be examined on special supports that were designed by a member of the Vatican Library, who was familiar with the delicacy of ancient documents like these. The garden belonging to the villa may have contained up to 60 statues cast in bronze, including a likeness of the Hellenistic ruler Seleucus Nicator.

The Villa of the Papyri at Herculeneum was so elegant and provided scholars with so much information that it was used as the inspiration and the physical model for the design of the Jean Paul Getty Museum in Malibu, California.

Such fragile finds as those priceless documents unearthed in the library are rarely discovered in sites which were abandoned and left to decay. They provide highly significant information for scholars seeking to obtain insight into life in an Italian provincial town during the 1st century AD.

VINDOLANDA

LETTERS FROM ROME

During the Roman occupation of northern Britain, a fort was established at Vindolanda close to the later line of the fixed frontier, Hadrian's Wall. The site came to the notice of antiquarians in the early 18th century, not least through the publication of a number of inscriptions which helped to confirm the Latin name of the fort and its settlement. A description by Christopher Hunter in 1702 mentioned the remains of the bath-house, with a "pavement . . . tinged black with Smoak." The first scientific exploration of the fort was in 1930 under the direction of Eric Birley. However, it was to be eclipsed by excavations elsewhere and was not renewed until after World War II, by Birley's son, Robin, who felt that the civilian settlement might have hidden secrets to reveal.

Discovery of the tablets

During Robin Birley's excavations in March 1973, he unearthed a trail of unusual wooden boards, some damaged by fire. Traces of ink could be made out on the boards, and Birley soon realized that these were writing tablets. He decided to study them under an infrared light in an attempt to make out the words, to see what the mysterious tablets could tell him.

It appears that in the late spring or early summer of AD 105, when the military unit, the 9th cohort of Batavians, was transferred to the Danube frontier to assist with the emperor Trajan's campaign against Dacia, the fort's archive of writing tablets was deliberately destroyed. Unfortunately for the person assigned to the task, it seems that the fire was lit on a windy day and some of the documents blew away from the fire onto the muddy ground in the fort. There they lay and were preserved for nearly 2,000 years. Moreover, it would appear that the bonfire itself, which even contained footwear, was extinguished by a storm and some 300 of the letters were found slightly charred but still readable. Although incomplete, this fascinating archive provided a useful parallel for the many literary and administrative papyri that had already been discovered in Egypt. Up to this

point, the Egyptian papyri had been the only source of detail about the daily workings of the Roman Empire, which rarely appeared in historical texts or formal inscriptions. The Vindolanda archive would add to this knowledge.

Careful study of the Vindolanda tablets – which were by now in excess of 1,600 documents – yielded more information. One of the tablets was dated precisely to May 18 (or in Roman terms, 15 days before the *kalends* of June); its archaeological context suggests a date of around AD 90. It mentions that the unit of the 1st cohort of Tungrians (the predecessors of the Batavians) had a unit strength of 752 men and 6 centurions (or officers). However, over 300 of the men were on detachment to Coria (probably the Roman fort at Corbridge to the east) and another officer was absent in London, which only left 296 men and one centurion at the fort of Vindolanda. The document also states that not all of them were in a fit state for combat: some were sick, wounded, or suffering from some sort of eye infection. It would seem that less than half the unit was available for active duty at Vindolanda.

Left: *Charred fragments of one of the 300 wooden writing tablets found preserved in the Vindolanda mud. This one mentions the writer's anticipation of a supply of socks and underwear. The personal nature of many of the letters offers a welcome insight into the everyday life of the mighty Roman Empire.*

Below: *Vindolanda from above; the remains of the fort can be seen in the centre of a walled enclosure. The civilian settlement, the area on which most archaeologists have focused, lies outside the fortress walls.*

In one of the letters found at Vindolanda, Lepdina, wife of the unit's commander Flavius Cerialis, received an invitation from the wife of a garrison commander at Kirkbride on the west coast of Britain to attend a birthday party on September 11 (the year is unknown). This might be one of the earliest letters written by a woman to have survived from antiquity.

Below: *The wives of soldiers posted to Britain kept in touch with friends by means of letters.*

Right: *Russell Crowe in the film* Gladiator *plays a Roman commander. Life for the common soldier in the outposts of the Roman Empire was often harsh.*

Another letter refers to a set of hides which were at Catterick to the south, but which could not be transferred to Vindolanda because of the poor state of the roads in between. A useful dating fix for the letters is provided by the mention of a man in one of the documents, Lucius Naeratius Marcellus, who is known to have been governor of Britain from AD 101 to 103. Some of the detail in the letters is quite personal – for example, one of the men was expecting a delivery of some woolen socks and undergarments, no doubt to help him withstand the rigors of a northern winter.

Mixed in with military documents were those relating to the family life of the unit's commander, Flavius Cerialis. He was a Roman citizen from Batavia. Clearly life up on the frontier was not entirely warlike; one letter to the commander of a neighboring fort begged for some nets so that he could go hunting. Some of the other Vindolanda letters provide insights into the Romans' attitude toward the local population who are referred to as *Brittunculi* which can be translated as "little Brits." These letters have provided new insights into written Latin as well as variations in spellings.

ORGANIC REMAINS

Excavations in the water-logged conditions at Vindolanda continue to uncover organic remains which have rarely survived elsewhere. One recent find is a large, complex, timbered building which originally had plastered walls. At least one

Above: *Reconstructed timber posts as they would have appeared at the fort site. Behind them stands a modern reconstruction of a stone wall with a turret and a milecastle.*

fragment of wall-painting has survived and, as it seems to be contemporary with the Hadrianic fort at the site (dating to AD 120–30), it has been suggested that this might have been accommodation for the emperor Hadrian himself, who had perhaps come to Vindolanda to supervise the construction of a fixed frontier, which became known as Hadrian's Wall.

A range of other organic material has been preserved on the site. For example, there appears to have been a tannery in operation at Vindolanda, using the hides of animals such as oxen, sheep, and dogs. The workshop appears to have made shoes as well as other leather items; the small size of some of the shoes found at the site suggests that they were intended for women or children. Elsewhere on the site fragments of textiles were discovered. One piece was decorated with a purple stripe, the mark of the Roman elite, and might have originally formed part of the wardrobe of the garrison commander.

Below: *Many artifacts have been found in the excavation of the civilian settlement, including this ornate metal belt accessory, with colored enamel decoration.*

Exciting finds at Vindolanda continue. For example, a recently discovered Latin inscription, probably from an elaborate mausoleum, mentions a soldier "killed in the war." Many scholars believe that this may allude to the uprisings in the early 2nd century AD which led to Hadrian's decision to construct his wall across northern Britain. In this and many other cases, Vindolanda is proving to be a major source for new documents which shed light on the Roman occupation of Britain.

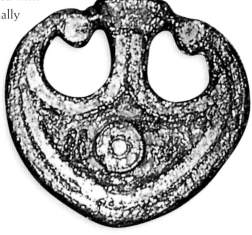

SUTTON HOO

SEAFARING KINGS

At Sutton Hoo on the River Deben in eastern England, between the town of Ipswich and the North Sea coast, lies a group of round burial mounds. In 1938, these were on the estate of Edith May Pretty, a widow who had traveled widely and had an interest in the past. Deciding that these mounds should be investigated, she engaged the services of Basil Brown, a self-taught local archaeologist who had many years of experience excavating in the soils of East Anglia. On June 20, Brown and two workers from Mrs. Pretty's estate started excavation.

Right: *Instigator of the dig, Edith May Pretty, observes Stuart Piggott, W.F. Grimes, Sir John Forsdyke, and T.D. Kendrick crouch in the dust of the Burial Chamber to examine the shoulder clasps unearthed there.*

GREAT
BRITAIN
● **Sutton Hoo**

Above: *Excavations proceed apace in 1939. The whole of the ship's hull area has been uncovered and the iron nails that once held the ship's planks together are visible. Using computer technology to plot the position of the nails (superimposed image) archaeologists have been able to accurately recreate the shape of the ship's prow.*

A slow start During the first season of excavations in June and July 1938, Brown and his assistants opened three of the smaller mounds, all of which were found to have been robbed in antiquity. Enough finds remained to establish that the mounds had covered cremation burials from the Anglo-Saxon period. Among the key finds were a number of iron bolt-like objects which Brown quickly identified as "ship rivets," which were used to hold together the planks of ships in the 1st millennium AD. Recognizing these and correctly inferring their purpose held considerable significance for future investigations at Sutton Hoo.

Although the results of the first campaign were disappointing, Mrs. Pretty was not discouraged. Thus, on May 8, 1939, another season of work began. Mrs. Pretty directed Brown to focus on a large mound that had been by-passed the previous year because it showed signs of disturbance. Within several days, Brown had uncovered a row of ship rivets in his trench. Brown deduced that he had uncovered the end of a buried boat whose wood had long since decayed but whose rivets had remained in their original locations, trapped by the matrix of soil. Ship burials were already known from Viking-age sites of the 9th and 10th centuries AD in Scandinavia and the British Isles, so finding a boat under a mound was not entirely unexpected. Nonetheless, tracing the evidence for a

Below: *Reconstruction of the prow of the ship made by the staff of the Science Museum, London.*

decayed boat without any of the wood still present required very careful and meticulous excavation. Brown established the outline of the boat rivet by rivet, then began to follow the rows of rivets down into the depths of the vessel, tracing the inner surface of the 88-foot (27-m) hull.

EXPERT HELP

Word spread among archaeologists of a ship burial in East Anglia and, in early June, Charles Phillips of the University of Cambridge visited the site. He was astonished by what he saw and alerted the British Museum in London. They soon decided to appoint a team of experienced archaeologists to continue the excavations, and Phillips was asked to take charge. In 1939, with World War II looming, it was not easy to assemble a team of archaeologists. Phillips, however, found volunteers who were, or would later become, some of the most distinguished figures in the field, including Stuart and Peggy Piggott, O.G.S. Crawford and W.F. Grimes. On July 8, 1939 he assumed control of the Sutton Hoo excavations. Brown apparently accepted this takeover with equanimity.

THE CENTRAL CHAMBER

Brown had not yet touched the central burial chamber, in which excavation commenced on July 13. Over the next 17 days, the most remarkable burial deposit ever found in Britain came to light, yielding 263 objects, many made from gold or decorated with precious gems. Mrs. Pretty decided the finds should be deposited in the British Museum. Most of the team returned to their vacations at the end of July; Phillips and Brown finished the documentation. On August 18, the Anglo-Saxon historian H.M. Chadwick visited the site and declared it to be the burial of Raedwald, King of East Anglia from AD 599 to 625. No one questioned this interpretation. Meanwhile, with the outbreak of war, the finds were stored in the safety of the London Underground. They were unpacked in 1945 by Rupert Bruce-Mitford, who would make the analysis of the Sutton Hoo finds his life's work until his death in 1994.

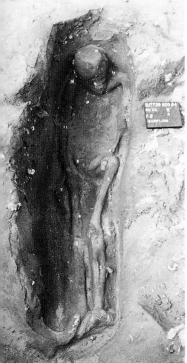

Above: In 1969, exploration of flat ground between the Sutton Hoo mounds revealed buried "sand bodies." These were corpses of people buried without coffins. As the flesh and bone decayed they were replaced by crusted sand, producing a lifelike but extremely fragile "cast" of the original body.

Right: A reconstruction of the silver and gold helmet that was found in the burial mound. The original helmet was found in pieces and may have been broken for symbolic reasons before being put into the grave.

Above: *Shoulder clasps made from gold, richly decorated with garnets and millefiore glass.*

Left: *A solid gold belt buckle, weighing almost 1 lb (450 g), is decorated with intricate lacing patterns with typical Anglo Saxon bird and animal motifs.*

The items uncovered in the central burial chamber of the largest mound included an iron helmet, coat of mail, axe-hammer, and sword; many different textiles, including wall hangings and cloaks; a wooden shield with bronze decoration; a solid gold belt buckle; gold shoulder clasps inset with glass and garnets; a purse with gold decoration that held 37 Frankish gold coins; a stack of 10 silver bowls; a large silver dish, 28 inches (70 cm) in diameter, that had the stamp of the Byzantine emperor Anastasius I (AD 491–518); silver spoons inscribed in Greek; drinking horns decorated with silver fittings; a large bronze bowl from North Africa with images of animals; a wooden lyre; three Celtic bronze hanging bowls; various wooden tubs and buckets; and a stone "sceptre."

Return to Sutton Hoo

Excavations were renewed in 1965–70 and in 1983–92. These investigations established that Sutton Hoo was the site of a cemetery for the Anglo-Saxon elite between the late 6th and late 7th centuries AD. The earliest burials were cremations placed in bronze bowls under mounds; one such mound is surrounded by flat burials, possibly those of retainers. Later, uncremated bodies were buried under mounds. Under one lay a young man in a wooden coffin with his weapons, a bucket, and a cauldron, while his horse lay in a separate chamber nearby. It appears that the mound excavated by Brown and Phillips was one of the latest burials, perhaps the final one.

In the last decade, archaeologists have retreated from the identification of the ship burial as that of Raedwald, but they all agree Sutton Hoo is the largest concentration of high-ranking burials in England. The occupants were probably Kings of East Anglia who flourished during the early 7th century AD. They were defiant pagans on the margin of the Christian Merovingian empire. Of particular interest is the evidence for their Scandinavian connections. The ship burial bears a resemblance to the chieftains' graves at Vendel and Valsgärde, north of Stockholm, as well as the royal grave at Gamla Uppsala in Sweden. The helmet and shield boss from Sutton Hoo closely resemble artifacts from these sites. This is not to suggest that the Kings of East Anglia came from Sweden, but that in both these areas the elite had similar ideologies. The sea was not a barrier, but a communication route linking these two regions as well as other points in Europe.

NOVGOROD
LIFE IN MEDIEVAL RUSSIA

Novgorod, situated where the Volkhov River drains from Lake Ilmen on its way north to Lake Ladoga, is one of the oldest towns in Russia. It was an important city on the network of rivers and lakes that formed major communication corridors during the first millennium AD. Its waterlogged clay soil has led to an extraordinary quality of preservation, not only of the structural wood that formed house walls and timber streets, but also of leather and wooden utensils, musical instruments, and even toys. These artifacts offer an invaluable insight into life in medieval Novgorod.

Viking trade During the 8th and 9th centuries AD, a series of fortified settlements was established along the Volkhov River. These were apparently trading centers that grew up as Viking merchants penetrated into the Russian interior and conducted business with the local Slavic peoples. At Gorodische, located about 1¼ miles (2 km) upstream from modern Novgorod, archaeological research has revealed the presence of a mixed Slavic and Scandinavian population. Known to the Vikings as Holmgård, this was a center of local craft production in addition to being a trading center. Amulets carved with runic inscriptions as well as pottery, beads, and combs in typical Scandinavian style confirm the Viking presence. The site of Gorodische/Holmgård has become identified in historical accounts with the Viking prince Rurik, who was invited in AD 862 to restore order in the region.

However, in about AD 930, the center of settlement along the upper Volkhov shifted downstream from Gorodische/Holmgård to Novgorod. Over the next several centuries, Novgorod emerged as a large, prosperous city situated on a major trade route between the Baltic and Byzantium. Its population continued to be a mixture of Slavs and Scandinavians. The Viking presence in northwestern Russia never took the form of a colonization, but the social elite were often of Scandinavian origin or descent. They adopted Slavic names and began to mix with the local inhabitants to establish the early Russian state.

RUSSIA

Novgorod

Excavations begin

Large-scale archaeological excavations of the city, and documentary evidence from early Russian chronicles, have enabled scholars to learn much about life in Novgorod in medieval times. Excavations began in 1929 under the direction of Artemii Artsikhovsky and have continued ever since under a variety of directors. Since 1951, the Novgorod excavations have been more or less continuous and have taken place in many parts of the town. The clay soil which lies beneath Novgorod impedes drainage, so the archaeological deposits in the city center, which are up to 20 feet (6 m) deep in some places, have been waterlogged. This has created ideal preservation conditions, especially of organic remains such as wood and leather. Analysis of the tree rings in the larger timbers, used for constructing house walls and timber streets, has resulted in the development of a chronology that permits the dating of structures to within 15 to 25 years.

Far left: *Sample of Cyrillic script written on birchbark from medieval Novgorod. It is a deed written out by a man named Mstislav on behalf of the Yyuryev monastery in around AD 1130.*

Below: *Excavations in 1967 revealed streets made from pine planks about 1 foot (30 cm) thick, lined with the remains of wooden huts and some grander mansions with private gated courtyards. Below the wooden walkway is the 11th-century layer of wood and stone chippings.*

TRADE LINKS

Between the 11th and 15th centuries, Novgorod was linked to a trading network that encompassed much of northern Europe and extended as far as the Indian Ocean. A remarkable array of goods passed through Novgorod, including wine, incense, spices, nuts, exotic woods, and cloth. The city was a hub of mercantile activity with Scandinavian merchants and Slavic artisans and traders.

The wealth and power that came from such commerce enabled it to emerge as the leading town in the north of the nascent Russian state. Products from this region, especially furs and wax, were traded to the west and produced immense wealth on the island of Gotland in the Baltic Sea, which had special ties with the Novgorod area. The wax trade was especially lucrative, due to the demand for candles in churches throughout Europe. Merchants from Visby, on Gotland, established a trading operation in Novgorod, while merchants from Novgorod maintained a similar center in Visby.

WOODEN STREETS AND HOUSES

A network of winding streets forms the plan of ancient Novgorod. Due to the damp conditions in the town, the streets were surfaced with timbers. The paving method involved first laying three or four lines of thin birch or pine poles down the length of the street. On this footing was laid a deck of split logs of about 16–20 inches (40–50 cm) in diameter side-by-side across the width of the street. As lower levels became wet again, the street was raised by adding another layer of logs. Along Saints Cosmas and Damian Street, a total of 28 paving levels have been identified and dated by their tree rings. The earliest street at this location was laid down in 953 and the latest in 1462.

Novgorod's streets were lined with timber buildings, and the remarkable preservation of their lower walls permits their reconstruction in some detail. The inhabitants dwelt in log cabins that were built in combinations of several basic modules. Some of these houses stood two or even three stories tall. They were organized into compounds that consisted of a house and its outbuildings – stables, storehouses, and workshops – around a yard. A stake fence separated the compound from the street and from adjacent buildings. Artisans who worked in these compounds manufactured leather goods, jewelry, shoes, metal and glass objects, and pottery. Specific crafts predominated in different districts in the city.

The manuscripts The most remarkable finds at Novgorod have been nearly 1,000 birch bark manuscripts, known as *beresty*, preserved in the waterlogged deposits. The *beresty* date from between the middle of the 11th century and the early 15th century, at the zenith of Novgorod's prosperity. The first of these manuscripts was discovered in 1951 in a level dating from between 1369 and 1409, but other manuscripts were later found in earlier levels. The *beresty* were made from pieces of birch bark that were first boiled to remove the coarse outer layers. The soft inner layers were then inscribed using styluses made from bone or metal, without ink. The *beresty* describe numerous aspects of life in Novgorod, from mundane household records and business receipts to legal, governmental, and commercial discussions. Since only about 2 percent of the area of ancient Novgorod has been excavated, archaeologists have estimated that over 20,000 *beresty* remain buried in the medieval layers under the modern town. Even love letters are among the texts found so far. These documents indicate that a large segment of the population could read and write, and provide a detailed glimpse of urban life in medieval Russia.

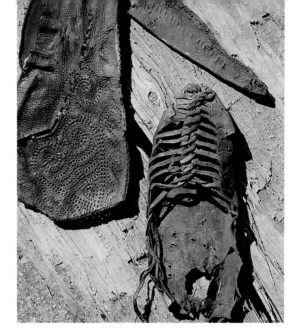

Above: *Fragments of a child's leather shoe, well preserved in the waterlogged soil of the area.*

Below: *Medieval Novgorod was divided into five autonomous settlements. It was in the Nerevsky settlement (on the bottom left of the plan) that Professor Artsikhovsky discovered the first of the famous birch bark manuscripts.*

Troy

Altai

Zhoukoudian

Çatal Höyük

Ulu Burun

Dunhuang

Ebla

Jericho
Jerusalem

Masada

Babylon
Ur

Mawangdui

Mehrgarh

Mohenjo Daro

Khok Phanom Di

SECTION THREE
ASIA

The continent of Asia is the region that will probably surprise us the most in future years. The fantastically rich remains of China and the former Soviet Union have, until recently, been inaccessible to the west, but are becoming better known, as more exploration and discoveries take place over this vast area. It may yet prove true that Africa was not the only cradle of humankind, and very early dates are already emerging from Asian hominid sites. Even in those parts of the continent that have long been the scene of extensive archaeological work, such as Mesopotamia and the Bible lands, new finds emerge at a rapid pace and are constantly changing our perception of the past, especially our understanding of the rise of agriculture and of cities, as well as the major role of trade and warfare in shaping the ancient world.

Asia has so much to offer, from fossil humans to Buddhist texts, from ziggurats to frozen Scythian tombs, and from the farthest outposts of Greek and Roman influence to the splendors of Angkor. Meticulous modern excavations such as that of Khok Phanom Di, in Thailand, exemplify the vast amount of varied information that even a single site can yield to the latest techniques of the archaeological detective.

PEKING MAN

DRAGON BONES OR HUMAN REMAINS?

In 1914 Johan Gunnar Andersson, a Swedish geologist, accepted a post as mining advisor to the Chinese government. The many geological deposits containing fossils that he examined in his work aroused his interest in China's past, and he sought and investigated both fossils and more recent remains. These investigations brought him to a vital link in the search for early man.

Dragon bones

Andersson's task of discovering fossil sites was made easier by a peculiar element of the Chinese pharmacopia. Ancient bones believed to come from dragons were ground up and used as a general remedy, and Andersson recognized that these so-called dragon bones were in fact fossils of many different varieties. He collected information on the location of deposits containing these "dragon bones" and sent his assistants to investigate those that sounded promising.

One site identified in this way was Chicken Bone Hill, a deposit yielding many bird bones in a quarry at Zhoukoudian, a village 28 miles (45 km) south of Beijing. After Andersson had been working there for a while, a local man told him that much better dragon bones were available elsewhere in the neighborhood. This information led Andersson to a series of caves containing deposits rich in mammal fossils. He also noticed quartz flakes and surmised that humans had lived at the same time as the fossilized mammals.

The fossils were taken to Sweden for study by their excavator, Andersson's assistant, Otto Zdansky. In 1926, he sent Andersson some startling information:

Above: *The caves at Zhoukoudian, where Johan Gunnar Andersson inadvertently discovered* Homo erectus *remains, which became known as Peking Man. A local man had recommended the cave to the Swedish geologist as a good source of medicinal "dragon's bones."*

two of the many teeth excavated at the site appeared to be those of a hominid, a human ancestor. This remarkable and, at the time, controversial find was a stimulus to more extensive work at Zhoukoudian, with funding from the Rockefeller Foundation. Finds from the site were now studied by Davidson Black of the Peking Union Medical College and, following his death in 1934, by his distinguished colleague, the German anatomist Franz Weidenreich. The initial identification of hominid teeth was confirmed by the discovery of many more fossilized human remains, including three skulls. Eventually the remains of 40 individuals, including 15 children, were recovered. The creature the archaeologists found became popularly known as Peking Man.

ANALYZING PEKING MAN

At the time of this discovery, the human family tree had huge gaps in it. The Neanderthals were known and accepted as recent humans and *Australopithecus* had recently been identified as the first step on the path dividing ape and man. Between these extremes there was a long period in which many changes had

Far right: *Reconstructed model of a male Homo* erectus. *It is thought that H.* erectus *stood upright, and was stockily built, but slightly shorter than average modern humans.*

Right: *Excavation continued near the original Zhoukoudian cave in 1980, in the hope of finding more fossil evidence. The grid of white chalk marks on the wall helps the diggers keep track of their discoveries.*

PEKING MAN VANISHES

To settle the cannibalism debate the bones from Zhoukoudian need to be re-examined. Sadly, this is no longer possible. In 1941, China was on the brink of a Japanese invasion. Scholars asked what was to be done with the Zhoukoudian material when the enemy came. Casts of the bones had been made and shipped to the American Museum of Natural History in New York. Would it be better to ship out the bones too, despite a previous decision that they should never leave China, or to risk them being taken by the Japanese? The staff of Peking Union Medical College were unable to decide.

At the eleventh hour, they decided to send the fossils to America. They were carefully packed and dispatched with a party of U.S. Marines who were due to sail home. The Marines were held up at several points on their journey and eventually captured by the Japanese. The precious fossils have not been seen since. Were they lost at some point on the journey? Were they discarded as worthless by Japanese soldiers at the time of the capture? We shall probably never know.

Above: *Casts of a hominid skull, classified as* Homo erectus, *made from bone fragments found in the 1930s by paleoanthropologist Franz Weidenreich (1873–1948).*

occurred but few fossils were known. Some decades earlier, the Dutch physician Eugene Dubois had discovered one such transitional hominid in Java, which he named *Pithecanthropus* – apeman. This creature had been so ill received at first that Dubois eventually lost his reason. Much more acceptable had been Piltdown Man, which later turned out to be a fake and a red herring, but at this time was bedeviling and confusing the understanding of the path of human evolution.

Initially called *Sinanthropus* (Chinese man), these new Chinese specimens showed strong similarities to Javanese *Pithecanthropus*. By 1939 both were recognized as a single species, known as *Homo erectus* (upright man).

The Zhoukoudian specimens represent nearly a third of all extant fossils of this species and are a large enough group for comparative studies to be undertaken on them. Detailed analyses revealed that Peking Man walked upright (as had his remote australopithecine ancestors). His brain was about two-thirds the size of the modern human brain and he had a large forward-projecting jaw with big teeth but no chin. Whether or not he could speak was much debated, but recent studies suggest that his capacity for speech was limited.

The life of Peking Man

When the bones of *Homo erectus* were discovered at Zhoukoudian, little was known about the lives of our early ancestors. Did they hunt? Were they capable of modifying their environment? Finds from the Zhoukoudian caves gave some clues. Substantial deposits of ash were excavated here, with the remains of burnt bone and other material. It seemed clear that Peking Man had succeeded in taming fire, an invaluable tool. Without fire for warmth it is unlikely that humans could have colonized temperate regions like northern China. The climate half a million years ago, when occupation of the caves began, was much as it is today. Fire also offered protection against wild animals, as well as the means to cook food, making it easier to digest. Zhoukoudian may still be the earliest documented use of fire, although some earlier claims have been made, but strong doubt has recently been cast on whether the deposits at the site do indeed constitute ash from fires.

THE CANNIBALISM QUESTION

The majority of the bones in the Zhoukoudian deposits came from deer and it is probable, though not certain, that these were hunted by the people who dwelt in the caves, along with other animals like pigs and sheep. As well as eating the meat, they split the bones to extract marrow. Fossilized feces show that they also ate berries, seeds, fruits, and nuts. Weidenreich's analysis of the bones from the site suggested another, startling, source of meat: *Homo erectus* themselves.

Was Peking Man a cannibal? Weidenreich believed so, for the skulls from the caves appeared to have been butchered, with the face removed and the base of the skull enlarged to extract the brain. Subsequent discoveries at sites elsewhere in the world have been interpreted in the same way. But there are strong doubts in most cases. At Zhoukoudian it is likely that the damage was inflicted by hyenas. The number of hyena bones found nearby show they were common in the neighborhood.

ÇATAL HÖYÜK

ARTISTIC CREATIVITY

Although they are working with evidence 7,000–10,000 years old, archaeologists researching the neolithic period in the Near East are searching for the roots of the modern world. The great prehistorian V. Gordon Childe spoke of the "neolithic revolution" and although recent scholars emphasize the more gradual, and even fitful, changes of the period, its consequences were truly revolutionary. In this phase of human history, people started farming and keeping animals instead of hunting and collecting food, and eventually settled in ever larger villages.

Early work in the Near East Interest in the neolithic Near East grew enormously after World War II, when excavations at early farming communities in Israel, Syria, and Iraq started documenting early steps toward village life. The newly invented radiocarbon dating technique placed these steps as early as the eighth and seventh millennia BC. Life seemed to be simple and perhaps precarious at this time – small groups of farmers living in basic mud houses in villages 2½–5 acres (1–2 hectares) in size, prosperous enough to acquire some exotic goods like sea shells or obsidian from distant sources, but still needing to hunt animals and gather wild plants to supplement the fruits of their agricultural labor. This picture corresponded to what we might expect of early farming life.

A LARGER SETTLEMENT

But then James Mellaart, a flamboyant and controversial British archaeologist, began excavating at Çatal Höyük in south-central Turkey, not far from the great medieval religious city of Konya. Çatal Höyük ("fork mound" in Turkish) covers about 32 acres (13 hectares) and rises 55 feet (17 m) above the surrounding plain. As Mellaart's excavations between 1961 and 1965 showed, the entire mound (aside from an ephemeral later occupation at its summit) represents the accumulated remains and debris of a town that had been continuously rebuilt and renovated for over a thousand years from its foundation around 7000 BC. This alone shows impressive and important contrasts with the small villages so far explored in lands to the south.

The contents of this town were even more astonishing. In the areas Mellaart excavated, he uncovered solid blocks of mud houses sharing party walls, packed so closely together that many inhabitants must have entered their abodes through doorways in the roofs. The blocks included small, scattered courtyards or a single large central courtyard or open space. Inside, the houses were divided into several rooms fitted with plastered benches, storage bins, hearths, and low platforms for special household activities. A great many rooms also contained elaborate and highly varied ornamentation. The horns of wild bulls might be set into the tops of clay pedestals, or on modeled bulls' heads fixed to the wall. Sometimes animals, especially large wild cats, were modeled in relief in clay on the walls, and then painted. Frequently the walls bore painted decoration, often repeated geometric designs but also scenes of animal hunts, great vultures, and possibly a landscape dominated by an active volcano. This outpouring of artistic creativity, and the rich body of symbolic and mythical

Left: *An example of a small statuette, dated 8th–7th millennium BC. Archaeologists found many such figurines buried along with community members.*

Below: *Excavation has revealed a cross-section of a house in Çatal Höyük. The family vaults can be seen clearly.*

The material opulence evident in the graves and in the living areas indicates an effective economic system, and the artistic labor evident in so many rooms suggests both ample leisure time to devote to art and a very refined sense of expression. Indeed, the apparent cultic emphasis of so many rooms suggests an exceptionally religious attitude.

Efforts to account for this striking anomaly in the neolithic work often emphasized economic factors – according to one popular idea, Çatal Höyük prospered because it controlled access to an important nearby source of obsidian, a naturally occurring volcanic glass that societies in the rest of the Near East desired greatly. Traders from Çatal Höyük peddled obsidian as far as southern Jordan, 312 miles (500 km) away.

Right: *Faintly discernible wall painting from one of the smaller houses at Çatal Höyük. Such rich decoration in even the more modest dwellings indicates that the town was home to a thriving, wealthy, and civilized society.*

meaning it represented, was unparalleled in the neolithic world as it was understood during the 1960s, and forever changed our perception of it.

OTHER ART FORMS

Other aspects of the Çatal Höyük community excited considerable astonishment. The neolithic artists turned out exquisite creations in other media. Among the figurines in clay are statuettes of seated naked women with large breasts, sometimes shown in childbirth. Some of these mother goddess figures sit in very formal straight-backed chairs, the arms of which are decorated with animal figures. The workers of stone and bone made elaborate jewelry of imported and semi-precious materials, intricately carved knife handles, and vessels. Large seals were incised with geometric designs, which were perhaps used to color-stamp textiles. Much of this wealth ended up interred with burials of community members. Even the more ordinary industries could be exceptional: skilled toolmakers crafted delicate stone knives, weavers used flax as well as wool to make clothing (small fragments of which survived in some of the burials), and workers of clay made pottery. This was crude at first, but their mastery of clay improved during a time when it seemed no other societies in the Near East were experimenting with this craft.

Neolithic discoveries

But the 1960s were still early days for research into the neolithic. Since then, a number of excavations in Israel, Jordan, Syria, Turkey, Iraq, and Iran – the Fertile Crescent plus Anatolia – have revealed surprisingly sophisticated communities in many places. Some communities stand out for their size, rivaling or exceeding Çatal Höyük. The tradition of closely packed houses appears common in Anatolia, sometimes in sites older than Çatal Höyük. Other sites across the region contain evidence of elaborate building technologies, early pottery experimentation, wide-flung trading connections, and skillful craftsmanship. And some sites, especially in northern Syria and eastern Anatolia, reveal vibrant artistic and cultic traditions – sophisticated cultic monuments in stone, wall paintings, elaborate and often communal burial rituals. We now know that, during the seventh millennium BC in the Near East, there was an incredible burst of cultural energy.

In these terms, then, Çatal Höyük can no longer be seen as an anomaly. Yet the place continues to exert considerable fascination, for its wall decorations and other symbolic artifacts remain the richest and best preserved witnesses to early neolithic attitudes. So powerful is its attraction that a British-American group began a new program of excavation and study there in 1993. With an enviable budget and hundreds of archaeologists and other specialists, this renewed investigation will provide new reasons to marvel at the riches of Çatal Höyük.

ÇATAL HÖYÜK'S POPULATION

The town probably held 5,000 or more inhabitants, an amazing concentration of people in a time of relatively simple technological capabilities. All in all, Mellaart's reports of Çatal Höyük overturned all expectations of neolithic society in the Near East.

MEHRGARH

EARLY FARMERS OR EVIDENCE OF TRADE?

The existence of prosperous agricultural communities in the Indo-Iranian borderlands during the 4th and 5th millennia BC has long been known to archaeologists, but their origins were a mystery until the chance discovery of neolithic Mehrgarh in western Pakistan in the 1970s.

An unexpected find

In 1974 Jean-François and Catherine Jarrige began excavating a Chalcolithic settlement at Mehrgarh in the Kachi Plain of western Pakistan. Originally extensive, the settlement had been eroded by a change in the course of the Bolan River. To their surprise and delight, when they examined the section cut by the river through the site, they discovered far earlier deposits, situated at a lower level. Evidence here revealed that agriculture in the region went back to around 7000 BC. Right from the earliest period in the settlement, the site yielded abundant remains of plants in the form of carbonized grain and plant impressions in the mudbricks of which the settlement's houses were constructed. These showed that the early inhabitants of Mehrgarh had cultivated both barley and a little wheat. They hunted local game, such as gazelle, but also kept some domestic goats. Later they began to rear domestic cattle and sheep, both of which became increasingly important through time.

Below: *The ruins of the neolithic settlement of Mehrgarh date as far back as 6500 BC. Numerous excavations have provided archaeologists with a clearer picture of how early cultures developed a number of technologies to improve early farming practices.*

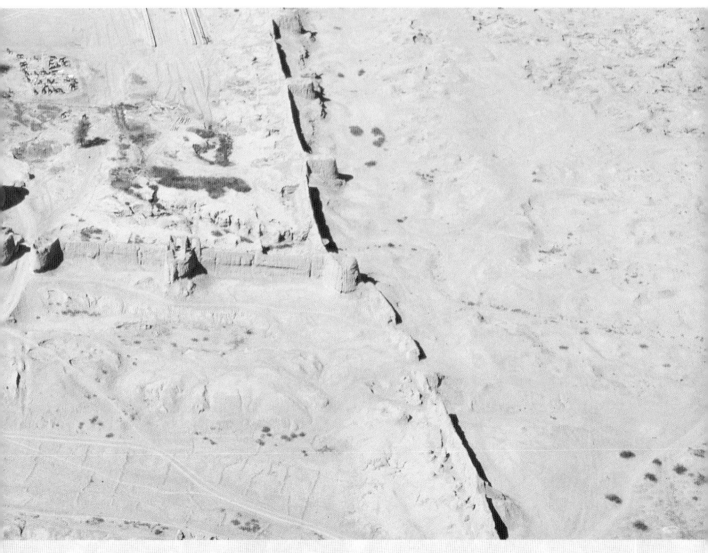

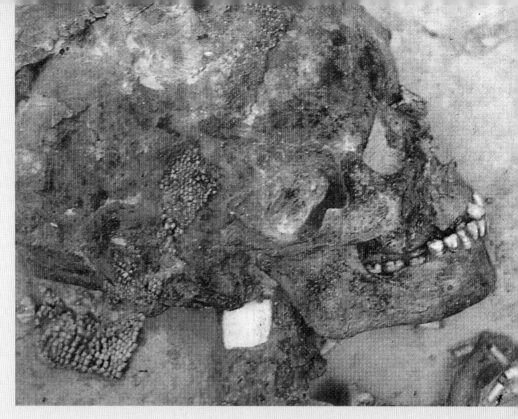

SEASONAL MIGRATION

The settlement of Mehrgarh was probably only occupied during the winter months. The region is hot in summer but mild in winter, while the adjacent uplands are the opposite. A pattern of seasonal movement still operates in the region; pastoralists graze their flocks in summer in the upland pastures of areas like the Quetta valley and congregate on the Kachi plain in winter. Before the development of animal husbandry, hunter-gatherers in the region would have followed wild herds in the same way.

LOCAL OR INTRODUCED?

Did the development of agriculture at Mehrgarh reflect local domestication or the introduction of domesticated animals and agricultural techniques from outside? By the time of the first settlement at Mehrgarh, farming was spreading from western Asia into adjacent regions. It was possible that western Asia was the source of farming in the Indo-Iranian borderlands. Or, this region might have been one where agriculture developed independently in the millennia after the end of the last Ice Age. Analyses of the local flora and fauna, and of finds from Mehrgarh, presented a mixed picture. The wheat and goats found in Period I must have been introduced from outside, since no local wild forms of these existed. It is possible that sheep were a local domesticate, although the local wild sheep were not Asiatic mouflon, the species ancestral to all modern sheep. Barley could have been domesticated in the region since it grows locally. About the cattle, however, there is little doubt: Indian zebu cattle, including those at Mehrgarh, derive from a local progenitor, *Bos namadicus*, and were locally domesticated.

So two different scenarios were possible: outsiders could have settled in the region, bringing domestic goats, wheat and perhaps barley, and gradually domesticating local plants and animals, too. Alternatively, plants and animals domesticated further west could have been introduced, through trade, into a community that was already beginning to practice agriculture using local plants and animals.

Could any evidence be found to support one of these scenarios and refute the other? Physical anthropologists studying the skeletons from burials at Mehrgarh and elsewhere were able to establish that the Mehrgarh people were of the same physical stock as other inhabitants of southern Asia in this period. In addition, jewelry from Period I included beads made of seashells and of turquoise and lapis lazuli from Central Asia. It was therefore clear that Mehrgarh formed part of a vast "interaction sphere" in which both commodities and ideas were exchanged between neighbors over vast distances. The current view, therefore, is that the farmers of early Mehrgarh were indigenous people who developed their own crops and domestic animals, raising these alongside imported domesticates.

Pottery innovations The painstaking investigation of the long-lived settlement at Mehrgarh has shed a fascinating light on local technological development, including pottery-making. During Period I at Mehrgarh, which lasted until around 5000 BC, the inhabitants of the settlement stored their grain and other produce in compartmented buildings—pairs of small mudbrick rooms separated by a central passage. For everyday purposes, they used baskets lined with bitumen.

Toward the end of this first period, coarse pottery began to appear. Some of these early vessels were made by coating the inside of bitumen-lined baskets with clay and firing it, burning off the basket and leaving a pottery vessel with clear basket marks on the exterior. Through time the pottery improved in quality, made first by building up slabs of clay and later by using a dabber. Finer, wheel-turned pottery had almost entirely replaced the other wares by about 4000 BC.

Alongside the manufacturing processes there was evidence of firing technology. One area of the settlement was covered with over-fired broken pottery. Observation of local practices in the region and analyses of these vessels and the area around them made it clear that these were the remains of a large bonfire kiln that had misfired. This simple technique involved setting many pots out in rows and covering them with fuel and then mud, with ventilation holes in it. The mound was set alight and left to burn for a day and to cool for three or four more, after which the ashes would be raked away and the vessels removed. In another part of the settlement, however, a permanent kiln was used repeatedly during the 4th millennium, showing that these two technologies thrived side by side.

A MINE OF INFORMATION

Eleven seasons of excavations at Mehrgarh and the work of many specialists have made the site an exceptional source of information on all aspects of life in the Indo-Iranian borderlands, as it changed from a simple community of mixed farmers and hunter-gatherers, moving seasonally, to a settlement of some thousand inhabitants on the brink of urbanization, with specialist artisans practicing a range of crafts, such as beadmaking, copper metallurgy, potting and figurine manufacturing. The strong traditions of the region have provided many points of contact with the activities of the settlement's inhabitants, throwing light upon them. Other information has been extracted from experimental work, such as the manufacturing of beads. Standing alone, this site has added 2,000 years to the prehistory of the Indo-Iranian borderlands, and has been one of the main sources of information on subsequent millennia.

Above: *This imprint of an ear of wheat made in the 7th millennium BC was found in building material at the Mehrgarh site. It reveals an outside influence, as no local forms of wheat existed in the region at the time the imprint was made.*

Above: *A rope of carnelian beads intricately etched in geometric patterns using an alkaline solution. Such craftsmanship characterized the Mohenjo Daro culture.*

MOHENJO DARO

THE LOST CIVILIZATION OF THE INDUS

By 1920 it was well known that civilization had emerged between 3000 and 1800 BC in Mesopotamia, Egypt, and China, the world's three most advanced areas at that time. Here, the features of civilized life first developed, including cities, complex political organization, and writing. Such features were known to have emerged at a later date in other regions of the world. In the Ganges Valley of India, for example, this had taken place by about 300 BC, relatively late compared with many parts of Eurasia. However, in 1921, archaeologists made an unexpected discovery that would soon challenge this assumption and introduced a whole new civilization to the world.

Far right: *White soapstone bust, thought to be an image of a priest-king. The statue would once have been painted various colors.*

PAKISTAN

Mohenjo Daro

The find In 1924, excavations on the 2nd-century AD Buddhist stupa at the site of Mohenjo Daro in the Ganges Valley revealed deposits that continued deep beneath the shrine. Artifacts found in these deposits indicated the presence of a society more advanced than archaeologists had expected. The finds showed remnants of substantial houses made of baked brick, with remarkable domestic sanitation and public drains. At the same time as the finds at Mohenjo Daro, excavations at Harappa, 400 miles (640 km) further up the Indus, yielded closely comparable remains.

It was clear to the archaeologists that they had discovered a new civilization of considerable antiquity – but how old was it? The finds included fine pottery, terra-cotta figurines, beautiful seals of carved steatite bearing an unknown script, and tools made of stone and copper or bronze, but not of iron, suggesting considerable antiquity.

Within days of the first announcement of the discoveries, scholars began to draw parallels between some of these objects, and artifacts from early Mesopotamian civilizations. By the 1930s, these impressionistic parallels had been replaced by concrete evidence of trade between the Indus region and Mesopotamia, pinning down the date of contacts and thus of the Indus civilization, as it was now called. More recently, radiocarbon dating has reinforced and refined the late 3rd millennium BC date indicated by Indus artifacts from Mesopotamian sites.

SKILLED ARTISANS

Among the Indus artifacts were distinctive etched carnelian beads and others of exceptional length, prized by the Mesopotamians and manufactured at Mohenjo Daro and other Indus sites. Recent studies of bead-working at Mohenjo Daro and of modern southern Asian bead-making has focused attention on the consummate skills of the Indus lapidaries, the culmination of a tradition that had begun at Mehrgarh, a major prehistoric site in Pakistan. Indus beads ranged from minute discs of fired steatite paste, about the size of a pin head, to slender biconical carnelian beads 5 inches (13cm) long, each one taking around two weeks to make.

Recent work at Mohenjo Daro has found a solution to a puzzle which reveals further evidence of the skills of the Indus craftsmen. The excavations at the site in the 1930s uncovered vitrified fragments of pottery vessels, clay, and terra-cotta bracelets, fused together into a black over-fired mass. Detailed examination and chemical and physical analyses revealed that these were the remains of a disastrous misfiring of a batch of highly sophisticated bracelets. Made of finely worked clay, they were created with elaborate care and placed in pairs within small lidded bowls sealed with clay. The bowls were stacked inside a larger vessel, which was sealed and then set carefully on heaps of terra-cotta bracelets within the kiln. This arrangement was designed to exclude air. When fired, bracelets of mottled gray stoneware were produced, virtually indistinguishable from fine-grained stone.

The citadel There are a number of references to Meluhha (the Indus civilization) in Sumerian texts. More is revealed by

Right: *This miniature bullock cart, complete with driver, is made from terra-cotta, a medium much favored by the Indus valley craftspeople. It may have been a sacred object, a child's toy or simply an ornament, but it does show that the wheel was a familiar object to this Bronze Age civilization.*

SILENT WITNESS

Both the stoneware bracelets found at Mohenjo Daro and the vessels in which they were fired bore writing – clearly their production was officially controlled and their function something beyond that of personal adornment. But what? Other than suggesting they might be badges of office, we can say little, for the Indus civilization remains the most enigmatic of the world's civilizations. One of the chief reasons for this is our inability to read the Indus writing.

Below: *The meaning of the characters on this seal, dating from 2500–1800 BC, is still not entirely understood to archaeologists.*

the structures and artifacts of cities such as Mohenjo Daro, which can help us to discover the nature of the political and social organization, the religion, and other aspects of the lives of the Indus people. Some clues are easy to read: delightful terra-cotta models of carts pulled by bullocks, for instance, directly reflect the way of life of ancient and modern farmers of the region. Official seals that depict boats offer some clues about the types of craft sailed by Indus travelers and fishermen. The well-preserved Indus houses with their brick-paved bathrooms and toilets, their central courtyards overlooked by upper stories, similarly reveal details of a pattern of existence that is familiar to us today in the region. But other evidence, such as the massive mound (known as the citadel) fortified by a baked brick wall, that towers over the western side of Mohenjo Daro, has proved difficult to interpret. The citadel is a place of substantial buildings, of which the most intriguing is the Great Bath. Surrounded by small rooms with their own bathrooms, the Great Bath has been taken to reflect India's religious emphasis on purity and ritual cleanliness. Yet few other structures in the city can be linked confidently with religious practices, and further evidence is elusive.

Sir Mortimer Wheeler, the British archaeologist who excavated here in 1950, felt he was on safer ground in interpreting the wall around the citadel, a mighty fortress like those attacked by the invading Indo-Aryans whose oral literature describes their violent early days in the northwest. Unburied skeletons in the streets of the city seemed to bear vivid witness to such an attack.

Fifty years on, however, little survives of Wheeler's interpretation. The city's defenses now appear more likely to have been built against the constant danger of flooding than against human foes, and, uniquely, the Indus civilization seems to have experienced no warfare. Furthermore, by the time the Indo-Aryans appeared on the scene the city had already fallen into ruins. And the analysis of the scattered skeletons and their locations shows that they were in fact more likely to be casual burials, in abandoned houses or streets, of individuals who were often the victims of disease.

THE ELUSIVE LANGUAGE

While the secrets of unknown scripts elsewhere in the world have gradually been unlocked, the Indus texts still remain stubbornly silent. Intensive studies by international teams of scholars, whether working with pencil and paper or with computers, have wrung scraps of information from the Indus inscriptions found on seals and other objects, the vast majority of which are frustratingly short. For example, some numerals have been identified, and it has been proved by examining the arrangement of the signs that the script was written from right to left and top to bottom. Some features of the language of the inscriptions have been determined, suggesting that the Indus people spoke an early form of Dravidian, but no words have yet been read, and it seems unlikely they ever will be, unless longer inscriptions are discovered.

Below: *The ruins of Mohenjo Daro, first excavated in 1924, reveal a highly organized and well-planned town. It was built on a grid pattern, with a sophisticated sewerage system, multi-story houses, and an industrial zone, where workshops were separate from residential buildings.*

CITY OF UR

SECRETS OF A ROYAL CEMETERY

When British archaeologist Sir Charles Leonard Woolley excavated the fabled city of Ur in modern-day Iraq, he made one of the most spectacular archaeological discoveries of the 20th century. Woolley's discoveries put flesh on the court life, and death, of a Sumerian city-state during the middle of the third millennium BC. Although other archaeological teams also discovered Sumerian cities and great works of art soon after, Woolley's results at Ur remain the most impressive and among the most important.

Above: *The impressive reconstructed ziggurat (pyramid-like tower) of Ur-Nammu, the first king of Ur, dominates the surrounding area.*

Discovery of the cemetery

Woolley first came upon the rich burials in what proved to be the Royal Cemetery during his first season of excavation in 1922. Realizing that he was on the verge of a special find, but feeling that he needed more experience with Ur before tackling the cemetery, Woolley postponed work in this part of the site until 1926. During this and the next three seasons he excavated over 2,000 burials, 16 of which he described as "royal." These 16, and some of the other tombs, contained a fabulous wealth of precious metals and semi-precious stones artfully worked into beautiful objects. They also contained grisly evidence of human sacrifices to accompany the prince or princess in death.

Woolley's discoveries made a big splash in the popular press, and Woolley himself quickly wrote several books about Ur and the ancient Sumerian society of which Ur was a part. He also managed to publish his technical report with an astonishing speed that few scholars could match. Appearing in 1934, his *Ur Excavations II: The Royal Cemetery* remains to this day a useful and detailed description of the tombs.

WOOLLEY'S FINDS

The cemetery, ironically, was located in a rubbish heap just outside the city walls. The rubbish had been accumulating for three or four centuries when the cemetery was first established, around 2600 BC, and it continued to collect while the cemetery was in use, until 2000 BC. The royal tombs date to the first hundred years or so of the cemetery's existence. Woolley identified these 16 tombs as "royal" by their architecture and by the presence of apparently sacrificed bodies. The tombs consist of a stone or mud brick structure (often with several rooms) at the bottom of a deep shaft, approached by a ramp cut from the side. The principal burial lay within the tomb chamber while remains of the sacrifice victims – up to 74 people, mostly bejeweled women, in a tomb – lay outside the chamber and along the ramp. Royal names inscribed on seals found in several graves identified some of the dead – Pu-abi, A-kalam-dug, and Mes-kalam-dug. Several of the other tombs, thought to be of the same age, lacked the structural features and the sacrificial victims, but they did contain an equally incredible wealth of precious grave goods.

The art that Woolley found in the Royal Cemetery includes many pieces that are typical of the Sumerian culture. These include the Standard of Ur (a wooden panel, inlaid with semi-precious stones depicting scenes of victorious warfare and rituals), the lyres, the figures of the ram caught in a thicket, the golden helmet of Mes-kalam-dug, and other splendid objects that today grace the British Museum in London and the University of Pennsylvania Museum in Philadelphia. Each represents the Sumerian tradition with an immediacy that few finds from other sites can match. The macabre practices that were revealed in the Death Pits of Ur color our perceptions of Sumerian royalty and political authority more than ancient documents or artwork ever could.

Archaeologists first encountered the Sumerians, the dominant people of southern Mesopotamia during the fourth and third millennia BC, when French archaeologists excavated at Tello during the last quarter of the 19th century. But the Sumerians remained shrouded in mystery until after World War I, when the new colonial masters of Iraq encouraged archaeological exploration of the country. Although many other teams from all over the world have discovered and excavated Sumerian cities, Woolley's findings at Ur remain among the most spectacular and revealing.

Right: *One of the most exciting finds was the Royal Standard of Ur, a magnificent double sided panel, inlaid with mother-of-pearl and lapis lazuli. On one side it showed scenes of war and on the other, shown here, scenes of peace, represented by kings and nobles amicably feasting.*

The secrets of the graves

Questions still remain about the Royal Cemetery despite the many details provided by Woolley. Did the graves really contain the remains of Sumerian royalty? Who were the sacrificial victims? Why did they die? Although the special nature of the tombs is clear, there is only slender evidence to indicate conclusively royal internments. The seals inscribed with people's names turn out not to be decisive in many instances. The seal of Pu-abi, for example, describes her as "queen" or "great lady" and Woolley found the seal in her burial chamber. So far so good – this is very likely the burial of queen Pu-abi. However, the seal of A-kalam-dug names him king, but the burial itself had been heavily disturbed and contained no body, so we are less sure that this grave was actually his. Other seals that have been discovered show the names of individuals but do not give them titles – maybe the tombs held royal internments, or maybe not.

The case of Mes-kalam-dug is especially difficult. A seal naming him king appeared (along with two golden daggers) in the remains of a wooden box that had been placed high in the burial shaft, not in the burial itself. A nearby burial that was extremely rich but without royal references included several vessels inscribed with the same name but without the title. So, was Mes-kalam-dug the king buried in the "royal" or in the ordinary burial (keeping in mind that "royal" refers to graves with architectural structure and slaughtered attendants)?

Below: *This ornate figurine of wood, shell, gold leaf, silver, and lapis lazuli found within a royal tomb shows a ram feeding at a bush. As an offering to the Sumerian fertility gods, it was probably intended to guarantee a trouble-free afterlife for the occupant of the tomb.*

SOCIAL STRUCTURE

The cemetery seems to have been reserved for the political establishment. In southern Mesopotamia at this time, palaces and temples were organized as large households to which were attached farmlands and farmers, animals and herders, weavers, smiths, potters, bakers, servants, commercial agents, bureaucrats, and priests in a hierarchy of power, duties, freedom, and wealth. The rich graves reflect high station in one of these institutions, the poor graves low station. So the "royal" tombs might include high priests or priestesses.

But here the distinctions between religious and secular office become blurred, for we know from records several centuries later that the king appointed a daughter as the chief priestess in the temple of Nanna, moon-god and patron deity of Ur. So might Pu-abi have been an important priestess from the royal family rather than a reigning queen? That the sacrificed servants gave up their lives for a dead monarch says something about political power in Ur; but if they died to accompany the human wife of the city's most important god, that says something else entirely about theological concepts.

The mortuary practices in the royal tombs are unparalleled elsewhere in Mesopotamia, and they seem to have been an aberration unique to Ur within Sumerian culture. Happily, these customs seem to have been short-lived, lasting only several generations. But the cemetery continues to withhold its secret meanings from us.

EBLA
THE DISCOVERY OF A NEW LANGUAGE

Near Eastern archaeologists, captives of habit and established tradition, have long focused their energies and intent on Mesopotamia (the lands of Iraq between the Euphrates and Tigris Rivers). At first, they excitedly uncovered Assyrian royal capitals in northern Iraq, then they shifted their attention southward to the area where the Sumerian civilization took shape between 4000 and 2500 BC. Lists of important firsts – writing, cities, state government, massive public buildings – typically focused on southern Iraq with other parts of the Near East merely inheriting this cultural bounty. This idea may soon change.

A marked exception

Excavations of more recent vintage have begun to temper, but not yet overturn, this intellectual bias. Northern Iraq and eastern Syria must now be considered a vital part of southern Mesopotamia's development toward civilization, while western Syria, along with adjacent lands between the Euphrates and the Mediterranean, remain largely places where important events occurred only after 2000 BC. With one striking exception: an Italian excavation at Tell Mardikh uncovered a mighty Syrian city dating to 2400 BC with a rich and unparalleled cultural heritage. The royal palace of this city, Ebla, contained a large archive of cuneiform tablets that reveals an unexpected and hitherto unknown society in the landscape of the Near East.

Tell Mardikh is a large mound that sits on the north Syrian plain halfway between the Euphrates and the Mediterranean. The site has a roughly trapezoidal shape with very steep sides, consistent with the massive ramparts of the middle Bronze Age (2000–1600 BC) city. A high-mounded acropolis dominates the center of the site. The Italian team began excavating there in 1964, at first finding only remains of the middle Bronze Age town – hardly surprising in light of the existing expectations. Almost exactly ten years into the project, patience rewarded the archaeologists when they came upon a much older, large building within the

Ebla
SYRIA

slopes of the acropolis. The following year, in 1975, they uncovered part of an archive of clay tablets which were written in a previously unknown version of cuneiform, the script of ancient Mesopotamia.

Above: *Ebla uncovered; work is still going on, and more secrets are waiting to be revealed.*

Below: *Miniature alabaster figure of a priestess dating from about 2600–2350 BC.*

THE ARCHIVE

By 1985 the archaeologists had exposed major sections of the early Bronze Age palace – the administrative quarter, a probable throne room, store rooms, and parts of several residential wings – and had recovered nearly 17,000 tablets and fragments of tablets. The latter had been stored on wooden shelves in the records office, and had been buried under collapsing walls when the palace was destroyed around 2300 BC.

The archive recorded palace affairs of a kingdom new to the annals of history. Specialists who deciphered the cuneiform at first had enormous difficulty making sense of the texts: although written in a fairly well-understood script, most of the texts were in a Semitic language not previously known to scholars of ancient linguistics. The uncertain reading of many passages at first produced some grave mistakes that made their way into the popular press. For example, some scholars claimed that the Ebla records contained references to biblical places as far away as Palestine, and that Ebla had ruled a very large empire.

The kingdom of Ebla More sober reconsideration showed that the kingdom had been much smaller, and that other principalities had thrived at the same time in western Syria. In addition to the royal seat, the Ebla state included a number of towns and villages in the region, the location of many of which still cannot be identified. As in all pre-industrial states, Ebla was founded on the rural labor of farmers and animal

Ebla was trading with cities from the northern Orontes River eastward across the plain of northern Mesopotamia. Perhaps it profited from its intermediate position on transportation routes that led to the mountainous regions of Lebanon and southern Turkey. These regions were the source of riches such as silver, copper, useful or semiprecious stones, fragrant resins, and other commodities desired by the ruling elite of societies to the east.

Below: One of the 15,000 cuneiform tablets found in the royal archives of the palace at Ebla. Most are concerned with commercial transactions or administration.

herders, but the lives of these people entered the written record only to the extent that palace bureaucrats took an interest in the fruits of their labor. In fact the palace directly oversaw the work of a great many people, directing the efforts of gangs of workmen, issuing supplies and rations (food and clothing) to workers and palace personnel, registering the disposition of animal herds, maintaining files on commodities in storage, and recording commercial transactions. The palace records from contemporary states in southern Mesopotamia have a similar flavor, and royal power in the Syrian state flowed along lines similar to those of Mesopotamian states.

TRADE RELATIONS

Ebla enjoyed relations with lands in a broad band stretching from the northern Orontes River (in modern Turkey) eastward across the broad plain of northern Mesopotamia. Societies in the latter region, the Jezirah, were undergoing a remarkable transformation at the time, as immense cities had been springing up almost overnight during the century or so following 2600 BC.

But Ebla's most important commercial and diplomatic relations were in fact oriented toward Mesopotamia, and especially with the city of Mari, which was situated on the Euphrates River (near Syria's modern border with Iraq), and with Kish near modern Baghdad, at the northern edge of the heartland of Mesopotamian civilization. The Ebla archive reveals struggles with Mari over territory, which alternated with diplomacy. The records mention royal gift exchanges of precious metals and finely woven garments; kings sending skilled craftsmen and entertainers (such as stone-cutters, smiths, carpenters, weavers, and singers) to foreign courts, students from Ebla attending scribal schools in Mari and Kish; treaties that secured rights of foreign trade; gifts to visiting merchants; and so forth. The records and artistic products of Ebla show that the Syrian society was deeply indebted to Mesopotamia for many things cultural as well as economic. But this conclusion does not imply that Ebla was totally derivative from a Mesopotamian prototype. Far from it: the basic Syrian character of the society remains clear throughout.

RECENT FINDS

We still know very little about Ebla before around 2400 BC. The archaeologists had to stop uncovering the early Bronze Age town – the massive buildings of the middle Bronze Age city had buried the older structures. Since 1985 they have continued working at Tell Mardikh, and in fact have made many extremely important discoveries within the younger city. And now, after 15 years of patient work, they are poised to discover more remains and cuneiform records of this remarkable culture. Indeed, during the later 1990s the team penetrated levels below the palace, discovering a royal tomb, alas thoroughly ransacked in antiquity, that probably belonged to one of the kings of Ebla. Just as intriguing, the team has already touched upon a tiny portion of a large building older than the palace and archive. These levels, and those even older, will eventually yield their secrets to the patient archaeologists. No doubt further surprises are in store, both at Ebla and at other ancient cities of western Syria. This western region of Syria was not the backwater once supposed, but rather was an integral part of the development of civilization in the ancient Near East.

EBLA'S WEALTH

The kingdom of Ebla relied on the work of the local farmers and animal herders for its wealth. They produced the grain, olive oil, and wine that fed the city, the wool and flax that clothed its populace, and the oil, wine, and textiles that its merchants traded abroad.

Left: *Fresco showing a priest pulling a sacrificial bull by a nose ring.*

TROY
FACT OR FICTION?

The city of Troy has excited imagination since time immemorial. Toward the end of the 19th century, the German archaeologist Heinrich Schliemann began excavations at Hisarlik in Turkey to search for Troy and prove the reality of the Trojan War vividly described in Homer's epics. Whether Schliemann was successful in this aim remains open to question, but he certainly discovered the remains of previously unknown Bronze Age civilizations which flourished around the Aegean in the 2nd and 3rd millennia BC.

Far right: *As Troy burns at the end of the war, the hero Aeneas escapes with his father Anchises and sets out to found a new Troy in the southern lands. Apparently, it was this engraving that so inspired the child Schliemann that he resolved he would one day find the lost city of Troy.*

Right: *Replica of a golden bottle found in the Trojan ruins. The real thing has been missing since the outbreak of World War II.*

Troy

TURKEY

Calvert's early work

Schliemann's interest, the actual location of the ancient city of Troy had long been debated. A large mound at Hisarlik in Turkey was suggested as one possible location, but there were several contenders. The true pioneer and early champion of Hisarlik was Frank Calvert, a businessman and diplomat whose family owned land close by. He was convinced that the mound concealed the ruins of Troy. In 1863 he began to test this theory through excavation. Moreover, he suggested to Charles Newton, curator of the Department of Greek and Roman Antiquities at the British Museum, that they should participate in these excavations. Although Newton refused this offer, Calvert continued his work, his trial trenches revealed the Hellenistic temple and part of the city walls. Yet the complex layers of habitation and the rich artifacts they contained eventually convinced Calvert that further work was not viable without a large sum of money and substanial manpower. There the matter might have rested, but in 1868 Calvert met Schliemann, a self-made millionaire who had come to Turkey to search for the lost city of Troy. Calvert shared his knowledge and beliefs with Schliemann and put his land in Hisarlik at Schliemann's disposal.

THE EXCAVATIONS

Schliemann's first excavations at Hisarlik took place in 1870, before he had been given a permit by the Turkish authorities, but it was not until 1871 that he began to explore the site in earnest, cutting a huge north–south trench over the center of the mound. He removed huge quantities of earth and large blocks of stone which he assumed belonged to the later Greek city, as he believed Troy was the first city on the site and would thus be found right at the bottom of the mound. However, it now seems more likely that these stones he threw aside were in fact part of the city he was searching for.

However careless his early digging was, once Schliemann was in the levels he assumed to belong to Troy he was very careful in keeping a record of what he found, including approximate locations and the depths of the artifacts. This method, crude though it was, foreshadows archaeological practice of the late 20th century, in which both the vertical and horizontal locations of the finds and features are carefully recorded.

By the end of the 1872 season Schliemann had uncovered the remains of substantial fortification walls and could identify a series of cultural strata representing the different cities that had occupied the site at different periods through time. However, the most successful campaign was in 1873 when

Below: *This stone ramp is part of the Troy of Homeric times, found at the sixth level of excavation.*

Schliemann uncovered a paved ramp leading into the city which he identified as the Scaean Gate mentioned by Homer in his epic poem. Nearby was a series of large rooms belonging to a substantial building which Schliemann identified, referring to the epic poem, as Priam's palace. There was also evidence of extensive burning, which Schliemann ascribed to the sacking of Troy. Schliemann was in no doubt that he had truly unearthed the remains of the fabled city.

Most notable among his finds that year was a magnificent cache of treasure found outside the city wall, comprising a copper bowl and cauldron, numerous gold, silver, electrum and bronze vessels, and fine gold jewelry. This was the first of some 19 caches of treasure that Schliemann found at the site at Hisarlik. These remains, belonging to a previously unknown culture, were found at a depth of 55 feet (17 m) and were correctly assigned to the second phase, or culture level, of Troy, which Schliemann ascribed to the city of Homer's epic. Yet he was unhappy at the small size of the city he had uncovered since he felt it did not correspond to the grandeur of the Troy described by Homer.

THE SCANDAL OF THE TREASURES

Schliemann soon became embroiled in a bitter legal dispute with the Turkish authorities over ownership of the treasure hoard which he had illegally removed from Turkish soil. In 1875, however, the treasures became his, and he later presented them to the city of Berlin. He returned to Troy in 1878 when, aided by French archaeologist Emile Burnouf, he was able to further refine his understanding of the city, identifying some seven occupation layers. Even so, the complexity of the different habitation layers still proved problematic for him.

However, now Schliemann's interpretations were beginning to display greater authority. Though he still strove to identify Priam's city, he moved away from identifying actual structures on the ground with those described in the epics – most notably Schliemann began to refer to a "royal residence" or "chieftain's house" rather than to Priam's Palace.

Following the 1882 season, the understanding of the site's many layers was again refined – the architect Dörpfeld identified nine major layers – and more of the settlement's architecture was uncovered. For example, in the center of the citadel three large rectangular buildings with porticos were excavated in the level of Troy II (Roman numerals refer to the different phases of the city's occupation). Moreover, the so-called chieftain's house was shown to be a peripheral structure.

Troy at last Schliemann's final excavations at Troy in 1890 were in some ways the most important. Under the influence of Dörpfeld, he excavated methodically and in Troy VI found two large porticoed buildings containing gray ceramics and Mycenaean pottery from the late Bronze Age. This meant Troy VI and not Troy II was contemporary with Mycenaean Greece and thus more probably the city of Homeric tradition. Certainly, the

impressively built stone fortifications and the larger size of Troy VI were more in keeping with Priam's Troy. It seems that previously Schliemann had missed Troy VI, partly in his rush to the lower levels but also because much of the sixth city had been levelled for later constructions during the Greek and Roman periods. The earlier city, Troy II, was in fact an important early Bronze Age city dating to the early third millennium BC.

Schliemann's earliest campaigns at Troy have been criticized for the unscientific way in which they were carried out. For instance, in his haste to reach lower levels he cut straight through and destroyed the levels most likely to be contemporary with the Trojan War. His work should, however, be viewed in its 19th century context when the science of archaeology was in its infancy and he had nothing with which to compare his finds, as there was no knowledge of the early civilizations that had flourished in the Aegean.

KHOK PHANOM DI

CLUES TO DAILY LIFE

Farming began in East Asia around 6000 BC. On the Yellow River millet was cultivated, while on the Yangzi the main staple was rice. Rice, however, is native to southern China and Southeast Asia, so might its cultivation have begun at an early date in these regions also? This question was one of the prime reasons that New Zealand-based archaeologist Charles Higham selected the site of Khok Phanom Di in Thailand for excavation in 1984.

A different study Earlier work on the substantial burial mound at Khok Phanom Di had revealed burials with traces of rice, believed to date to the fifth millennium BC. However, excavation in a larger area, 33 feet (10m) square, revealed that the settlement was not nearly as old as previously thought and that it could not provide answers to the question of local agricultural origins. Yet, although it offered no clues about agriculture, the substantial cemetery and the surrounding region promised a detailed picture of life and death in the settlement, and how it changed through time.

REGIONAL SETTING

A variety of data were used to reconstruct a picture of the immediate environment and of the Bang Pakong valley as a whole. Cores taken from the local sediments yielded microscopic clues to local vegetation, such as pollen grains, leaf fragments, and fern spores, and how it had changed through time. From the site itself came ostracodes and forams – minute aquatic organisms with specific and restricted habitats. These also gave very clear information about the natural environment. Somewhat broader in their habitat preferences, the plants, animals, fish, and birds whose remains were recovered in the excavation gave a general impression of the local environment and how it changed with the years. They also provided considerable information on the diet of the people of Khok Phanom Di.

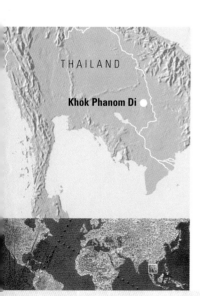

THAILAND

Khok Phanom Di

The site was first occupied around 4,000 years ago. The microfauna recovered from this period were species that occupied a marine or estuarine habitat, while larger creatures included crocodiles and birds that inhabited the open coast. The settlement lay beside, but slightly above, an estuary where abundant shellfish and crabs could be collected at low tide on the mudflats and offshore coral reefs. In the estuary and the waters beyond, the settlement's inhabitants caught fish from canoes, using nets or lines with bone fishhooks – many of these were found in the lower deposits of the settlement.

Rice was an unexpected find in this period, since the saline coastal environment was not suitable for its cultivation. Therefore the rice must have been brought in from elsewhere, probably exchanged with inland groups who also supplied stone tools, in return for the decorative pottery made by the women at Khok Phanom Di.

Left: The deceased were wrapped in cloth shrouds and placed on wooden biers in the graves at Khok Phanom Di.

Below: One of the grave clusters showing adult and infant remains. Pottery vessels and anvils for shaping pots often accompanied female burials.

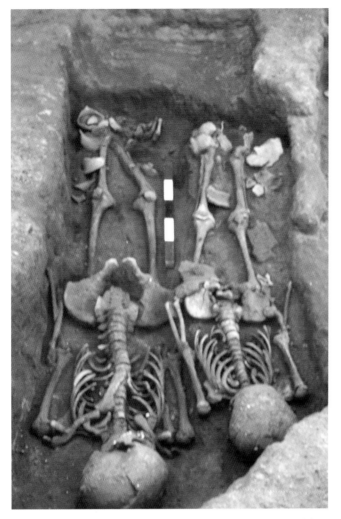

LIFE EXPECTANCY

Throughout the life of the settlement, infant and child mortality was high. Evidence of sickle-cell anemia, a serious hereditary condition that gives some protection against malaria, reflected the prevalence of malaria in this mosquito-infested environment. Individuals who survived into adulthood generally died between the ages of 20 and 30. Despite their poor life expectancy, however, the people were well nourished and strong.

Changing times

In later levels, the faunal remains indicated major environmental change. The settlement was now surrounded by marshland and mangroves, with freshwater ponds nearby. The mangrove swamps provided a rich environment for plants and animals suited to its brackish but fertile waters. Shellfish from the intertidal mudflats and the mangrove swamps were still important in the diet, but hunted game like wild pig and macaque was on the increase.

Gradually, coastal shellfish gave way to swamp and freshwater species, as the silting of the estuary moved the coastline progressively further from the settlement. Sea fishing declined – only a single fish-hook was found in the deposits of this period. But striking evidence that fish still had a place in the diet came from the burial of an individual whose stomach contents included partly digested fish bones and scales, along with rice chaff.

The local change from saline to freshwater swamps enabled the people of Khok Phanom Di to cultivate rice. Their tools now included granite hoes, and shells sharpened for use as knives. Experiments with modern replicas of these knives allowed the wear patterns to be compared with those on the original knives, to see what they had been used for. Many uses were ruled out. The best match was for their use as sickles for harvesting grasses such as cultivated rice.

This phase of rice-growing was quite short-lived, however. An alteration in the course of the river soon left the site surrounded by dry land. Local rice cultivation was no longer possible, and the shell knives ceased to be used. Dry-land plants, animals and micro-fauna, particularly forest species, reflected this change. Not long after this, around 1600 BC, the site was abandoned.

EVIDENCE FROM BEYOND THE GRAVE

In the relatively short time that the settlement was occupied, a massive mound of occupation debris developed. The constantly rising ground surface made it easy to establish the relative chronology of

Left: *Overhead view of the site, showing archaeologists at work recording their finds. The settlement's superimposed layers form a mound 23 feet (7 m) deep.*

Above: *One of the pieces of pottery that the women of Khok Phanom Di made. The pots were exchanged for food, such as rice.*

the 154 burials in the settlement's large cemetery, providing a unique opportunity to study the population of a settlement through time.

The burials were arranged in clusters, probably the burial plots of individual families, each surrounded by a wooden structure indicated by postholes. It proved possible to reconstruct the genealogy of two family clusters over about 20 generations. Genetically determined features of skulls and teeth shared by suggested members of the same family supported the proposed family trees. So did the patterns of decorative tooth removal, with related individuals often sharing the same pattern.

The skeletons also revealed much about the health and physical activities of the settlement's inhabitants. In the earlier period when sea fishing was important, the men had strong, well-developed arms but also suffered joint degeneration as a result of the strenuous activity of paddling their canoes. Later, the men had less robust physiques but also showed less stress on their joints. Evidence of strong wrist and arm muscles in the women reflected their important role as potters, producing decorative pottery here not only for local use but also for trade.

SOCIAL HIERARCHY

Statistical analyses conducted on the grave goods showed little evidence of social hierarchy. Some graves were more richly furnished than others. The finest example was the "Princess" who was buried wearing more than 120,000 shell beads. None of her family was accorded such rich furnishings, however, so wealth and status were evidently not inherited but acquired on personal merit.

ULU BURUN

THE WORLD'S OLDEST SHIPWRECK

Some time during the Late Bronze Age, a 50-foot (15m) cargo ship, laden with valuable goods, left Cyprus bound for the Aegean. Just off the southern coast of Turkey disaster struck and the ship sank, preserving beneath the water an involuntary freeze-frame image of life on a 14th-century trading vessel. The Ulu Burun wreck — the world's earliest known shipwreck, dating to the 14th century BC — provides impressive confirmation of the extent and complexity of Bronze Age marine trade routes.

TURKEY

Ulu Burun

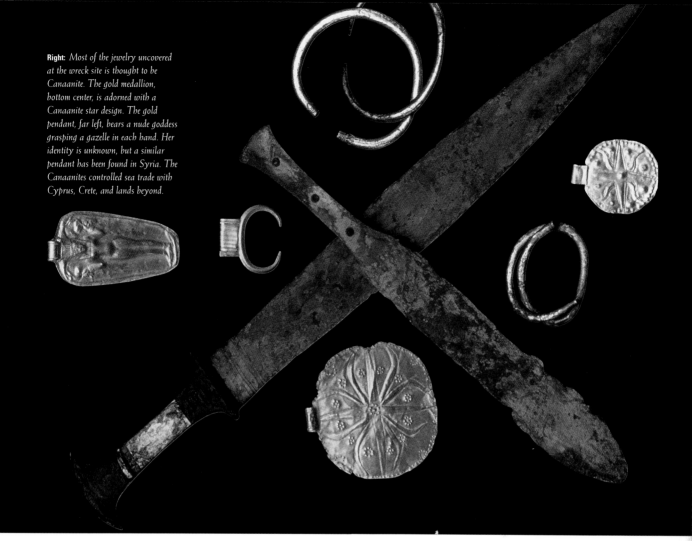

Seabed discovery

The Mediterranean coast is known to be home to hundreds of ancient wrecks. Locating these vessels, however, poses a problem. Underwater surveys involving sonar and magnetometers are extremely expensive, and it is simply not feasible to conduct a detailed search of every inch of the seabed looking for archaeological debris. Fortunately, Turkey has its own unique band of underwater professionals. During the summer months, sponge divers work along the Turkish coast, combing the seabed daily in their search for valuable sponges. Recognizing their expertise, marine archaeologists associated with the Institute of Nautical Archaeology (INA) at Texas A & M University, recruited local sponge divers as unofficial surveyors, teaching them to look for the characteristic signs of an ancient wreck.

In 1982 this policy paid off when a young diver, Mehmet Cakir, working near the promontory of Ulu Burun, discovered a collection of strange "metal biscuits with ears" lying on the seabed at a depth of 150 feet (45m). He reported his discovery to the captain of his boat who correctly identified the "biscuits" as Bronze Age copper ingots and passed the information on to the Turkish Museum of Underwater Archaeology in Bodrum. A joint team of divers from the Museum and the INA investigated, and quickly confirmed the discovery of an undisturbed

Far left: Amphoras, copper ingots, and other priceless relics are tagged and catalogued by members of the dive team. Only short dives could be made to the wreck site, which lay 170 feet (56m) down, and each diver could stay on the bottom for only 20 minutes because of the danger of nitrogen narcosis from breathing oxygen at such depths. Hundreds of dives were made to bring up all the material.

POTTERY CLUES

The pottery recovered from the ship was mainly Canaanite, and may be divided into three classes: pottery used to store foodstuffs and trade items, pottery used by the ship's crew, and valuable pottery which was itself intended for trade. One large "pithos" vessel has yielded a carefully packed collection of eighteen Cypriot pots which were clearly regarded as valuable cargo.

Above This group of artifacts testifies to the diversity of cultures represented by finds at the wreck site. A Canaanite sword rests on a Mycenaean sword, fronted by a pair of musician's finger cymbals. At the back, from left to right, stand a Mycenaean kylix, a Cypriot bucchero jug, and a Canaanite pilgrim flask.

Bronze Age ship. The ship had been just one of many that regularly traversed the Mediterranean. Such ships took full advantage of the tides and winds to sail in a counterclockwise circuit, during which they visited the ports of Ugarit (Syria), Cyprus, and Greece or Crete, then crossed the sea to Egypt before returning to the Levant to complete the circuit.

UNDERWATER EXCAVATION

In 1984, following a preliminary season of survey work, the planning and excavation of the ship started in earnest. Under the experienced directorship of George Bass, a research center was established on land while a boat, the *Virazon*, was moored directly above the wreck. From here the archaeologists were able to embark on dives of no longer than 20 minutes twice a day. The depth of the wreck, 140–170 feet (43–52m), made longer dives dangerous. The high pressure and the buildup of nitrogen at this depth meant that each dive had to be followed by a lengthy period of decompression. To complicate matters further, the seabed at this point dips steeply and is irregular, making the mapping of the wreck particularly difficult. To assist the divers, and form an emergency shelter, an air-filled plexiglass booth was set on the seabed and fitted with a telephone line which would allow communication with the *Virazon*. A balloon system was also installed to help lift heavy artifacts to the surface. Under these far-from-ideal conditions, work on the wreck progressed with surprising speed, with the team averaging a thousand dives per season. The artifacts recovered from the seabed are now housed in Bodrum Museum.

A rich cargo It soon became obvious that the fragile wooden upper parts of the ship had long since vanished, although some of the lower timbers remained preserved by sediment, allowing the archaeologists to plan the outline of the ship and determine that the fir planks of the hull had been fitted with mortise and tenon joints. The non-organic part of the cargo was substantially intact with metal making up the bulk by weight. When she sank, the ship was transporting over 250 copper ingots weighing some 6 tons (5.4 metric tons); subsequent analysis indicates that the copper in these ingots had been mined in Cyprus even though many of them are cast into a distinctive shape – rectangular with elongated corners or handles – more typical of Syria. Tin ingots, too, have been found, and although their origins are as yet unproven, archaeologists have drawn on textual sources to speculate that they may have originated as far away as Afghanistan. Copper and tin were at this time highly prized commodities, essential for the manufacture of the new-style bronze artifacts which were rapidly replacing the old-fashioned stone and copper tools.

Other raw materials found in the wreck include blue glass, ebony, hippopotamus and elephant ivory, pigment, amber, and ostrich eggs. More obviously valuable to modern eyes are the gold drinking cup, gold and silver jewelry, and bronze tools and weapons recovered. Included among these precious items was a gold scarab inscribed with the name of the Egyptian Queen Nefertiti. Some of the items appear to have been the personal property of the crew; it is tempting to speculate that a hinged wooden writing tablet designed to be fitted with a wax writing surface may well have belonged to the long-lost captain.

With such a mixture of contents, we cannot be certain whether the Ulu Burun wreck was an independent merchant ship or an official royal trading vessel. Nor can we determine its port of origin, since the objects so far recovered come from at least seven different cultures. Instead the wreck and its cargo offer confirmation of the truly international nature of Bronze Age trade.

BRONZE AGE PIRATES?

With so many cargo ships criss-crossing the Mediterranean, the threat of attack had to be taken seriously. It may well be that the weapons found within the wreck, which include a dagger, swords and spearheads, represent the ship's own defense against pirates.

Left: *George F. Bass, founder of the Institute of Nautical Archaeology, examines a Cypriot bowl brought up from the wreck site. A mass of artifacts from different cultures has left the archaeologists guessing as to the nationality of the vessel.*

JERICHO

WHO WERE THE ISRAELITES?

Archaeologists have a difficult time with negative evidence, deciding when a lack of evidence is simply due to looking in the wrong place, and when its absence really is a sign that something was missing in the past. Negative evidence usually proves to be misleading, but in some cases it is meaningful, especially when it fits a pattern of negative evidence across a region. The town of Jericho and the origins of the Israelites is an interesting example.

Biblical stories Most people are familiar with the biblical stories of how the Israelites fled the oppressive Pharaoh, wandering for 40 years in the wilderness of Sinai before crossing the Jordan River into the Promised Land under the leadership first of Moses and then of Joshua. For many today, these stories are unassailable, a true account of actual events. For others they are the stuff of legend and myth. Skeptics can marshal many points in their favor, notably that archaeological evidence does not support the stories.

One point of inconsistency concerns the conquest story, when the Israelites crossed the Jordan River under Joshua's leadership and conquered Canaan as their promised land. Most scholars accept that these events must have happened in about 1200 BC, the time of upheavals that marked the transition between the late Bronze Age (1550–1200 BC) and the early Iron Age (1200–1000 BC). But in this context, Jericho, the walls of which the Israelite army famously brought down with its trumpets and shouts, offers a clear case of negative evidence.

ARCHAEOLOGICAL EVIDENCE

The first archaeological work at Jericho, conducted at the beginning of the 20th century, concluded that the place had no wall and was in fact unpopulated at the relevant time. Later excavations during the 1950s confirmed and refined these findings. A wall had surrounded and protected Jericho during several epochs of

ISRAEL

Jericho

JORDAN

Above left: *Foundations of a massive stone tower, dating from 8500–7300 BC. At 30 feet (9 m) in height it formed part of the 12-foot (3.6-m) town wall which may have been built as flood defence.*

Above: *The rugged and inhospitable terrain of Wadi Qilt, the desert surrounding the oasis of Jericho.*

the town's long history, but not during Joshua's time, when the place was at most a village or more likely uninhabited altogether. Maybe archaeological evidence alone is not sufficient to cast doubt on the conquest story – perhaps archaeologists simply missed the wall. Yet the same lack of evidence distinguishes other walled towns that the Israelites supposedly destroyed. For example, Joshua's next conquest, the town of 'Ai, had been a small walled town more than a thousand years earlier, and would become the setting of an Israelite village soon after the conquest, but did not exist at the time for Joshua's army to destroy.

The archaeological testimony gives mixed support for the conquest stories. Of the towns that the Israelite forces were said to have destroyed, some were unoccupied, some were occupied but not clearly destroyed, and others were both occupied and destroyed at the relevant time. But similarly mixed evidence emerges for conquered towns that the Israelites apparently spared from destruction.

A WAY FORWARD

Some people react to these observations by clinging to the literal truth of scripture, while others feel free to dismiss the entire account as fiction. The most responsible reaction is a proposal of alternative interpretations that fit the known facts and that can be supported or rejected by new evidence. Archaeologists face a difficult challenge. To talk about archaeological evidence for the early Israelites, we have

to know how to identify Israelites to begin with – this issue is long debated and is still unresolved. Nevertheless, we can speak with confidence about major changes in culture and lifestyles happening during the century or two after 1200 BC, changes that seem to correlate, at least generally, with the appearance of the Israelites and other new peoples.

During the late Bronze Age, imperial powers had struggled for dominion over Syria and the eastern Mediterranean, and Egypt had retained a strong grasp over Palestine for several centuries. This was a time of decline for the Canaanite cities that had so vibrantly flourished during the previous four centuries. Urban decay was especially noticeable in the hill country away from the centers of Egyptian power. Jericho illustrates this trend: during the centuries before the late Bronze Age it was a prosperous small town surrounded by a massive wall, but the settlement deteriorated into an impoverished village before disappearing altogether during the late Bronze Age. The decline of urban conditions and the stresses of the Egyptian empire encouraged people to seek alternative lifestyles, and texts of the time speak of many herding groups and of brigands living outside the grasp of the remaining towns.

The still poorly understood crisis of 1200 BC weakened Egypt's control, sweeping away the previous imperial world order and the ancient Levantine culture of Canaan. In its place emerged new peoples: the Philistines along the coast near Gaza, the Phoenicians arising from the ashes of Canaanite societies in Lebanon, the Aramaeans in parts of Syria, the peoples of Ammon and Moab east of the Jordan River, and the Israelites in the central hills (Samaria and Judah). Numerous villages sprang up in the central hill country, and the region turned again onto a path leading to prosperity, this time founded on a rural rather than urban culture.

Debating Israelite origins

This general background frames two interpretations of Israelite origins that are popular among those who believe that the biblical conquest stories should not

BURIED UNDER BUILDINGS

The first farmers at Jericho (8000–6000 BC) often buried the skulls of their dead separately from the other bones. The skulls seem to have been part of an ancestor cult, and by 7000 BC they were sometimes plastered and painted in the image of the honored dead. The children, like this one, were more usually buried intact.

Left: *Skeleton of a child found under a house in Jericho. It was the custom to bury the dead under the house floor, sometimes separating the skull to decorate and keep above ground.*

be accepted as history. One of these ideas suggests that the Israelites were descendants of those fleeing the political authority of towns to become brigands, mercenaries, and villagers in the hills. Although they were Canaanite by origin, these "peasants in revolt" gradually formed communities with a new cultural identity – the Israelites – as the authority of cities disappeared.

The other idea looks to the animal herders who were living on the fringes of Bronze Age urban societies. People in Near Eastern societies have long moved back and forth between farming and herding, according to changing political and economic factors that favor one way of life over the other. In this view, the Israelites were pastoralists on the eastern fringes of the Mediterranean who settled down in the central hills as part of the aftermath of the crisis at the end of the late Bronze Age.

Although opinions vary, and the question cannot yet be decided, scholars agree on several points: the origin of the Israelites lay in populations who had long been resident in the region; those populations themselves had a Canaanite background; the villages that filled up the central hills constitute an archaeological signal of the Israelites; and these events are part of long-term developments in the regional political and economic situation. Both the archaeological and historical evidence as currently understood stand a long way from Moses on his way to the Promised Land.

These reinterpretations of Israelite origins, whether right or wrong, began with the negative evidence from Jericho and other biblical sites. The negative evidence itself implied that the biblical stories were not accurate historical accounts, but did not, and could not, supply another way to see those events. For that we needed to stand back and look at other sites and the wider world, and perceive connections between events through time, connections that take into account the facts we already know and that can be tested against new facts as they are discovered.

Far left: *The traditional Bible version of the fall of Jericho, complete with Joshua and a band of powerful-lunged trumpeters, can be seen on one of the ten panels that decorate the huge bronze doors of the Baptistery of San Giovanni in Florence. It took sculptor and goldsmith Lorenzo Ghiberti (1378–1455) 27 years to make them, and they were finally installed in 1452. Michelangelo considered them "worthy of Paradise."*

SOLOMON'S TEMPLE

THE SEARCH BEGINS

Wise king Solomon was a great builder, according to the biblical accounts of his reign. Many monuments uncovered at archaeological sites in Israel have been attributed to Solomon's reign of the 10th century BC, yet none has remained unchallenged. While most archaeologists still accept that Solomon built the massive city gates at Megiddo, Hazor, and elsewhere, the stables at these sites are now usually reassigned to the 9th-century BC kings of Samaria. Still Solomon's most important buildings remain undiscovered in Jerusalem.

Detective work Solomon greatly expanded his capital to the north of the City of David, and here he erected his palace and temple. These royal structures will probably never be uncovered because they most likely lie beneath the Muslim Dome of the Rock or just to the north of it. The biblical description of these monuments is lovingly full (1 Kings and 2 Chronicles) but also ambiguous and confusing at many points. Yet archaeologists have worked to piece together the clues and can now describe with considerable confidence what these buildings must have looked like, despite the fact that they have never been able to find them.

The biblical description of Solomon's temple says that it was an elongated rectangle with inner measurements of roughly 35x110 feet (10x35 m), and stood 50 feet (15m) high. A porch at the east of the building, 16 feet (5m) deep and flanked by outward projections of the side walls, gave entry to the sanctuary. Two bronze pillars, probably ornamental rather than structural, framed the entrance.

The interior space was divided into a large antechamber and a smaller inner room. The latter, a 33-foot (10-m) square space against the back of the building, was the "holy of holies" that housed the Ark of the Covenant. Carefully shaped stone blocks formed the foundations of the structure; its upper walls were made of either rough stone or mud brick. Solomon's craftsmen paneled the interior

walls with cedar, covered with gold and decorated with cherubim and elaborate plant images. Banks of store rooms abutted the sacred space of the temple; here Solomon deposited the treasury of his father David and the temple's ritual objects.

SYMBOLIC IMPORTANCE

Solomon built this temple soon after David had established the Israelite state, and many people continued to resist the growing centralization of power in Jerusalem. The temple itself was an assertion of central authority, since it was supposed to supplant the rural open-air shrines and provincial temples. When Solomon's kingdom split into Judah and Israel (Samaria), the temple represented the claims of Jerusalem to righteous rule over all the Israelites, even after the Assyrians had destroyed Samaria and deported its people in 722 BC. And when Jerusalem in turn suffered destruction at the hands of Nebuchadnezzar in 586 BC, the Israelites in Babylonian exile saw rebuilding the temple as a symbol of re-establishing the Davidic state. Indeed, the Israelite community reconstituted the

Below: *The massive stone gates in the ancient walls of Megiddo, once known as Armageddon, are concrete evidence of Solomon's monumental building style.*

temple on returning from half a century of exile. Later expanded by Herod the Great and today represented by the Wailing Wall, this second temple remained the focus of religious life in the city until its destruction by the Romans in AD 70.

Physical evidence

We cannot dig up the temple or palace of Solomon; nevertheless we can almost photograph them. The rich biblical description closely matches temples and palaces excavated elsewhere in Syria and the eastern Mediterranean. Solomon's temple in fact belonged to an architectural tradition with an already venerable pedigree; soon after 2000 BC peoples in western Syria and then in Palestine began building temples of this sort.

Many of the oldest examples of these temples were squat, almost square, with impressively thick walls. These structures were usually divided into two spaces: a front porch framed by forward projections of the side walls and fronting, and a single interior room. A pair of tower-like structures sometimes marked the corners of the porch, and the rear wall of the room often bore a niche or bench which presumably accommodated the focus of worship, whether it was a statue or an altar.

In some examples, the inner room was divided into two areas by a cross wall and, in these cases, the building usually took a more elongated rectangular shape. In all cases, however, the entrance from the porch to the interior was in the center of the wall, and the building was laid out with a high degree of symmetry along its long axis. Biblical descriptions of Solomon's temple correspond in detail to these Bronze Age sanctuaries – Solomon had in fact built a Canaanite temple, ultimately of western Syrian origin, for himself.

Other aspects of Solomon's construction projects at Jerusalem also bear strong resemblance to contemporary and older practices found in western Syria. For example, Solomon built his temple and palace side by side, an architectural and political juxtaposition that had been common during earlier times in Palestine but seems to have disappeared

Left: *Modern Muslims gather for prayers at the Dome of the Rock on the last Friday of Ramadan, the month of fasting. The Dome stands directly above the site of Solomon's temple, precluding any hands-on archaeological exploration.*

Right: *A finely detailed reconstruction of Solomon's temple, based on the description given of the building in the Bible and on the layouts of similar temple complexes built in Syria.*

Below left: *An engraving of Jerusalem, made in 1815, shows clearly the prominent and central position of the Temple.*

THE PALACE

The scriptural descriptions of Solomon's palace are considerably less clear than those of his temple. Nevertheless several details suggest that in this, too, Solomon followed a Syrian design known today as *bit hilani* after its Assyrian name. In palaces of this kind, a colonnaded central porch leads directly to the throne room, with residential suites, administrative offices, store rooms, and courtyards arrayed around and behind the throne room. The palace at Tell Tayinat took this form, as did those in other Iron Age Syrian towns. Here too the architectural concept had its roots in Bronze Age practices of western Syria.

after 1500 BC. But this tradition continued in western Syria, where comparatively small temples were often built just outside massive palaces. To take examples from just one corner of ancient northwestern Syria (the Amuq plain, which is in modern-day Turkey), the site of Tell Atchana provides examples of this juxtaposition during the middle and later Bronze Ages (roughly 1700–1400 BC), while the adjacent site of Tell Tayinat contains another pair from around 800 BC. The temple at Tell Tayinat was identical to Solomon's in concept, although it was rather smaller in size.

According to the account in the Bible, Solomon employed Phoenician master craftsmen, supplied to him by the king of Tyre, in the construction and outfitting of his temple and palace at Jerusalem. The biblical descriptions of the gold and wood decoration and the bronze accoutrements of the temple make clear their essentially Phoenician character, and these descriptions can readily be matched with objects from Cyprus and other parts of the Phoenician world. Perhaps Solomon also borrowed from Phoenician or Syrian architects the concepts and ground plans for his temple and palace. But however he came by these ideas, Solomon accepted the architectural heritage of the Canaanites that were so heartily despised in the Bible.

Although Solomon's temple and palace have never been discovered in Jerusalem, archaeologists have been able to combine documentary evidence of the structures with physical evidence from known sites of the same tradition to construct a detailed picture of the king's most renowned handiwork.

BABYLON

THE MYSTERY OF THE HANGING GARDENS

Antipater of Sidon, a writer in the 2nd century BC, created a long-standing notion when he singled out seven tourist attractions as "wonders of the world." His list included the statue of Zeus at Olympia, the temple of Artemis at Ephesus, the Colossus of Rhodes, the Mausoleum at Halicarnassus in western Asia Minor, the lighthouse at Alexandria, the Great Pyramids at Giza, and the hanging gardens of Babylon. Though some are long since destroyed and others extant, the location and character of these wonders are well known – except for the hanging gardens of Babylon.

Literary references investigated

The hanging gardens of Babylon were described by writers of the classical period as a marvelous garden planted on a vaulted structure like an artificial hill and fed constantly with water raised from the river by a hidden mechanical system. One author stated that the garden rose in a bowl within the hill slope, similar in shape to a Greek theatre. Construction of this marvel was usually attributed to Nebuchadnezzar, who built the garden on the artificial hill to please his queen, a native of the mountains east of Babylonia.

The pioneering German archaeologist Robert Koldewey excavated continuously at Babylon between 1899 and 1917. Koldewey focused on the ceremonial heart of the city, where he found the famous Ishtar Gate and the monumental buildings that lined the Processional Way – Nebuchadnezzar's palace, the temple of Marduk (the chief god of Babylonia), and the adjacent ziggurat (the tower-like

IRAQ

Babylon

stepped platform upon which sat a temple), the temple of the war goddess Ishtar and other monumental buildings of the city center. This city was the creation of Nebuchadnezzar (604–562 BC), who had restored Babylon to its former glory and had cast its net across much of the Near East.

Nebuchadnezzar's palace, set against the inner city wall just inside the Ishtar Gate, contained a massive structure of partially underground vaulted chambers, their thick walls liberally laid with bitumen, or natural asphalt. One of the chambers housed a deep well, and Koldewey proposed this structure as the site of the hanging gardens. He suggested that the vaulted chambers were foundations for the artificial hill upon which grew the garden trees. The water for the garden, he speculated, came from the well within.

Koldewey's suggestion met only partial acceptance. The structure itself did not seem to fit the descriptions of the hanging garden, and it was never clear how the garden would have thrived on this spot. Some archaeologists, observing bitumen-lined drainage ways within ziggurats of Mesopotamian cities, proposed that these stepped temple towers had been planted with trees and other plants; Babylon's hanging garden would then simply be the most grandiose of a common arrangement. But this idea does not seem probable. The drainage ways were a necessary engineering feature of these solid mud brick structures, not installed to drain excess irrigation water. And no Mesopotamian image of a ziggurat depicts it covered with vegetation.

Another, more common, reaction to the hanging garden problem has been to doubt the veracity of the classical authors, and to dismiss this wonder of the world as more legend than reality. Indeed, Herodotus, the proverbial father of history, and many other widely read classical authors failed to mention the gardens in their descriptions of Babylon, and the Babylonians themselves did not boast, whether in literature or in art, of the glories of their gardens.

Far left: *The Ishtar Gate marks the beginning of the Processional Way of the city of Babylon. It has been reconstructed using glazed and molded bricks, as the original.*

Left: *Robert Koldewey's version of the hanging gardens, suggesting that they might have been a grandiose vaulted terrace.*

THE MYSTERY MECHANISM

Cuneiform scholar Stephanie Dalley adds a new twist to the whole hanging gardens question. According to his inscriptions, Sennacherib was deeply interested in new technology, including water systems. His aqueduct was fitted with automatic sluices, the nature of which escapes us today. He also describes an innovative mechanism for raising water from the river that flowed through Nineveh up to the top of his garden.

Dalley proposes that this innovation was a screw, the invention customarily attributed to Archimedes four centuries later. Interestingly, at least one classical author states that water reached the hanging gardens by means of just such a screw. Sennacherib's description of his device is far from clear, and Dalley's proposal cannot be proven. But if she is right, then the hanging gardens of Nineveh were indeed a wonder of the ancient world.

An alternative theory However, the kings of another ancient Mesopotamian people did revel in their gardens. The Assyrians in the region north of Babylonia had dominated the Near East for 300 years before succumbing to the rising power of Babylon at the end of the 7th century BC. The Assyrian rulers used the wealth of their empire to build on a lavish scale, periodically founding new capital cities, constructing grandiose palaces, and expanding the glory of their temples. These kings took great pride in their construction projects, boasting of them lovingly in their inscriptions and depicting them in the justly famous wall reliefs that ornamented the palaces themselves. Assyrian kings possessed a dichotomous nature, revelling in the hideously cruel treatment they meted out to their adversaries, but seeking out beauty, knowledge, and tranquility in their lives at home. Gardens filled with exotic trees and plants, and stocked with unusual animals from around the empire, were the delight of these rulers.

The king Sennacherib (704–681 BC), whose unsuccessful siege of Jerusalem is depicted in the Bible, built his capital on a grand scale at Nineveh. While his "Palace without a Rival" was the crowning jewel of all his creations, he also built temples, fortifications, gates, and an elaborate aqueduct system to transport water to his city. Sennacherib also made a garden next to his beloved palace. A palace wall relief, carved half a century after his reign, depicts this garden as a hill-like mound surmounted by a colonnaded pavilion, its slopes covered with

trees of various kinds and streams flowing down from an elevated aqueduct. The carved image in fact corresponds very closely with the descriptions that classical authors left us of the hanging gardens of Babylon. And indeed even today a bowl-like depression marks the ground immediately adjacent to the remains of Sennacherib's palace at Nineveh.

NEW SUPPORT

When this wall relief was discovered in the 1850s, several scholars suggested that Sennacherib's gardens were the real hanging gardens or at least the inspiration for the later Babylonian version. But so powerful is the authority of the written word that the former possibility was forgotten even after Koldewey's excavations at Babylon failed to produce a convincing garden site. Recently, British cuneiform scholar Stephanie Dalley has resurrected the idea of the hanging gardens of Nineveh, and has marshalled additional arguments in its favor. She points out that in the Hellenistic world (Greece, Egypt, and the Near East after Alexander the Great), the historians frequently combined Assyria and Babylonia into a single heroic past, and also confused Nineveh and Babylon. So a traditional story like the hanging gardens of Babylon might easily be a confused rendering of the hanging gardens of Nineveh. This conclusion itself does not settle the matter, but does open the door. If both cities are possible venues for the hanging gardens, then Nineveh has the far stronger empirical claim to the title.

Above: *An artist's view of the palace built by Sennacherib along the banks of the River Tigris at Nineveh.*

Above left: *Six hundred people were employed in the excavations of Babylon, of which 100 alone worked on this 40-foot (12-m)-deep trench in search of the royal palace.*

Above, far left: *A copy of an Assyrian stone tablet shows king Sennacherib relaxing with his queen in sumptuous garden surroundings. This could well be further evidence for the hanging gardens of Nineveh.*

ALTAI

THE TOMB OF A PRINCESS

The Altai Mountains lie in Russia and Kazakhstan on the borders with China and Mongolia. Today's geopolitics have rendered this a remote and forbidding part of the world, but around 2,500 years ago these high grasslands were home to horse-riding nomads who amassed tremendous wealth, raising sheep and horses on the wind-swept treeless grasslands. These pastoralists buried their aristocracy in richly equipped tombs, and the freezing conditions led to some of the burial chambers and their contents remaining remarkably well preserved.

Preserved in ice   Today, several dozen icy burial mounds are known from the Altai region, and it is likely that more remain to be discovered. Archaeologists are most familiar with two groups of mounds. The first group was discovered in the Ust Ulagan valley in 1929 by Russian archaeologist Sergei I. Rudenko. These graves are commonly known as the Pazyryk graves after the local word for "burial mound." The Ust Ulagan group consisted of five large and nine small burial mounds. Rudenko excavated the first large mound in 1929, and the remaining four mounds from 1947 to 1949.

It is the chambers that are the secret to the preservation of the tombs. Humid air was trapped in them during their construction; its water vapor then condensed

on the stones in the tomb shafts and trickled back into the mounds. More water percolated into the tombs from rainfall, mountain mists, and melting snow during the first summer and autumn. The corpses and their accompanying grave goods became saturated, and during the frigid Siberian winter that followed, the moisture froze, encasing the burial chamber in a block of ice. From then on, the thickness of the burial mound and its covering of stones insulated the ice block, or "lens," from the heat of over 2,000 summers that followed.

Such natural refrigeration would have allowed the contents of the tombs to be perfectly preserved were it not for the activity of ancient grave robbers, who dug down into the burial chambers, removing many of the finer objects. Disturbance

Above: *The Frozen Princess of Ukok in her grave, a sleeping beauty found again after more than two millennia preserved in a block of ice.*

Far left: *A felt wall-hanging, almost perfectly preserved, from Barrrow 5 of the Pazyryk graves. Horses, very important in nomadic culture, were honored with burials similar to those of their human masters.*

of the ice lenses also resulted in the defrosting and decomposition of many of the organic objects within the tombs. We can only speculate about the richness of these burials when they were intact.

Mound 2 at Ust Ulagan, excavated by Rudenko in 1947, had suffered the least at the hands of the ancient robbers, probably because it was so solidly frozen. Its timber chamber was lined with felt curtains and within it, the embalmed bodies of a man and a woman had been placed together in a coffin made from a hollowed-out larch trunk wrapped in a woolen rug. The man's arms and part of one leg were covered with tattoos depicting real and imaginary animals such as griffins, rams, birds, snakes, and deer. The burial chamber also contained more textiles and clothing, wooden furniture, gold and silver ornaments, and mirrors.

Recently, high-precision radiocarbon dating of wood from Mound 2 has established its date to within a few years of 300 BC, somewhat later than had been previously believed. The other mounds in the Ust Ulagan group had a similar level of richness, although they had been looted more extensively and much of the organic material had decayed.

New discoveries

Little, if any, further field research was carried out in the Altai until the summer of 1990, when Russian archaeologist Natalya Polosmak began to search on the high Ukok Plateau near the Chinese border. Three years later, in the summer of 1993, she found and excavated an unlooted frozen tomb at Ak-Alakha. In a larch coffin, encased in ice, Polosmak found the preserved body of a twenty-five-year-old

Right: *Detail of the tattooed arm of the man buried in Barrow 2 with his wife. Mythical beasts, including griffins, mingle with rams, birds, deer, and snakes. Tattoos were discovered on other bodies from the same area.*

Above: *Scientists in Moscow examine the body of the Warrior, found in 1995, buried with his horse and weapons. The long braids of his red hair are very well preserved.*

woman wearing an elaborate wooden headdress. Although the skin of her face had decayed, enough skin on her arms and hands remained to reveal swirling tattooed figures of mythical beasts. Her body had been carefully embalmed in preparation for burial, her brain and internal organs had been removed and her body had been packed with fur, wool, peat, and bark. Just outside the chamber that held the Frozen Princess, as she became known, were the remains of six relatively old horses. Each had been killed with a blow to the head. Patches of their chestnut-brown manes and their felt saddle had been preserved by the ice.

In 1995 Natalya Polosmak's husband, Vyecheslav Molodin, found another frozen tomb not far from his wife's 1993 discovery. Under 7 feet (2 m) of ice, the body of a young man of about twenty-five to thirty was found in a wooden coffin with his weapons – a bow and arrows, an axe and a knife. The Warrior, as he was named, wore his hair in two large braids which reached almost to his waist, and his woolen hat, embroidered trousers, and sheepskin coat were very well preserved. The skin of his upper arms and torso is in remarkably good condition, and he bears a large tattoo of a deer on his right shoulder. Alongside his coffin was his horse, whose harness was decorated with animal figures carved in wood and covered with gold foil.

The bodies of the Ukok Princess and the Warrior have been taken to Moscow to be conserved at the Biological Structures Research Institute, which also looks after Lenin's embalmed remains. Local authorities in the Altai region, however, were disappointed that these finds were taken off to Novosibirsk and Moscow. In late 1995, they banned further excavations of frozen tombs. Recently, however, frozen tombs have been reported from neighboring parts of eastern Kazakhstan, offering some hope that more such spectacular burials will come to light.

THE PRINCESS' POSSESSIONS

The objects buried with the Ukok Princess included clothes, leather items, and wooden salvers with cuts of mutton and horsemeat. They were everyday items that showed signs of use. She was wearing a silk blouse which may have come from India. Coriander seeds, perhaps burnt to cover unwanted odors, were found inside the coffin. Larvae in the stomach of one of the buried horses points toward a late June burial date. Radiocarbon dating places the find at around 450 BC.

MAWANGDUI
AN UNUSUAL AUTOPSY

Life and times in the Chinese Han Empire are well documented, with literature on a wealth of subjects, many tombs decorated with bricks bearing everyday scenes, and models of domestic structures. But there is always something new to be discovered, and the excavations of the tombs of a once noble household at Mawangdui richly proved this.

A noble family The archaeological site around the modern Chinese town of Changsha, called Mawangdui, has more than a thousand ancient mounded tombs. Although most were plundered in the past, a 65-foot-high (20 m) mound proved too daunting for tomb robbers, and it remained undisturbed until 1972 when it had to make way for a hospital. As excavators dug into the first of three shafts beneath the mound, they learned that its size was not its only unique feature. The thick layers of clay and charcoal used to seal the burial chamber had combined to preserve its contents virtually intact. A wealth of organic artifacts and the uncorrupted body of its female occupant lay beneath the mound. The burials of two men in the other two chambers were also lavishly furnished. Clay seals on bamboo objects and inscriptions on lacquerware identified them as the property of the household of the Marquis of Dai. Historical sources state that Li Cang, prime minister of Changsha state, was first granted this title but it was also enjoyed by two further generations of the family. Which of the three successive marquises was buried here?

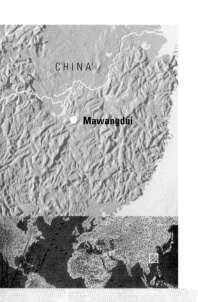

CHINA

Mawangdui

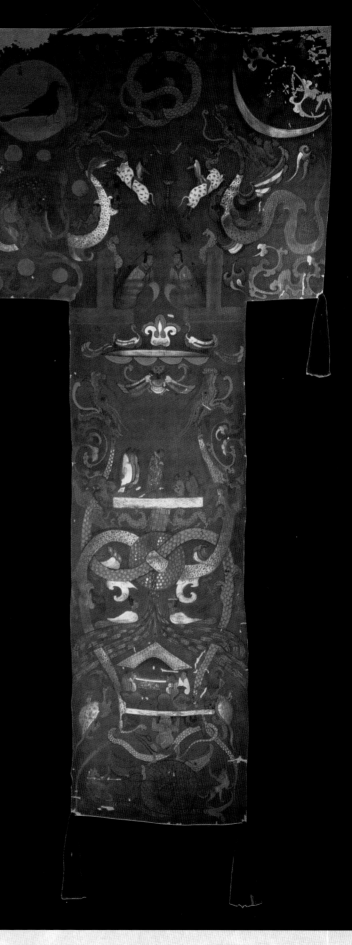

Left: *The intricacy of this bowl and the fact that it is made of lacquer reflect the importance of its owner – a member of a noble family. The poorer classes would eat off terracotta, wood, or bamboo.*

Right: *This sumptuously decorated silk banner was found with the innermost coffin during the excavations at Mawangdui. The images all symbolize significant religious and spiritual occurrences.*

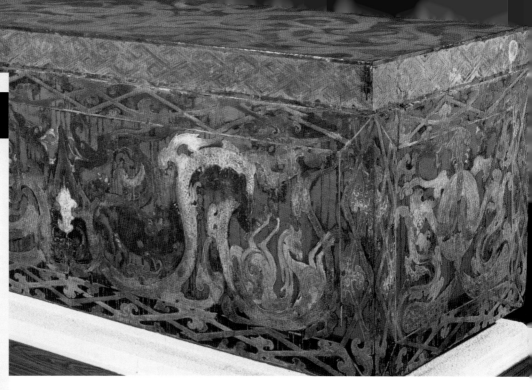

Food was probably a favorite interest of Lady Dai. To enable her to eat well in the afterlife, she was provided with pottery, bamboo, and wooden boxes containing a great selection of food – rice, millet and wheat, plums and pears, eggs, carp, hare, chicken, dog and other meat and fish. She had a superb collection of lacquerware off which to dine – chopsticks and spoons, bowls and cups, some inscribed with an invitation to drink wine, ladles and serving dishes. The finest collection of lacquer known from China, it also included many domestic objects such as a toiletry box with cosmetics, brushes, combs, a hairpiece and a mirror.

Below: *The extraordinarily well-preserved tomb of Lady Dai shows how she was buried seated next to a tray comprising a meal of vegetable and meat dishes. Subsequent analysis revealed how she died of a heart attack, most likely due to a lifetime of overindulgence.*

Three intact seals found in the grave of the elder man named him as Li Cang, so it could now be determined that this burial had taken place in 186 BC. A document found in tomb 3 recorded that the younger man was buried in 168 BC, three years before the death of the second marquis, so this was probably his younger brother, son of Li Cang and his wife Xin Zhiu, the occupant of tomb 1. Both men were well provided with the requirements of life, including amusements such as the popular board-game liubo, played with 12 pieces and an 18-sided die. Silks and lacquerware were also present, but the finest collection of these was found in the tomb of Xin Zhiu, Lady Dai.

RICH FURNISHINGS

In tombs of the earlier Shang and Zhou periods (16th–3rd centuries BC), important people were accompanied into the grave by their attendants, but by Han times (206 BC–AD 220) human sacrifice had been abandoned. Real people were replaced by modeled figures, lifesize in the case of the magnificent terra-cotta army that guarded the tomb of emperor Shi Huangdi. Lady Dai's arrangements were on a less ambitious scale but nevertheless sumptuous – 162 small figures carved from peachwood. Some were painted, others dressed in clothes of real silk. Along with the substantial quantity of clothing belonging to the lady herself buried in the chamber, these provide a detailed picture of costume in the Han period, right down to the ladies' silk slippers and embroidered gloves.

Music was regarded as a means of communicating with the spirit world, so a number of the figures were of musicians, with their pipes, mouth organs, and zithers. Genuine instruments were also included among the grave offerings. From finds like these it has been possible to build a much clearer understanding of ancient Chinese music.

A collection of superb lacquered coffins guarded Xin Zhiu's mortal remains. Scenes painted on the sides of the coffins represented the Netherworld, with its demons and benevolent spirits, while other scenes illustrated the celestial realms that lay above. These scenes were also depicted on a T-shaped silk banner that was found draped over the innermost coffin, providing new insights into the Chinese Otherworld. The lowest register of the banner shows Lady Dai's family making offerings next to her shrouded body, while images of fish symbolize the dark watery netherworld below. Lady Dai herself, leaning on a stick, waits in the middle register to be escorted to the mountainous celestial realms above, a world inhabited by dragons and other auspicious creatures.

Within the inner coffin was Xin Zhiu herself, wrapped in 20 layers of silk brocade bound with silk cords. The state of her body was quite extraordinary. It was perfectly preserved, her skin and joints were still supple and her long black hair remained neatly arranged. A subsequent autopsy showed that the insides of Xin Zhiu's body were equally well preserved, even to the extent that blood was still found in her veins.

Radiography and other methods of analysis revealed an extraordinarily complete picture of her health and physical condition at the time of her death. Contrary to the widely held belief that obesity is a modern Western disease, Lady Dai was overweight and had in fact died of a heart attack, most likely brought on by her excessive diet. To support this theory, herbal remedies for heart disease, made from cinnamon, peppercorns, and magnolia bark, were among the finds in her tomb. These were prescribed in medical texts of the time and are still recommended by Chinese herbalists today. During her life she had suffered from lumbago, gallstones, and tuberculosis. The effects of childbearing were also apparent and a fracture on her right forearm had been poorly set. She was also infested with internal parasites including whipworms. Nevertheless, at fifty she had enjoyed an unusually long life for the period.

Far left: *Scenes showing mythical creatures painted on the side of a coffin found at Mawangdui represent the Netherworld and Otherworld of Chinese mythology.*

Below: *Women of noble birth, such as Lady Dai, would use beautifully crafted cosmetic boxes and cases such as these. The compartments were used to store the different cosmetics.*

MASADA

SUICIDE OR MASSACRE?

The siege of the mountain-top stronghold of Masada forms the climax of the Jewish historian Josephus' account of the revolt against Rome. After the fall of Jerusalem and the sack of the temple in AD 70, one group of Jews held out deep in the remote desert to the west of the Dead Sea. Josephus told how the Roman general, Flavius Silva, took a force south to find them, probably in the winter of AD 73. At Passover AD 74, after a siege lasting several months, the general and his soldiers finally entered the walls, only to find that the garrison had committed suicide en masse.

ISRAEL

Masada

JORDAN

The site of the Masada stronghold had first been found by Edward Robinson and Eli Smith in 1838. Robinson was Professor of Biblical Literature at Union Theological Seminary in New York. Smith was a missionary, who had trained, like Robinson, at Andover Theological Seminary in Massachusetts. Together they made a number of topographical studies in the Holy Land, which were published in 1841 as *Biblical Researches in Palestine*. They located Masada on a high plateau known as es-Sebbeh rising some 1,300 feet (400 m) above the Dead Sea, yet below mean sea level. The first recorded ascent of Masada from the east, along the Snake Path described by Josephus, was made by British explorer Charles Warren in 1867. In the 1930s, American scholar William Albright tried to scale Masada's precipitous northern crags without success. It was only after the establishment of the modern state of Israel in 1948 that serious excavation of Masada was conducted, much of it between 1963 and 1965, by a team of archaeologists led by Yigael Yadin.

THE FORTRESS

The fortress had been developed by Herod the Great from 36 to 30 BC to serve as a secure base. He had equipped it with arsenals and storehouses to withstand a siege, and with palaces used in the winter to avoid the cold of Jerusalem. Josephus described the palaces and baths, including an intriguing passageway which led "to the very top of the mountain" through which people could move without being observed from outside. At first scholars thought the palace was located on the west side of Masada, but in the 1950s they realized it was on the northern end, built onto a series of precipitous terraces facing the Dead Sea. Excavations have shown that Herod decorated his palace in the elegant Roman style with Corinthian pillars and colorful wall-paintings.

During excavations of one of the rooms built into the outer walls of the fortress, Yadin's team found a series of Hebrew scrolls close to coins that had been minted during the Jewish revolt against Rome. One of the scrolls contained the line, "The song of the sixth Sabbath sacrifice on the ninth of the second month." Yadin realized that this was similar to the text on one of the Dead Sea scrolls found at Qumran, which lies at the northwestern end of the Dead Sea. Some scholars believe this indicates that residents of the community at Qumran, possibly a group known as the Essenes, joined the revolt and formed part of the garrison at Masada. Other scrolls discovered at Masada included the Hebrew text of the Book of Ecclesiasticus, which up to that point had only been known through the Greek translations.

Below right: *Herod's bath house, part of the king's complex and sophisticated palace-fortress at Masada. It was three storeys high and sited on the northern tip.*

Below: *Massive and impenetrable, the rock of Masada on the shore of the Dead Sea proved a very successful strategic position for a fortress strong enough to withstand the might and cunning of the Roman army.*

The siege

During the siege, the Romans built a series of eight camps around Masada, with an almost continuous 2-mile (3.5-km) wall, strengthened by towers. The earliest study of the siegeworks was made in 1909 and subsequent surveys have identified the internal details of the camps. As they excavated the sites, the archaeologists designated the camps A through H. Camp H is situated on a high bluff to the south of Masada from where all activity within the fortress could be observed. Notable features include the in-turned curving entrances known as *claviculae*. The largest of the camps (F) was located on the west side of the Masada ravine, parallel to the northern palace on its terraces. This was probably the headquarters of General Silva. Josephus described it as "an agreeable

Left: *Part of one of the Dead Sea Scrolls, discovered in a cave on the northwestern shore of the Dead Sea. This is the earliest known copy of the text of the Book of Isaiah.*

Below: *An aerial view gives a clear perspective on the remains of the Roman camp at Masada.*

THE DEAD SEA SCROLLS

One of the scrolls found at Masada bore a similar text to one of the Dead Sea scrolls. These were found in caves close to Qumran, on the northwest corner of the Dead Sea, in the early 1950s. Members of the Qumran community appear to have been obsessed with ritual washing – there was a large number of pools where ablutions could have taken place. One of the upper rooms in the complex at Qumran seems to have been used as a *scriptorium,* where some scholars have suggested the scrolls could have been prepared; inkwells were also discovered there. It seems likely that the people who lived at Qumran hid the scrolls in the caves for safety, perhaps during the troubled times of the Jewish revolt.

place . . . at which place the rock belonging to the fortress did make the nearest approach to the neighboring mountain." Excavation of Camp F showed that the Roman troops built low benches inside their tents which were used for eating and sleeping. Together the camps could have accommodated 9,000 men. Traces of a civilian encampment have been found outside the walls of Camp F. No doubt enterprising individuals camped out in the wilderness, conveniently located to provide for the needs of the troops.

The culmination of Josephus' account of the siege is a stirring speech by the Jewish commander Eleazer, and the mass suicide of the garrison which consisted of some 960 Zealots. But excavators were puzzled by the lack of bodies on the site. Remains of three individuals were found in the north palace (a young man with armor, a woman, and a child), and some 25 skeletons in a cave on the south side. Radiocarbon dating of textiles found close by indicated that the bones were placed there at roughly the time of the Jewish revolt. Yet the presence of pig bones, an animal considered "unclean" by Jews, has suggested to some scholars that these might be the remains of the Roman garrison established at Masada after its fall. Despite the discovery of Masada, the truth behind Josephus' vivid account still remains shrouded in mystery.

THE SIEGE RAMP

The western approach to Masada is dominated by a massive siege ramp, inclined at 20°, which the Romans built to gain access to the fortress. In the dry atmosphere of Masada the wood used in the ramp still protrudes, and has recently been studied to provide environmental information for the 1st century AD. At the foot of the ramp the Romans leveled an area to prepare the materials needed in its construction. Roman catapults would have limited attempts by the defenders to oppose its construction. The fact that the height of the ramp had not quite reached the height of the surrounding walls indicates that the fortress may have fallen before the ramp was completed.

Above: *A Roman siege ramp built on the western side of Masada. The builders were protected from attack by means of catapults.*

DUNHUANG
THE SECRET MANUSCRIPTS

Sir Marc Aurel Stein, a dauntless and intrepid scholar, Hungarian by birth, devoted many years of his life to exploring and documenting the ancient history and geography of Central Asia. His most exciting, most difficult, and most dangerous explorations were in the region of the Taklamakan desert where, through inspired detective work, he searched for remains of the military border which protected the western territories taken under Han Chinese control between 121 and 90 BC.

Dunhuang

CHINA

Detection and competition

Much of the military road was defended by a wall constructed from bundles of reeds held together with stamped clay. Aurel Stein was able to trace its course partly by inspired reading of the topography, which allowed him to judge where the ancient Chinese would have chosen to build the wall, and partly by spotting the remains of the ancient signal towers. On one occasion he followed a trail of small coins that had evidently trickled out of a pack in an ancient Chinese baggage train. Finds from Aurel Stein's excavations in the garrison posts, supply depots, and signal stations painted a detailed picture of life in this lonely outpost region. Aurel Stein also uncovered burials of well-preserved bodies, clad in fine textiles. The Swedish explorer Sven Hedin, the Germans Grunwedel and Von Le Coq, and the French sinologist Paul Pelliot were also exploring Central Asia in the same years of the early 20th century, and competition among them was intense.

Left: *Painting from Cave 217 of the Mogao Caves at Dunhuang, entitled "Western Paradise of the Pure Land."*

Right: *Twin towers guard the Mogao Caves at Dunhuang.*

MANUSCRIPTS IN OTHER LANGUAGES

Although far fewer in number, the non-Chinese manuscripts from Dunhuang were of exceptional interest. These included Tibetan Buddhist scriptures and Buddhist and medical texts in Indian Brahmi script. They rendered not only Sanskrit, the Classical Indian language, but also various Central Asian languages, among them the previously unknown Khotanese and Kuchean languages. The Iranian language of Sogdiana, with its own script, was also represented, as was a book of divination stories written in the rare Runic Turkish script.

Above: *A copy of the Diamond Sutra, produced in the mid-9th century, one of the earliest printed works in the world. It is in the form of a scroll 16 feet (5 m) long.*

THE CAVES OF THE 1,000 BUDDHAS

Dunhuang was one of the principal outposts in the Han Western Protectorates, a major caravan town on the international Silk Road. Twelve miles (20 km) from the oasis town, in steep cliffs overlooking a valley, Buddhist shrines and monastic cells dating from the 4th century AD onward were excavated. Embellished with paintings and stucco sculptures, the complex enjoyed its greatest prosperity under the Tang dynasty, in the 7th–10th centuries.

When Aurel Stein was exploring this region in 1907, he heard rumors of a cache of ancient manuscripts found at Dunhuang some years earlier. Forestalling his competitors, he visited the caves and began the delicate task of winning the confidence of the guardian of the cave in which the find had been made, a Taoist priest named Wang Fazhen. Wang was a timorous and uneducated man, devoted to the embellishment and protection of his cave shrine. At first he resisted the subtle negotiations of Aurel Stein's Chinese secretary, Jiang Siye, but was won over when he discovered that his respect for the Chinese pilgrim Xuan Zang was shared by Aurel Stein. In the early 7th century Xuan Zang had traveled extensively in Central Asia and India, where he had amassed a large collection of manuscripts, statues of the Buddha, and relics. Aurel Stein convincingly argued that, since their mutual hero had collected sacred scriptures to bring them to a place where they would be respectfully and reverently studied, Wang should allow his western visitor to do likewise.

Reluctantly, Wang allowed Aurel Stein and Jiang into the sealed chamber that was the secret repository of the ancient material. They were amazed by what they saw. Many thousands of manuscripts lay in a heap 10 feet (3 m) high, along with many paintings on silk, stored or hidden there in the 11th century AD.

A rapid examination revealed that the majority of the manuscripts were in Chinese, but there were some in Sanskrit and other Indian and Central Asian languages, some of them unknown.

In return for a generous donation for the embellishment of his shrine, Wang allowed Aurel Stein to take away 29 cases of manuscripts and silk temple banners which he eventually shipped to the British Museum. Pelliot visited Dunhuang in the following year and was able to take more of the manuscripts, which now reside in the Bibliothèque Nationale in Paris. A great part of the remaining material was taken by Chinese officials to Beijing, where it is housed in the National Library.

HEAVY WORK

The 7,000 manuscripts sent to the British Museum were entrusted to the care of Lionel Giles, who began sorting, cataloging, and studying them. This was an arduous task that took many years and was, as he commented wryly, physically challenging too, since the total length of the paper manuscripts he had to unroll and roll up again amounted to some 20 miles (32 km). Once sorted, the collection was assessed and studied by specialists in particular languages. The majority of the texts were Buddhist scriptures, many already well known, but even among these familiar works some treasures were found, including a copy of the Diamond Sutra. Dated AD 868, it is one of the earliest printed books to survive in the world. Taoist and Confucian texts were also present. Two manuscripts shed important light on the hitherto little-known Manichaean religion, a blend of Christian, Buddhist and Zoroastrian beliefs: the hymns relating to Jesus have attracted particular interest.

Above: *Aurel Stein (1862–1943), whose meticulous records, both written and photographic, enabled later scholars to continue work on the discoveries at Dunhuang.*

What the manuscripts revealed

The abundance of carefully dated manuscripts provided invaluable information about changes in types of paper and styles of handwriting through time, an important tool for dating other manuscripts, and data of considerable interest in their own right. The earliest paper from Dunhuang, dated AD 406, was made of the inner bark of the mulberry tree; China-grass was also used in the 5th century. Earlier paper documents were found by Stein at another site near Dunhuang, including letters written by merchants, complaining, among other things, about the postal service and the rate of exchange.

In addition to the sacred texts, some of the Chinese manuscripts dealt with secular matters. These included medical treatises and calendars used for predicting lucky and unlucky days. Little new historical material was present, however. One manuscript of a previously unknown work frustratingly ended after the preface and first five columns of text. But other subjects were better served. For example, one document is a fascinating tourist guide to Dunhuang in the 10th century AD. Poetry, manuals of advice on various subjects, and personal letters were also present, including a model letter to apologize for bad behavior when drunk. These provide many illuminating insights into Chinese daily life. Truly the Dunhuang secret chamber had proved a treasurehouse for scholars.

L'Anse aux Meadows

Olsen-Chubbuck

Pecos Pueblo

Cacaxtla

Palenque   Copán

Sipán

Machu Picchu

Chinchorro

Rapid

SECTION FOUR

NEW WORLD AND OCEANIA

T hese islands are the "latecomers" to human history, since they were colonized by humankind far later than the rest of the world. On present evidence, Australia was first occupied around 60,000 years ago. The same may well be true of the New World – the myth that big-game hunters first settled the Americas only about 12,000 years ago has been shattered by more ancient finds. Human colonization of the Pacific islands was completed around 1,000 years ago.

The Pacific regions have a rich archaeological record, ranging from the rock art in Australia to the enigmatic stone statues of Easter Island. But it is the Americas which have long caught the public imagination with their exotic civilizations. From the Arctic to Tierra del Fuego, the New World offers a wealth of ancient civilizations, and countless problems to solve.

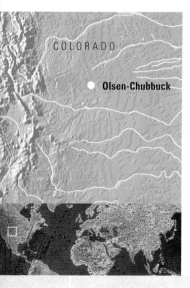

OLSEN-CHUBBUCK

THE SECRETS OF THE HUNTING GROUNDS

Scattered throughout the wind-blown Great Plains of North America are literally thousands of kill sites. These are the places where Native Americans killed the now-extinct mammoth and later the bison, or buffalo. They can be as small as the remains of a few animal bones or as large as the massive buffalo jumps, where, over thousands of years, whole herds of bison were driven off cliffs to their deaths below. Besides the animal bones themselves, archaeologists have studied the tools found at the sites, used to kill and butcher the animals. It wasn't until Joe Ben Wheat's groundbreaking work at Olsen-Chubbuck that archaeologists realized these kill sites held many more secrets about the Native Americans and their lives.

COLORADO

● **Olsen-Chubbuck**

The background   Beginning in the 1930s, kill sites across the Great Plains became important sources of information for archaeologists trying to uncover the remains of the earliest Americans. In Colorado and New Mexico, sites like Blackwater Draw, Folsom, and Lindenmeier provided fascinating glimpses into how these ancient Americans lived. They also proved that the North American continent, as a whole, had been occupied by humans for at least 11,000 years. As Great Plains archaeology became a modern scientific discipline, archaeologists wanted to find out how long the area had been occupied, how people had lived in the past, and what changes in culture had occurred. In trying to answer these basic questions, Great Plains archaeologists concentrated on studying the tools found at kill sites across the Plains. While stone butchering tools such as choppers and scrapers were found at many sites, it was the projectile points (spear and arrowheads), used to kill the animals, that were found in greatest numbers. Archaeologists studied these projectile points and their stylistic changes through time in an attempt to build up a "culture history."

They realized that kill sites, particularly sites that had been used on numerous occasions in the past, were invaluable for providing good samples of projectile points, whose changing styles could help with the construction of culture histories. Up through the 1960s, the primary reason for excavating kill sites was to obtain good samples of the Native Americans' weapons.

THE REVOLUTION

However, in 1958, Joe Ben Wheat, an archaeologist at the University of Colorado Museum in Boulder, decided to excavate a kill site for somewhat different purposes. And in so doing, Wheat helped usher in a revolution in Great Plains archaeology.

Far left: The Buffalo Hunt *by 19th-century American artist Paul Kane. Buffalo (American bison) were the main sustenance of the Plains Indians before the arrival of white settlers. The herds were hunted to extinction by the settlers to deliberately remove the Native Americans' main source of food and clothing.*

Below: *Using a giant sieve, archaeologist Dennis Stanford, of the Smithsonian Institution, sifts through the findings at a dig in the San Luis Valley, Colorado.*

There are three basic types of point. The earliest, the spear point, was in general use until about 7,000 years ago, when it was replaced by the so-called atlatl (an Aztec word for spear thrower) which was used with a throwing stick. Sometime in the first millennium BC, the bow and arrow were introduced. Within these three major groupings, archaeologists recognized that through time and from place to place the particular shape, or style, of the points also changed. These different styles are invaluable in formulating culture histories for specific regions.

The Olsen-Chubbuck site is located in eastern Colorado; it takes its name from the two amateur archaeologists who had found the site and conducted excavations there. About 8,500 years ago, a band of ancient hunters stampeded approximately 200 bison (the now-extinct *Bison occidentalis*) into a steep-sided gully about 12 feet (3.5 m) wide and 7 feet (2 m) deep. As the herd stampeded, it lost its ability to change direction. The rear animals drove the lead animals closer and closer to their doom. The bison were either killed by the fall, squashed to death by other animals, or killed by the hunters themselves.

Wheat's discoveries

Wheat began by determining the ages of the dead animals. The presence of bones from calves only a few days old led him to believe that the kill, which must have been over in a few minutes, took place in late May or early June (bison have a short and predictable annual birthing season). He was even able to tell the wind direction, based on the fact that the hunters must have approached the herd downwind and he knew in which direction the herd had been stampeded.

By carefully excavating the three distinct layers in which the animal bones were deposited, Wheat concluded that the first animals into the gully had been

left unbutchered (13 complete skeletons comprised this layer), presumably because they were just too difficult to get to, buried as they were under thousands of pounds of dead bison. Above this layer were skeletal remains that showed some signs of butchering. The top layer comprised numerous single bones and articulated segments of the skeletons themselves, indicating that these animals had been heavily butchered.

Wheat estimated that about 100 people could have butchered the entire kill in about half a day. Wheat was also able to analyze specifically how the animals had been butchered by carefully identifying the cut-marks and breaks on the bones themselves. This gave him invaluable clues to what meat cuts were preferred by the hunters and their families – tongues and the rich meat of the bison humps seemed to have been particularly prized cuts. Furthermore, Wheat was able to project from the amount of meat available from the kill the number of people who could have been fed. He estimated that about 150 people could have lived for about a month off the approximately 28 tons (25,000 kg) of meat (not to mention fat and internal organs) that the kill provided. This was based on an abnormally high consumption rate of 10 pounds (4.5 kg) of meat per person per day. A lower and more realistic consumption rate, allied with the Native Americans' ability to dry the meat for later use, would mean that the kill could have lasted considerably longer.

The questions that Wheat asked of this site – all of which dealt with the human behavior involved in both making the kill and then butchering the animals afterwards, rather than just with the projectile points and other stone tools found there – are now common in Great Plains archaeology. Wheat touched off a revolution in Great Plains archaeology, simply by asking questions that others had not considered before.

Left: *A buffalo stampede. Plains hunters would goad the animals to stampede, directing their charge so that they fell over steep cliffs where they could be slaughtered* en masse, *to provide food, skins, and bone.*

Right and above: *Archaeologist Peggy Jodry uncovering the butchered bones found at the site. Examination of the way the bones were cut up yielded evidence about the way the Plains people used their primary food source.*

CHINCHORRO MUMMIES

QUESTIONS RAISED BY THE DEAD

At the turn of the 20th century, archaeologists discovered a number of elaborately prepared and perfectly preserved mummies along the coast of northern Chile. The stiff human figures wore strange clay masks and modeled clay breasts and genitalia. The Chinchorro mummies were so well preserved that archaeologists assumed they were prepared by a sophisticated race of people. Yet recent research shows that these mummies are the oldest purposefully mummified human remains in the world and were made by small groups of hunter-gatherer fishermen using only simple techniques.

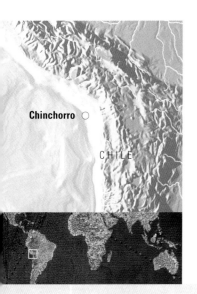

Right: *Detail from one of the mummies; although they are about 7,000 years old, the trunk and head are extremely well preserved, particularly the teeth and hair.*

Chinchorro ○

CHILE

Above: *These six mummified bodies were found interred together at tomb 7 of the El Morro 1 site at Arica. The remains of both adults and children were found in the same tomb, perhaps indicating that all the members of one unlucky family had died or been killed in the same incident. Other scholars suggest that the bodies were buried at different times, but in the same family grave.*

Initial reactions

The Chinchorro mummies were discovered along the south-central Andean coast, one of the driest areas of desert in the world, at a time when antiquities were gaining interest in the Americas. Early newspaper accounts described them and their fresh-looking appearance, but gave no indication of their true age. Both local scholars and foreigners took interest in them, but it would be half a century before radiocarbon dating would reveal their antiquity, or much else about them. Their near-perfect preservation made it hard to believe that they could be more than a few years old, and they appeared to be so elaborately prepared that it seemed likely they were produced by the most technologically and medically sophisticated people.

THE STUDY BEGINS

The German scholar Max Uhle studied a group of the mummies in the late 19th century, and his detailed research laid the foundation for all future work. At the time, there was no reliable way of determining how old the mummies were. Based on comparisons with other areas, Uhle believed that they dated to the early years AD, and were no more than about 2,000 years old. Yet he noted that the tools found with the mummies were relatively primitive in comparison with the technology produced by the civilizations of Peru.

Uhle studied the mummies carefully. He noticed a good deal of variation among them and attempted to make sense of it by classifying the mummies by appearance and by what he could see of the way they had been prepared. He noted that some of the mummies appeared to be naturally mummified, and treated only on the outside, while others had been eviscerated and had been reconstructed using mud or clay, sticks, and grasses. Excavations revealed that the mummies were generally found in small groups, often including adults, children, and babies, and scholars began to wonder whether the Chinchorro might have been buried in family groupings.

Left: *A close-up of one of the clay masks that characterize the Chinchorro mummies. Detailed research shows that when new, many of these masks would have been painted with red or black pigment.*

FURTHER QUESTIONS

Although we have made significant discoveries about the age of the Chinchorro mummies, about how they were made and by whom, we still cannot answer with any degree of certainty why they were made.

Were the ancient fishing peoples of northern Chile trying to preserve the bodies of their family members so they could be transported from camp to camp?

Were they preserved so that they could be part of group ceremonies?

Were they kept preserved until some key group or family member died so they could be interred together? Or was there some other reason? We may never know, though work is continuing on the Chinchorro.

DATING THE MUMMIES

Continuing archaeological investigations on the coast of northern Chile allowed researchers to develop the rudiments of an archaeological sequence, even before radiocarbon dating provided the necessary absolute dates. Relative dating, based only upon the relationships among objects found in the ground, and usually on the assumption that items found lower down must be older than those above, indicated the presence of two or more archaeological periods before the beginning of pottery use in the area. It became clear that the Chinchorro mummies were associated with these early periods, and not with later periods characterized by the use of pottery, metals, and other materials, settlement in formal villages and towns, and close contact with other regions of the Andes. The Chinchorro mummies, it seemed, were older than Uhle imagined.

As radiocarbon dating became widely available during the 1950s and 1960s it became possible to date organic materials from archaeological sites. Even then, however, very few radiocarbon tests were run on Chinchorro and other early materials from Chile, and the first few mummies to be subjected to the process were not among the earliest. So although archaeologists now knew that the mummies were much earlier than Uhle had believed, they assumed they were only 3,000 to 5,000 years old.

The mystery solved

It was only in the early 1980s that the true antiquity of the Chinchorro mummies was finally established. An in-depth study was performed on 96 mummies, including dissection, detailed description and analysis, and radiocarbon dating. This study provided concrete evidence that the Chinchorro mummies were up to 8,000 years old. Further radiocarbon dates were run on the mummies throughout the 1980s and 1990s and these built up a more detailed picture, showing that around 9,000 years ago the people of northern Chile started to bury their dead stretched out and wrapped in the position now known as Chinchorro. Although these earliest burials were not artificially mummified, there is evidence of artificial mummification beginning around 7,000 years ago, roughly 5000 BC.

Ongoing archaeological research into the Chinchorro mummies continues to reveal fascinating new facts about them. One of the most exciting new techniques being used is the study of ancient DNA, which may soon tell us if, indeed, the Chinchorro were buried in family groupings. The answer to that question, when it comes, will surely open up a whole new set of questions, keeping archaeologists busy with the Chinchorro for years to come.

LIFE AFTER DEATH?

Of the 282 or so mummies discovered so far (of which almost half are the result of natural preservation due to the dry coastal climate) many artificially preserved Chinchorro mummies were buried with the various everyday artifacts that had sustained them through life.

This has led to many questions about the belief systems, particularly regarding the afterlife, of these mysterious people.

Below: *Items found during the excavations included a bola stone for hunting, bone tools most likely used for prying shellfish from rocks, rope, and a fragment of mesh, possibly from a bag in which the tools were packed.*

Left: *One of the mummies in the laboratory, where extensive forensic testing was carried out. Beside the body lies the reed mat that had covered it during its time in the tomb.*

SIPÁN
THE LOOTED TOMBS

Dramatic new discoveries that change our understanding of an entire civilization are rare. The ongoing looting of archaeological sites around the world makes them even less common, since grave-robbers not only remove ancient treasures, they also destroy information that is even more valuable than the priceless objects they steal. The discovery of the Royal Tombs at Sipán, which changed forever our view of the Moche civilization of Peru and provided a glimpse of the richest tombs ever found in the New World, almost never happened.

Alva's telephone call

One night in February 1987, a telephone call from the local police awakened archaeologist Walter Alva, director of a small museum in the town of Lambayeque, Peru. He went down to the police station, little expecting that it would radically change the course of his career, making him famous and determining how he would spend the next decade or more of his life. What the police showed him changed everything.

Lambayeque is located on the coast of northern Peru, in the middle of the territory once inhabited by the great Moche civilization, one of the earliest states in the Andes. The Moche ruled the area between approximately AD 100 and 700, building huge pyramids of mud bricks in which they buried their rulers and upon which they practiced elaborate ceremonies that included the sacrifice of human prisoners. There were major Moche pyramids in each of the river valleys that cut through the coastal desert of Peru.

Walter Alva knew that many of the local archaeological sites were being looted for their treasures, but there was little he could do about it. Still, he did what he could to protect the sites in the region, and he developed a relationship with the local police, helping them with looting cases and encouraging them to do what they could to uphold the law. So when a local man denounced his comrades for looting and helped police to recover some of the items they had stolen, the police called Walter Alva to identify the materials and confirm that they were, indeed, ancient artifacts.

ECQUADOR

Sipán

PERU

THE TREASURE TROVE

Alva was astounded to find not the usual pottery and other items, but 30 of the finest gold, silver, gilded copper, and other metal objects he had ever seen. He knew from the style that they had been made by the Moche, and the looters' trail led to Sipán, to a little-known Moche pyramid called Huaca Rajada.

When Alva and the police arrived at the site, there were villagers everywhere. They had all heard of the discovery of a treasure trove of gold and silver and many had come to look for themselves. It was no easy task for the small local police force and the archaeologist to convince people to give up their treasure hunting and leave the pyramid, but they finally did, leaving Alva to set to work inspecting the site. Although the rich tomb the looters had found was almost completely destroyed, a few clues were left to indicate its form and size, and a few objects were still there. And although the confiscated objects provided evidence of rich Moche burials at Sipán, it was clear that there was still a lot more Alva could learn about the site.

Above left: *The startling circular golden head found at the site was just one of many precious artifacts. The riches sealed in the tombs were a constant temptation to looters.*

Above: *Archaeologists stand inside the Sipán sarcophagus to gather as much detail and information as possible. Discoveries at the site transformed the way scholars perceived the structure and complexity of the Moche culture.*

LOOTING IN PERU

Most of the pyramid sites on the coast of northern Peru were looted during the Spanish colonial period (16th–19th centuries) in a feverish search for gold. A few had been subject to some scientific investigation, but most were poorly protected in the turbulent 1980s when terrorism, crime, and a lack of funds kept archaeologists away from the region. Local people looted Moche sites at will, selling finds to middlemen and collectors. It was by far their best source of income, even when all they found was a few pottery vessels and an occasional metal piece.

Alva's painstaking excavation work that followed led to the discovery of other major tombs at Sipán, and the careful exploration of these tombs dramatically changed our understanding of the ancient Moche civilization. The first royal tomb was to reveal startling new facts about the nature of Moche rulership, Moche ceremony, and Moche technology and craftsmanship. Careful excavation of this and later tombs made possible a reconstruction of burial rites more detailed than any that had been done before.

Grave goods in the Royal Tombs

Conditions at Sipán were difficult. As local people kept watch, the archaeologists began their careful search for clues to the structure of the pyramid, and for more tombs. It took weeks of careful excavation, but finally they unearthed the skeleton of a man wearing a gilded copper helmet and carrying a copper shield. His feet were missing. Excavations continued, and not far below the skeleton the remains of 17 parallel wooden beams were found. The beams had been about 13 feet (4m) long, and they clearly formed the top of something, probably a room or a chamber. Below the beams, a chamber was indeed discovered, in the center of which archaeologists identified the remains of the most elaborate Moche coffin ever found. It had been made of wooden planks held together with copper straps.

Inside the coffin were the disintegrated remains of three large textiles that had served as shrouds. Under these, a treasure trove of burial goods was found, including a feather headdress with a gold ingot on top of it. The headdress looked like those worn by men depicted on Moche pottery and other art, providing the first clue that the remains being excavated might be linked to some very well known Moche iconography. Next came layers of textile banners with sheet metal figures sewn on. Items like this had never been found before, but again, they were recognizable as being similar to objects held by figures in Moche art. In fact, as the hundreds of fine textiles, beadwork, featherwork, and metal objects continued to be found, it became increasingly clear that most of these items were similar to known images from Moche art. This was unprecedented.

UNDERSTANDING OF MOCHE ICONOGRAPHY

The drama at Sipán was increasing, and causing excitement among scholars who had dedicated their careers to the study of Moche iconography, identifying recurring figures depicted in fine line painting scenes and in architectural friezes. These figures, identified by the distinctive items they carried, appeared in the art scenes to be participating in a variety of ceremonies including hunting rituals, warfare, the taking of prisoners, and the sacrifice of their captives. In one of the most chilling scenes, the blood of the sacrifice victims is presented to a warrior priest who is shown wearing items like those found in the first tomb excavated at Sipán. The richest tomb ever found in the Americas appeared to hold the mortal remains of a man who had been the central figure in the Moche sacrifice ceremony – was this the tomb of a warrior priest?

Continued research at Sipán, as well as work at other Moche sites in nearby valleys, led to the discovery of more royal tombs, containing individuals identifiable as other participants in the Moche sacrifice ceremony. The pyramids held not only the rulers, but often other members of the Moche elite classes, particularly warriors.

Archaeological research supports the proposal that many of the elite burials found in Moche pyramids in northern Peru are of hereditary rulers as well as warriors, priests, and priestesses who performed complex ceremonies that are depicted in Moche art and iconography. It was the exciting discoveries at Sipán that first revealed this pattern, and made possible a dramatic revision of our understanding of the ancient Moche.

Left: To uncover the skeletons intact, work undertaken by archaeologists is painstaking and precise.

PROTECTING SIPÁN

The gold fever that had swept the town of Sipán after the looters' discovery meant that if the site was not immediately protected, it would probably be completely destroyed by treasure hunters. To protect the site, Walter Alva set up a camp there while he began work. Four armed guards protected the pyramid and the archaeologists day and night.

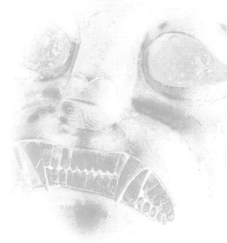

CACAXTLA

THE BIRD WOMAN

Archaeologists and art historians of Mesoamerica were shocked when, in 1975, brilliant polychrome murals of Maya color schemes and design elements were found at the highland Mexican site of Cacaxtla. These murals portrayed the defeat of Maya warriors by an army arrayed in jaguar insignia. Though Cacaxtla is far from the Maya heartland, the murals are painted in Maya artistic style, and, even more perplexing to scholars, the Maya army is represented in defeat.

The site Cacaxtla is located on a hilltop in the Puebla/Tlaxcala Valley, a high plateau east of Mexico City. It consists of a large man-made acropolis built between AD 600–800, immediately following the collapse of the great highland capital of Teotihuacán. While the Cacaxtla acropolis was probably the dwelling place of the political elite, the adjacent hill known as Xochitecatl seems to have had a more religious purpose, centered on its Temple of the Flowers, dedicated to female earth and fertility principles.

Although the archaeology of Cacaxtla-Xochitecatl is relatively recent, 16th-century historical accounts describe the site as the capital of a small kingdom dominated by the Olmeca-Xicallanca ethnic group, with its origins on the southern Gulf Coast where Chontal Maya now live. The Olmeca-Xicallanca were ruled by dual leaders, the Aquiach associated with the sky and the Tlachiach associated with the earth. Painted figures stand on either side of the doorway to Building A, one dressed in bird costume and the other in jaguar costume, standing on the back of a feathered serpent and jaguar serpent respectively. The discovery of these figures led researchers to infer that these were the Aquiach and Tlachiach in their regal attire.

THE MURALS

The murals feature life-size figures in elaborate costume and with finely detailed weapons and other objects, including two-headed ceremonial bars strongly reminiscent of Maya emblems of office. Painted hieroglyphs name important individuals, though in this case the writing system is not Maya but can be linked to

MEXICO

Cacaxtla

Above: *Detail from the so-called Battle Mural. The wall painting, in the polychrome Maya style, shows battle raging between warriors depicted as birds and jaguars. The large bird, shown here, is thought to represent a woman.*

highland Mixtec and Xochicalco styles. A stratigraphically early mural depicts the Maya merchant god "4 Dog/God L" wearing his characteristic sombrero and a carrying rack (like a modern backpack). This contained exotic trade goods from the Maya lowlands, including precious green quetzal feathers. Rising above the merchant god, following an ascending staircase, the artists depicted corn plants with small human heads in place of the cobs. The heads feature cranial deformation that mimics the form of a corn cob in a style that was characteristic of Maya representational art.

By far the most complex and perplexing part of the artistic program is the Battle Mural, painted on either side of a central staircase in a building that faces the main patio of the acropolis. The stairs divide the action into two different points in the conflict. The right side of the mural depicts the final moments of a

MARRIAGE BETWEEN LINEAGES

Marriage alliances were a common political strategy in ancient Mesoamerica. They linked distinctive and even antagonistic lineages to secure trade relations, unify geographic regions and make peace. By merging the highland Mexican jaguar lineage and the lowland Maya bird lineage into a joint dynasty, the artists of Cacaxtla were proclaiming their "international" roots while recording the city's history. Chronicles of the colonial period retain elements of this incursion of lowland Maya groups into the highlands. Gulf Coast groups such as the Olmec, Xicallanca, and Nonoalca established enclaves at highland centers such as Cholula, Tula, and Xochicalco.

violent battle while the left side represents its aftermath. In both cases jaguar warriors are represented as victorious, while the bird warriors are in defeat; many are dead or dying while others are shown naked, a sign of humiliation that the Mesoamericans used to symbolize defeat and capture for sacrifice.

The mystery woman

But two prominent figures in the costume of the bird warriors remain standing, and are dressed in the most elaborate clothes of any of the figures shown. They wear long triangular capes known as *quechquemitls*, and knee-length skirts, both with detailed woven patterns. These are typical clothing styles of women in the pre-Columbian world. Furthermore, the figures lack the typical male loincloth worn by the other warriors in the murals, further suggesting that these were females. They also wear leggings made of cloth secured with shell ties, and both wear the large bird helmets that are the insignia of their respective armies. One even wears a balloon headdress typical of Maya warrior-chiefs.

In both cases the women are confronted by a jaguar warrior with glyphic elements naming him as "3 Deer Antler" and with a mask representing Tlaloc, the Mexican Rain/Storm god. Since the two female images appear on either side of the central staircase, the archaeologists concluded that it is likely that this is the same woman depicted twice. On the earlier, right side she is wounded, with an

arrow or dart embedded in her cheek. In the other scene she is shown as a captive, with her hands bound in front of her.

The elaborate costume of the bird woman is in contrast to the nudity of the other captive warriors, suggesting a different fate. Instead of death by sacrifice, the bird woman was probably captured to become the bride of Lord "3 Deer Antler," the leader of the jaguar clan. The union of the bird and jaguar lineages would have created a new dynasty, as indicated by the flanking bird and jaguar lords depicted around the door of Building B.

If the central bird woman of the Cacaxtla Battle Murals is recognized as a key element in the action, the scene can be interpreted not simply as ethnic conflict, but rather as the capture of the founding queen of the bird/jaguar dynasty. Archaeological detective-work has been employed to consider all of the evidence in order to develop a complete and comprehensive reconstruction of the past.

Above: *The Merchant God, with his dog-shaped sombrero and backpack for carrying exotic goods.*

Above left: *Detail from the Battle Mural showing a prisoner being attacked by victorious soldiers.*

Below: *Restoration work on the Cacaxtla murals began in 1993, and continues today.*

PAKAL'S TOMB
A MAYA MYSTERY

Palenque's Temple of the Inscriptions is among the best understood and most romantic of Classic Maya structures. It is certainly the most famous. Named after the three hieroglyphic panels found inside its sanctuary, this nine-tiered temple dominates Palenque's skyline, towering above the sprawling Palace and the evocative Group of the Cross. Its forest-covered surroundings on the western Maya lowlands in Mexico, its sweeping view of the humid northern plains, and its aura of concealed mystery have captured the imagination of scholars and laymen alike since its rediscovery late in the 18th century.

MEXICO   **Palenque**

The excavations conducted by the Mexican archaeologist Alberto Ruz from 1949 to 1952 not only cleared and reconstructed the temple, but also uncovered a rubble-filled stairway leading deep into its unknown heart. For four grueling seasons, the archaeologists patiently followed the stairway's plunging shaft, tantalized now and again by small offerings that materialized from the earth matrix beneath their tireless trowels. Finally, just when it seemed that they must hit bedrock, they came upon a landing and a brief corridor, at the end of which was a large stone coffin containing the remains of six dismembered human skeletons. These sacrifices spoke to the archaeologists of something guarded and mysterious which lay just beyond a massive triangular slab of stone.

On June 15, 1952, the archaeologists removed the slab and were stunned by what they saw. An even larger chamber lay beyond the opening: a spectacular tomb, decorated with baroque stucco images, housed a huge, monolithic limestone sarcophagus covered with hieroglyphic inscriptions and intricate sculpture. The archaeologists had found the final resting place of K'inich Janaahb' Pakal I, greatest of all of Palenque's kings.

THE MAIZE GOD

Inside the sarcophagus was a tall male skeleton covered in cinnabar, a crimson mineral whose color the Maya associated with blood and life. A jade mosaic portrait mask covered his face, and intricate jade and shell earplugs lay to either side of this mask. The carved hieroglyphic texts spoke of secrets whispered into the ears of the great king by avatars of the god of rain. In each hand he held a large jade bead. Another bead had been carefully placed in his mouth. His body was bedecked in the heavy jade necklace, rings, and skirt of the Maize God – a deity which the deceased emulated both in life and in death – and a small jade statue representing the Maize God had been placed at his feet. The Maya associated jade with ripe maize, so its abundance in Pakal's sarcophagus extended the association of the king

Left: *A death mask, thought to be that of Pakal. It looks like the stucco heads of the ruler found under his sarcophagus.*

Far left: *The staircase leading down to Pakal's magnificent tomb in the Temple of Inscriptions, painstakingly unearthed by Alberto Ruz and his team.*

The name-glyphs of K'inich
Janaahb' Pakal I illustrate
the complex variation that
characterizes the Maya script. In
the first example of this name,
each sign is logographic, and
representative of a whole word.
The signs K'INICH, JANAAHB',
and PAKAL together spell K'inich
Janaahb' Pakal. Alternatively,
purely syllabic signs could be
employed, as in the second
example, where ja, na, b'i, pa, ka,
and la together spell Janaahb'
Pakal. Various combinations of
logographs and syllables are
possible within the same name,
which proved a bewildering
problem for earlier researchers,
and these contribute to the
mystery and fascination of the
New World's only fully phonetic
writing system.

with this most sacred plant and, most importantly, with the story of the Maize God. Both ancient and modern Maya myths of creation speak of a primordial ballcourt which was the place of the Maize God's burial and eventual resurrection. It is for this reason that Pakal's tomb was I-shaped, approximating the form of a ballcourt. The face of the sarcophagus itself further extends this metaphor, for it bears an elaborate depiction of the king at the moment of his rebirth from the underworld. Pakal is dressed as the Maize God, and the torch that penetrates his forehead speaks of his apotheosis as this deity. Combined with the long text describing the death and resurrection of the previous eight generations of Palenque's rulers, it is clear that the entire tomb was designed to invoke the apotheosis and resurrection of this great king.

A mighty ruler

The inscriptions in the tomb tell us that K'inich Janaahb' Pakal I was born on March 26 in the year AD 603, into a city devastated by warfare. By his eighth birthday, Palenque would be attacked three times by the neighboring "super-state" of Calakmul and her allies, and much of the ruling lineage of the city would be killed. Pakal himself became king of the beleaguered capital on July 29, 615. He proved to be a cunning ruler, and surrounded himself with trusted advisors and strong allies. By AD 645 he had extended his kingdom as far north as Comalcalco and the Gulf of Mexico, and by 659 as far south as the Usumacinta basin. As the tribute from these subjugated centers poured into Palenque, Pakal began a huge construction

Right: *The Temple of the Inscriptions at Palenque (c. AD 688) is the final resting place of Palenque's greatest king, K'inich Janaahb' Pakal I (603–683).*

program, commissioning the Templo Olvidado, Houses A, C, and E of the Palace and, eventually, the Temple of the Inscriptions itself. To the extent that we can trust the truthfulness of the hieroglyphic histories, Pakal seems to have been a great war leader, patron of the arts, and builder. He ruled Palenque for 68 years and died at the age of 80 on August 28, 683.

PROPAGANDA OR IMPOSTOR?

Palenque's explicit historical record and the legacy of earlier archaeological work made Pakal and his tomb the focus of a modern-day mystery that has required almost 50 years of painstaking detective work to resolve. A preliminary osteological examination conducted soon after the tomb's discovery reached the conclusion that the skeleton was a male in his mid-forties, a consideration which fit with contemporary opinions on the length of pre-Columbian lifespans. However, hieroglyphs in the tomb were soon deciphered and a puzzle arose. It became clear that not only the hieroglyphs found in association with the tomb, but also all of Palenque's written history and the history of other known Maya sites, demonstrated that the mighty Pakal was over 80 years old when he died.

At first there seemed no way to reconcile these two sets of data, and some scholars actually conten-ded that all inscriptions were therefore untrustworthy and examples of propa-ganda put out by the Maya elite. Thankfully, osteologists then reexamined the procedures that had been employed to age the king's remains and concluded that they had been inadequate and untrustworthy even for the time they were performed. A new examination has recently been conducted by an international team of osteologists, and their findings indicate that Pakal's remains are most definitely those of an old man who could well have lived to be 80. In future, contemporary hieroglyphic records of ancient lifespans will help us to refine our osteological aging methods and to calibrate them for pre-Columbian populations.

Above: *On the exquisitely carved sarcophagus lid, Pakal is depicted as the Maize God at the moment of his resurrection, in a posture otherwise restricted to scenes of birth and portraits of babies. He is ejected from the gaping skeletal maw of the underworld into the numinous realm of the gods. Flanking bands of celestial symbols situate the event in the heavens, and hieroglyphs at the top and bottom of the composition are the signatures of the sculptors who wrought this masterpiece.*

Left: *A jade-mosaic portrait mask of the great king, inlaid with eyes of obsidian and shell, was placed over his face to eternally evoke his appearance in life.*

COPÁN

THE MACABRE TOWER OF BATS

Copán, in modern-day Honduras, has yielded more hieroglyphic inscriptions and monuments than any other Maya ruin. The awe-inspiring pyramids, palaces, and plazas which make up the city were once the seat of the Maya king and his court. Scholars have conducted multidisciplinary studies, making Copán the most investigated of all Classic Maya sites and solving the mystery of the macabre Tower of Bats.

HONDURAS
Copán

Piecing together the past

Such is the growing understanding of ancient Copán that modern archaeological investigators, sharing their specializations and insights, have been able to reconstruct the appearance and comprehend the significance of even long-vanished structures in the city. Consider, for instance, the remarkable detective work brought to bear on Structure 20, a mysterious tower on the Copán Acropolis. The tower was destroyed by gradual erosion and flooding of the Copán River soon after the turn of the last century. Yet early reports and excavations of the structure, coupled with surviving fragments of its façade sculptures, allowed a group of archaeologists led by William Fash of Harvard University to solve the mysterious puzzle of Copán's Tower of Bats.

According to the 16th-century explorer Diego Garcia de Palacio, "on one side of this structure was a tower . . . very high, and overhanging the river which flows at its base." Indeed, by all accounts, this tower once dominated the skyline of Copán's Acropolis, and must have been an extremely important building. As well as its imposing height, however, it seems the tower also displayed a grim and frightening façade. Members of the Peabody Museum and Carnegie Institution expeditions of the 1890s and 1930s respectively, reported that a number of large sculptures of the killer bats of Maya mythology originally decorated the tower's

Above left: A building block in the shape of a skull, a reflection of the bloodthirsty nature of the culture and rituals of the ancient people of Copán.

Far left: The expedition to Copán led by John Stephens and the English surveyor Frederick Catherwood in 1839. Catherwood's meticulous drawing and surveying, and his almost intuitive ability to understand the function of a structure, however ruinous, laid the foundations for the interpretation of the Maya city.

PORTRAIT OF A CITY

Heirs to a diverse landscape with some of the richest soils of Central America, Copán's ancient farmers fed a population of 25,000 people at the city's Late Classic height (AD 700–850). The complicated construction history of the palaces and other buildings represents around 400 years of occupation. The fits and starts of this architectural record are a sensitive barometer of the relations between the elite and the commoner throughout Copán's history.

Above: *Some of the Maya ruins at Copán.*

Below: *Dramatic gargoyle features on a plinth found among the ruins.*

exterior. Using these descriptions of the bats, Fash and his team deduced that fragments of stone bats found in a pile of sculptures on the Acropolis must originally have come from the tower. They probably were moved into a pile during an excavation of the tower performed by Alfred Maudslay in 1886.

But there were other unidentified pieces of sculpture as well. Like a gigantic jigsaw puzzle in stone, some 25,000 fragments of mosaic sculpture were scattered about the site: some where they fell but others moved many times over the past 150 years of investigations. By meticulously comparing the size, style, and depth of relief of these fragments against those known to be from the tower, the investigators found that at least six of these bats originally decorated the tower's roof. Designed to be viewed from the court below, the bats appeared like the hideous gargoyles on a medieval cathedral. Moreover, they were clearly designed to provoke fright, with their collars of extruded eyeballs and large fangs which relate to Maya tales of the Underworld. The tower itself had been decorated with row upon row of extruded eyeballs and blood scrolls. Its entrance may once have been framed by the gaping maw of a monstrous bat.

MAYA MYTHOLOGY

To Fash and his team, the lost tower evoked certain dark tales of Maya myth. In the Popol Vuh, a 17th-century Maya holy book, the Hero Twins were imprisoned by the Lords of Death " . . . inside Bat House . . . a house of snatch-bats, monstrous beasts, their snouts like knives." There was no escape from this prison, for in the book the bats stood watch and eventually beheaded one of the twins. That Copán's tower reflected this myth seemed certain, but how perfect was the analogy? Was there anything, for instance, to suggest that the tower might also have been intended for use as a prison, as the Bat House was in the book?

Further clues came from an account of Alfred Maudslay's partial excavation in 1886. He described a tall central staircase that led to a second-story chamber.

Left: *Archaeologists examine ongoing work on the excavation of Temple 22 at Copán.*

BALLGAME SACRIFICE

Maya kings vied for the control of one another's kingdoms in many ways throughout the Classic Period (AD 250–900) – but perhaps the grimmest of all was the capture and torture of an enemy monarch. Weakened and demoralized, such kings were forced to play a life-or-death ballgame against their well-rested captors. Classic Maya texts and imagery depict what inevitably happened next. The vanquished king was decapitated, and his head placed in a skull rack especially erected beside the ballcourt.

Such deaths, although horrible to contemplate, deified an ancient mythical character from the *Popol Vuh*. The death of the Hero Twins' father by ballgame sacrifice made his rebirth as the Maize God possible, which was the central parable of ancient Maya religion. The decapitation of enemy monarchs was the ritual reenactment of this myth, and was considered necessary for the nourishment of the captor's realm.

Above: *The ballcourt at Copán. The ball with which the game was played may often have been the head of an enemy or sacrificial victim.*

Most importantly, he discovered that the tower was designed to be secured from the outside, not the inside. Thus the tower may have indeed been a prison.

Moreover, the ethnographic record is replete with accounts of such prisons, all designed for the holding and torture of prisoners. Besides the above example from the Popol Vuh, it was also known that the Yucatec and Lacandón Maya customarily confined prisoners and future sacrificial victims in wooden cages. Guards slept on top of the prisoners' cages throughout the night. So, might the upper chamber of the Tower of Bats have housed watchful guards?

A sticky end The sculptural style of the Tower of Bats, plus evidence from the construction history of Copán's Acropolis, demonstrates that the Tower was commissioned by one of the city's most illustrious kings, Waxaklajuun U B'aah K'awiil. He ruled from AD 695 to 738 and erected most of the stelae in the Great Plaza as well as the final version of the Great Ballcourt, the setting for a ritual Maya game, in which two teams of players scored points by hitting a solid rubber ball. Ironically, inscriptions record that this king was himself captured in warfare and beheaded – probably in an act of ballgame sacrifice – by the former puppet monarch K'ahk' Tiliw' of Quirigua, on May 3, 738.

The multidisciplinary approach of a new generation of archaeological detectives has made it clear that Copán's famous Tower of Bats was an imposing structure evoking themes of death and sacrifice central to Maya mythology. It was designed primarily for the imprisonment and demoralization of captives at the behest of the king. It may also have been the place of their eventual decapitation, perhaps in conjunction with ballgame sacrifice. In conception and general purpose, archaeologists have concluded that this early 8th-century Maya building functioned as a tool to curb courtly intrigue, safeguard potent political prisoners, and mete out kingly justice.

PECOS PUEBLO

A CONTINUOUS CULTURE

The deserts of the American Southwest are home to some spectacular archaeological ruins. Beginning over a thousand years ago, ancient Native Americans constructed large towns and villages of sandstone, wood and plaster. Some, such as Pueblo Bonito in northern New Mexico, have more than 400 individual rooms. These ruins, together with their magnificent pottery and well-preserved organic artifacts, ranging from baskets to yucca sandals and food remains, provided wonderful specimens that graced the museums of the East Coast and attracted 19th-century archaeologists and treasure-seekers.

COLORADO

● Pecos Pueblo

Left: *This photograph of the ruins at the Pecos National Historical Park, New Mexico, clearly shows the individual rooms.*

Search for understanding

In the 19th century the region was still inhabited by Native Americans who were descendants of those who had constructed these magnificent ancient ruins. So archaeologists and anthropologists were provided with a kind of living cultural laboratory for the study of native cultures. By the end of the 19th century, the study of these sites had led to sophisticated knowledge and understanding of the ancient cultures in the Southwest. The sheer quantity of information was outstanding, and new techniques and theories were being developed that would help scholars to understand the past.

However, as the store of information grew, archaeologists were increasingly frustrated by the difficulties of finding ways to organize these facts into meaningful classifications. It was important for them to develop frameworks that

Far left: *Painted pottery bowl from Pecos Pueblo, believed to be about 800 years old.*

would help them to date the cultural developments of the past. One of the leading Southwest archaeologists of the day, Alfred Kidder, decided to try to solve these problems by undertaking excavations at Pecos Pueblo, southeast of Santa Fe in northern New Mexico. His excavations, which lasted from 1915 to 1929 (interrupted by World War I and ended by the financial crash of 1929), were the largest archaeological project up to that time and remain a milestone in Southwestern archaeology.

THE SITE AT PECOS PUEBLO

Pecos Pueblo has two major concentrations of ruins that were occupied from approximately AD 1000 through to the 19th century. The overall complex had over a thousand individual rooms, although they were never all in use at the same time, because the pueblo was continuously being added to and altered. Kidder concluded that the pueblo had reached its maximum size in the 16th century, estimating that its population at that time was about a thousand people.

The large number of different occupation levels at Pecos Pueblo, which were inhabited during different periods of time, gave Kidder the chance to develop and refine a number of chronological cultural sequences. He analyzed the changing pottery styles over time at the site, and used his findings to evolve a chronological framework. His record of changing pottery styles over a long period at Pecos Pueblo was an important tool in the process of developing comparable chronologies for other sites.

Because the site was not abandoned until 1838, Kidder also had the chance to use the so-called Direct Historical Approach. A close study of the historic tribes of the area thus enabled him to compare and connect their culture with the strictly archaeological cultures he was investigating. Pecos' location, close to Plains cultures to the east, also enabled Kidder to study the cultural relationships between two major areas of settlement – the Southwest and the Great Plains.

Right: *Pecos Pueblo, one of the richest architectural sites in America, now a National Historical Park.*

Kidder's approach One of the most important features of Kidder's work at Pecos is that in the first season he avoided digging in the ruins themselves, something which earlier Southwest archaeologists had found virtually irresistible. He concentrated instead on the middens – the rubbish dumps left by the pueblo's occupants. Because of this exploratory work in the first summer, he was able to construct a detailed record of the different levels of habitation over time, finally identifying eight different pottery types that served as useful markers for the changing culture of Pecos. He also began the excavation of what, by 1925, totaled over 1,800 human burials. The quantity of these burials allowed physical anthropologist Ernest A. Hooton to compile a seminal study of the disease, pathology, and demography of the pueblo and their changes through time. Kidder even used the fledgling tool of aerial photography in his study of the site. In this, he was helped by the famous aviator Charles Lindbergh and his wife, Anne.

THE PECOS CLASSIFICATION

After six years of successful excavations at the site, in 1927 Kidder invited prominent Southwestern archaeologists to his headquarters at Pecos to try to synthesize Southwestern archaeology. The result of this seminal meeting was the so-called Pecos Classification. The archaeological past of the Southwest was divided into eight developmental stages, which were called Basketmaker I–III and Pueblo I–V. The sequence was marked by increasing sophistication in architectural techniques, technology (especially pottery manufacture and decoration), and an increasing reliance on agriculture (primarily maize, beans, and squash).

However, by 1936 it was clear that this sequence was applicable only to the northern Southwest, and so Kidder proposed that the term Anasazi be coined for this northern sequence. Similar terms, called Hohokam and Mogollon, were later used to describe the rest of the Southwest culture area.

Left: *Pottery photographed outside the ruins of the Pecos Mission. By carefully studying the various types of pottery, Alfred Kidder was able to create an accurate chronological record of the site.*

L'ANSE AUX MEADOWS

SEARCHING FOR VIKINGS IN THE NEW WORLD

The Vikings, who originated in present-day Scandinavia in the 8th century AD, were one of the greatest seafaring peoples of all time. Their sagas — as well as years of archaeological investigations — tell us they were farmers, skilled craftsmen, traders, and, of course, pillagers. For many years, scholars had suspected that the Vikings had made contact with North America, but direct evidence had eluded them until a husband and wife archaeological team excavated a site that opened up a whole new window on the past. The site at L'Anse aux Meadows showed that inhabitants of the Old and New Worlds had been in contact 500 years before the European colonization of North America.

CANADA

L'Anse aux Meadows

Above: *Typical Viking longhouses reconstructed at Epaves Bay, L'Anse aux Meadows. The existence of the longhouses establish the Scandinavian claim to be the first Europeans to reach the American landmass.*

Bold adventurers The Viking sagas tell us that in AD 982, Erik the Red, who had been banished first from Norway and then from Iceland for murder, sailed west and landed on Greenland where he established a series of colonies. His son, Leif Erikson, followed in his father's entrepreneurial footsteps. He acted on rumors of forested land even further to the west, and established a short-lived colony in an area that he called Vinland. This region was long thought to lie somewhere along the coast of northeast America, but attempts to locate the place by using geographical references and descriptions in the sagas proved unsuccessful. This is where archaeology came into play.

In 1960, Dr. Helge Ingstad, who had once been the governor of Greenland, decided to search for Vinland. Ingstad sailed north from Rhode Island, checking the local landscape for any similarities with the saga descriptions. Arriving at L'Anse aux Meadows, a small isolated fishing village on the northern coast of Newfoundland, Ingstad asked the villagers if they knew of any ancient ruins in the area. The location was marked on a 17th-century map as "Promontorium Winlandiae" (a name that Ingstad thought resembled "Vinland"). The villagers immediately took him to Epaves Bay, close to the village itself. There, on a rocky promontory, Ingstad saw a series of grass-covered ridges, suspiciously similar to the Viking villages in Iceland and Greenland. Ingstad believed that he had found a Viking settlement.

Left: *A 19th-century view of life aboard a Viking longship shows Leif Erikson sighting the coast of North America after an epic voyage across the northern Atlantic.*

Radiocarbon dating was used to date conclusively the finds at L'Anse aux Meadows. This method provides an age estimate for carbon-containing materials, such as charcoal, wood, bone, and shell, younger than about 40,000 years old. All living organisms contain small amounts of the radioactive form of carbon known as carbon-14. After an organism dies, the amount of carbon-14 present gradually decreases at a known rate until there is none left. Measurement of the amount of carbon-14 in material from an archaeological site can thus indicate how much time has passed since the death of the organism, and thereby provide a date.

Radiocarbon dates are expressed in radiocarbon years BP, meaning "before the present." The present actually refers to "before 1950," because the ratio of three different forms of carbon known in the atmosphere at that time is used as a reference point by general agreement. Radiocarbon years do not correspond exactly to calendar years, because the relative quantity of carbon-14 in the atmosphere is known to have fluctuated slightly over time. To solve this problem, archaeologists compared the dates of tree rings of known age with their radiocarbon dates, and established correction factors, which must be used to convert radiocarbon dates into corresponding calendar dates.

VINLAND REDISCOVERED

Going back the following year, Ingstad and his wife, Anne Stine Ingstad, an archaeologist, initiated full-scale excavations of the area that lasted until 1968. The Ingstads were fortunate to have modern scientific techniques of archaeological excavation and analysis and the more recently developed technique of radiocarbon dating available to them. These tools enabled them to obtain reasonably precise calendar dates for the organic materials that they excavated, including the charcoal and turf.

What the Ingstads found were the undeniable remains of a Viking village of the 11th century. L'Anse aux Meadows probably served as a base for exploring the Atlantic coast both to the north and the south. It was made up of three groups of houses (a total of eight), a smithy, and a charcoal kiln. The houses were made of layers of turf. Each group of structures comprised a longhouse, which followed the classic Viking plan, and smaller buildings. One longhouse measured just under 90 feet (27 m) by 13 feet (4 m). There is evidence of workshops for iron forging, carpentry, and weaving.

The Ingstads also found typical Viking artifacts. These included part of a spinning wheel, a hollowed stone oil lamp, a bone needle, and a bronze pin. Iron rivets were also found. All of these items were totally different from those of the contemporary Native American cultures of the area. Numerous samples were dated using the radiocarbon dating technique, and these all pointed to a period of occupation sometime around AD 1000, which agrees with what the sagas tell us. It is now certain that this village was a part of the region described in the sagas as "Vinland" (which translates as "vine-land"). Although the climate of the region was far too harsh for grape growing, it does produce many types of wild berries, which might have been used for the making of berry wine, a drink well known to Viking peoples – hence the name Vinland.

It is clear from the excavations that the occupation of L'Anse aux Meadows was fairly short, perhaps only 30 years at the most (for instance, the middens – the refuse heaps of the village – were relatively shallow). Although we are not sure exactly why the site was abandoned so soon after it had been founded, it is likely that it was just too remote even for the Vikings to feel safe (especially if they had planned on having their families live there permanently). Moreover, even under the most peaceful conditions, eking out an agricultural living in such a land and climate would have been difficult for these settlers.

Above: *Replica of a Viking house at the L'Anse aux Meadows National Historic Park. Eight original buildings were found, three of which were houses built from layers of turf supported by a wooden framework. The largest of them had five rooms.*

In context The significance of the Ingstads' excavations goes beyond simply confirming Viking contact with North America; this had been alluded to in the sagas, although in this instance the importance of the archaeological finds dwarfs the documentary evidence. Moreover, archaeological excavations further to the north have uncovered Viking artifacts at numerous native Inuit sites that date later than the L'Anse aux Meadows occupation, suggesting a much more complex contact between the Vikings and native North Americans than had once been surmised.

More importantly, though, the discovery of L'Anse aux Meadows has shown indisputably that 500 years earlier than the famous, well documented colonization of the New World by the imperial powers of Spain, England, and France, independent Viking explorers had set in motion the long process of colonizing the New World and hence bringing it into the world economic system. This has profound implications for how the descendants of those later European settlers see themselves. The Scandinavians were the first to reach the New World, not the Spanish, the English, or the French.

Left: *A modern replica of the kind of long-prowed, shallow draft ship used by the Vikings for exploration and warfare. These ships were light enough to be dragged overland and would have been brought up to the settlement for repairs.*

MACHU PICCHU

THE HIDDEN CITY

Machu Picchu is one of the most famous archaeological sites in the Americas. Tourists visit the ruins by the thousands, attracted by the site's beauty and aura of mystery. Tour guides often reinforce the idea that the site is a mysterious, unknown, and magical place. But in fact it is one of the most studied sites in the Andes, and research continues today, revealing ever more of its secrets.

The discovery of Machu Picchu

Machu Picchu was first brought to the attention of the world by the American explorer Hiram Bingham in 1911. This breathtaking site is located in the Urubamba River valley, Peru, about four days' walk from Cuzco, the ancient Inca capital. The Urubamba region is filled with Inca settlements, and virtually every square inch of it had been sculpted into agricultural terraces with elaborate irrigation systems. The Urubamba River itself was canalized and controlled in many places by masonry walls that still survive today. Bingham was led to the site, which was buried in the remote Peruvian jungle, by a local farmer while he was searching for the city of Vilcabamba, the last Inca capital and stronghold against colonial Spanish rule.

Bingham had the site partially cleared in 1911, and returned with a team to study the ruins in 1912. He cleared and mapped the ruins, excavating small portions of them, and photographed many spectacular architectural features and details. Bingham's research made the site famous around the world, and it formed the foundation for the archaeological work that was to follow. It also led to widespread interest in the mystery of Machu Picchu: the architecture, location, structure, and artifacts that Bingham uncovered clearly showed that the city was built by the Inca. But he raised one burning question: Why was such a significant settlement so inaccessibly sited? Did it have a specific purpose?

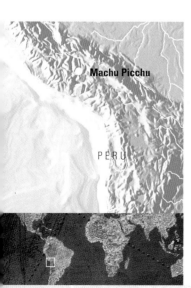

Machu Picchu

PERU

Much of the information that archaeologists have on Machu Picchu has
been derived from early colonial Spanish "chronicles," some of which are located in museums in Lima, Peru, while others are in collections in Spain. From these
sources, many of which were reports sent by the conquistadors to Emperor
Charles V of Spain, archaeologists have discovered that different Inca emperors
constructed estates in certain favorite areas. These tended to be beautifully built
royal complexes with fine architecture, royal residences, and religious structures.
Such compounds differed from many other Inca sites around the empire, which
include regional and provincial administrative capitals. In attempting to understand who built Machu Picchu and why, researchers sought out the chronicles
that discussed the area in which Machu Picchu was found. They discovered a
series of 16th-century documents, based on Inca accounts, suggesting that
Machu Picchu had been built as a royal estate by the emperor Pachacuti Inca

Below: *The ruins of Machu Picchu,
at once the most mysterious and the
best known of Inca sites.*

Yupanqui (1438–71), and that the lands surrounding the site formed part of this estate. Archaeological, architectural, astronomical, and topographic studies of Machu Picchu and its location support the idea that the site was of great significance to the Inca.

AN ASTRONOMICAL SITE?

Along with the remains of royal residences, pools and baths once fed by running water, temple complexes, and the observation points that abound at the site, Machu Picchu also contains a number of beautifully carved stones. Some of these were incorporated into buildings, but others were freestanding. Early interpretations of the latter labeled them as calendar or sun stones, but these ideas were hard to prove until researchers discovered more about the customs of the Inca. Many non-western societies developed sophisticated methods of recording the changes in the seasons that mark the appropriate times for planting and harvesting.

It was known from the Spanish chronicles that the Inca had built elaborate sun observation systems around Cuzco, and that Inca priests used them to measure the movements of the sun and thus maintain an accurate calendar. Scientific study of the site, including detailed mapping, identification of the orientations of stones, buildings, and windows with respect to angles of the sun and other astronomical bodies, suggested that several of the mysterious stone structures had been used to make astronomical and calendrical observations. Finally, observations made during solstices and equinoxes confirmed that a number of architectural features had been placed and built so that daggers of light would point to key dates in the Inca calendar.

A mountain retreat While both the historical and archaeological evidence indicated that Machu Picchu was a royal estate, visited by the Inca emperor and his entourage, when the site was excavated the human burials found were those of ordinary people, not of the elite or of royal individuals. How could this be if the site was built for the emperor and

BUILT TO LAST

The Inca are known for their remarkable stone masonry, characterized by the use of large worked stone blocks, which fit together without mortar so precisely that they have survived the seismic activity of the Andes for hundreds of years. This is in contrast to more recent Spanish constructions, which have been destroyed with each successive earthquake in the region.

Below: *Precision Inca wall-building.*

occupied by him and his entourage? More clues come from the cultivated fields at the site. Although it is difficult to be sure, since the jungle has taken over large areas of what might once have been cleared agricultural fields, there is little evidence of the production of food on a scale sufficient to support a large full-time population.

Drawing on all these clues, archaeologists now believe that Machu Picchu was most likely built by Pachacuti as a royal estate that was used as a short-term retreat, perhaps principally for meditative and religious reasons. When the emperor was away, the site was probably inhabited only by a small group of caretakers and retainers. When, however, the emperor visited Machu Picchu, hundreds of people, including priests, family members, and retainers, probably accompanied him. This would account for the city's size – it could have accommodated perhaps a thousand people. Since no one of any status in the empire lived there permanently, none was buried there. The burials found were probably of people who permanently inhabited the site, maintaining it for the emperor while he was absent, and serving as retainers when he was there.

AN ABANDONED CITY

When the Spanish arrived in Peru, Machu Picchu was no longer a major city – in fact they seemed unaware of its existence. No artifacts found at the site date to the colonial period, leading archaeologists to the conclusion that Machu Picchu may have been abandoned before or soon after the arrival of the Spaniards. Most likely, the site was maintained after Pachacuti's death by his descendants, but was not used by later emperors. It continued in use for a number of years, but was effectively abandoned by the time the Spaniards arrived, most likely due to a prolonged spell of very dry weather. They, in turn, ignored the area, as they were far more concerned with finding the last Inca capital, which was actually further down river at Vilcabamba. Today, research continues at Machu Picchu, where tourists flock to see the mysterious and beautiful site so long forgotten in the jungle.

Far left: *A doorway in one of the buildings of Machu Picchu shows the same kind of skill with masonry that the Inca demonstrated in their walls and paved roads.*

Below: *A freestanding stone amid the Inca ruins, believed to have been some form of astronomical calendar.*

THE RAPID

A CACHE OF CLUES

In the 18th century, the west coast of Australia was the first landfall for ships from the western hemisphere following the fast southerly route to the East Indies and China. "East Indiamen," large merchant sailing ships used for trans-global trade, would round the Cape of Good Hope and strike out across the southern Indian Ocean, heading for Australia's northwest Cape. They would then sail northward along the dangerous coast to Java and on to China. Many ships foundered on the treacherous reefs, especially around Point Cloates, which was incorrectly charted as an island until 1820.

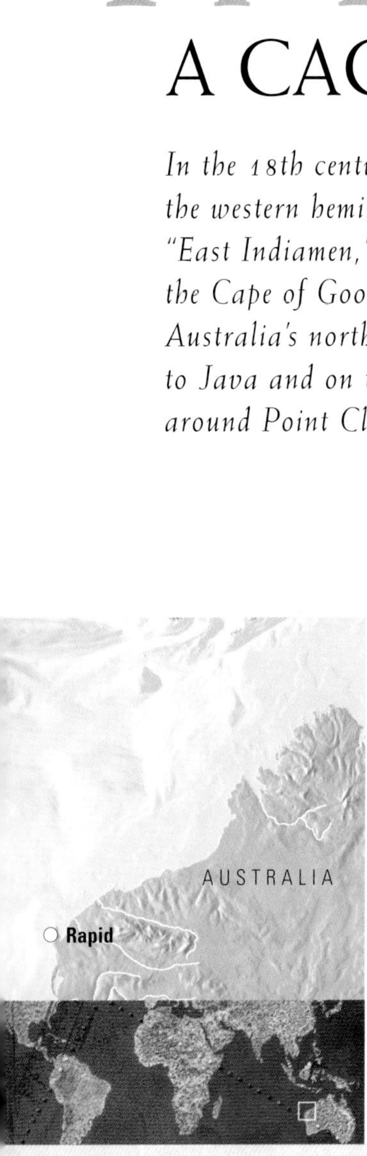

The mysterious wreck Archaeologists investigating western Australian shipwrecks have built up a detailed picture of European trade with the East. This has mainly been derived from Dutch merchant ships, such as the *Batavia*, the *Zuytdorp*, and the *Vergulde Draeck*. The first wreck of an American China trader ever reported was found in 1978 by a party of spearfishers at Point Cloates. At the time, the identity of the ship was a complete mystery. It took a grueling three years for archaeologists from the Western Australian Maritime Museum, led by Graeme Henderson, to finally piece together sufficient clues to identify the ship.

COLLECTING EVIDENCE

The first excavation took place in 1978–79. It showed that the ship had sunk in a sheltered spot on the landward side of an offshore reef. Clearly, her captain had deliberately sailed inside the reef, perhaps to reach sheltered water, enabling the

AUSTRALIA

○ **Rapid**

crew to disembark safely. Burnt timber and glass, and globules of once-molten lead showed that the ship had been on fire when she was wrecked. The mystery ship was obviously large and well armed. The size of the largest of the three anchors suggested the vessel was about 492 tons (500 tonnes). She carried eight cannons and a quantity of canister shot, a necessary defense against pirates during this period.

To identify the ship, it was crucial to establish the date of the wreck and its port of origin. Without these key facts, searching shipping records and other archives would be an impossible task. Many structural features of the ship, such as the copper sheathing on the hull, were characteristic of ships built toward the end of the 18th century. The cargo provided a more precise clue. About 19,000 silver coins, mostly Spanish silver dollars or pieces of eight, were recovered from the stern. They ranged in date from 1759 to 1809. This suggested the ship was wrecked soon after 1809.

The Spanish coins did not indicate the nationality of the ship since Spanish currency was widely used for international trade at this time. There was no sign of cargo apart from the silver. Outward-bound East Indiamen commonly sailed in ballast with a supply of currency and returned home fully laden. Analysis of the barnacles on the wreck suggested that she had been sailing northward when disaster struck. This confirmed that she was outward-bound.

MORE CLUES

Among the silver coins found in the stern were 13 United States silver dollars. These could have been part of the silver consignment, or they could have belonged to the captain and officers who would have had cabins in the stern. Small denomination coins found in the forecastle, where the crew would have been quartered, included six copper United States one-cent pieces and a single brass Chinese coin.

Other clues also indicated that this might be an American ship. A shard from a stoneware jug was stamped BOSTON. Some of the copper fittings were stamped with the name J. Davis. Archival research revealed that a Jonathan Davis was a shipbuilder in Bath, Maine, from 1785 to 1819. Most of the 22 ships he is known to have built were smaller than the Point Cloates shipwreck. However, he was also a merchant and ship's chandler and may well have supplied the fittings to the shipbuilder.

The most revealing clue, however, came during the second season of excavation in 1980. Then the archaeologists found an intact barrel of salt beef. The lid was stamped MESS BEEF BOSTON MASS. In all probability, this barrel would have been taken aboard at the port of origin.

A RED HERRING

The guns found on the wreck were stamped GR3 and IC. This indicated they were made in Britain, probably by the Christopher family of gunsmiths, in the reign of George III (1760–1820). Like the coins, however, this did not help to establish the nationality of the ship, since guns made in Britain were exported to many other countries at this time.

Left: *Coins and other small artifacts are sent up to the excavator ship via a vacuum tube while a second diver records the finds and bags them up.*

Dating the wreck

Identifying the ship as American was extremely helpful, as it further narrowed the possible date of the wreck. The War of 1812 between Britain and America interrupted trade with the East, so the ship probably left Boston sometime between 1810 and 1812.

A search through the Boston newspapers turned up a report of the loss of the *Rapid* on the coast of New Holland on January 7, 1811. She had sailed from Boston on September 28, 1810, in ballast with 280,000 Spanish pieces of eight, bound for Canton, on her second voyage to the East. She struck a reef at Point Cloates on January 7, 1811. The crew took to the boats the very next day, setting fire to the ship as they left so that she would burn to the waterline and hide the valuable cargo of coins from passing ships who might be tempted to loot it. The survivors then traveled northward in three small boats, reaching Java after a difficult and dangerous 37-day voyage covering more than 625 miles (1,000 km) of open sea. All of them were alive, although some were so weak that tragically they died shortly afterward. Captain Dorr and some of the survivors eventually sailed home in another ship.

THE MISSING SILVER

The final mystery was what happened to the rest of the silver, since only 19,000 of the 280,000 coins were found in 1978. Archival research provided a partial answer. In 1813, the *Meridian*, sent by the Boston Marine Insurance Company, insurers of the *Rapid*, managed to salvage about 90,000 dollars. A further 5,000 turned up in Java at about the same time. The remainder must have been salvaged by a passing ship that spotted the wreck, or perhaps salvors from Java reached the wreck first, with the help of the surviving crew members.

As the first American East Indiaman to be archaeologically investigated, the *Rapid* helps to fill in the details of this trade with the East. She has also contributed extensively to our understanding of early 19th-century American shipbuilding methods and techniques.

RETRACING THE PAST

From the earliest hominid sites to a 19th-century shipwreck, this timeline plots all of the sites from the book both chronologically and within the four geographic areas. You can see the dates when each archaeological site was occupied at a glance, and see which others were contemporaneous elsewhere.

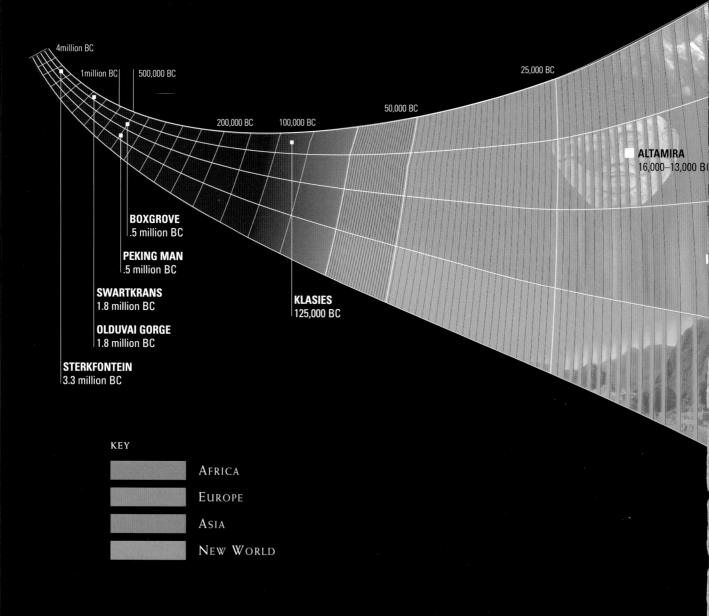

4million BC

1million BC | 500,000 BC

25,000 BC

50,000 BC

200,000 BC | 100,000 BC

ALTAMIRA
16,000–13,000 BC

BOXGROVE
.5 million BC

PEKING MAN
.5 million BC

SWARTKRANS
1.8 million BC

KLASIES
125,000 BC

OLDUVAI GORGE
1.8 million BC

STERKFONTEIN
3.3 million BC

KEY

AFRICA

EUROPE

ASIA

NEW WORLD

AD 1000

GREAT ZIMBABWE
AD 1300

1000 BC

0

GOLDEN MUMMIES
570 BC

TUTANKHAMEN
1323 BC

AMARNA
1350 BC

NOVGOROD
AD 900–1000

SUTTON HOO
AD 500

CERVETERI
500 BC

MYCENAE
1600–1500 BC

VINDOLANDA
AD 105

ICEMAN
3300 BC

HALLSTATT
700–500 BC

AKROTIRI
1630 BC

HERCULANEUM
AD 79

CORTAILLOD
4000–2000 BC

KNOSSOS
1200 BC

ATHENS
460 BC

TALHEIM
5500–5000 BC

EGTVED
1400–1100 BC

DUNHUANG
AD 406

JERUSALEM
1000 BC

MEHRGARH
7000 BC

TROY
1500–2500 BC

MASADA
74 BC

ATAL HÖYÜK
0,000–7000 BC

JERICHO
1200–1000 BC

EBLA
2400 BC

MAWANGDUI
186 BC

UR
2600 BC

ULU BURUN
1400–1300 BC

ALTAI
300 BC

MOHENJO-DARO/HARAPPA
2800 BC

KHOK PHANOM DI
2000 BC

BABYLON
700 BC

CHINCHORRO
5000 BC

COPÁN
AD 738

OLSEN-CHUBBUCK
6500 BC

RAPID
AD 1810

MACHU PICCHU
AD 1200

PALENQUE
AD 683

L'ANSE AUX MEADOWS
AD 1100

CACAXTLA
AD 600–800

SIPÁN
AD 100–700

PECOS PUEBLO
AD 1000

WHO'S WHO

BLEGEN, CARL WILLIAM (1887-1971)
American archaeologist known for his research at the site of Troy. Blegen began his research career under the auspices of the American School of Classical Studies in Athens in 1913, and remained active until his death. As a professor at the University of Cincinnati (1927–57), he directed numerous excavations of major Classical Greek sites. His research at Troy (1932–38) included a detailed stratigraphic study that identified 46 phases in the construction of the site. One phase revealed evidence of widespread violence, and is thought to substantiate the story of the sack of Troy as described in Homer's *Iliad*. In 1939 Blegen discovered some of the earliest known examples of European inscriptions, dating to approximately 1250 BC.

BOYD HAWES, HARRIETT (1871-1945)
American archaeologist known for her extensive research on the Greek island of Crete. After her graduation from college, Boyd Hawes made several trips to Crete in search of archaeological sites. Although the island was dangerous, she undertook these expeditions either alone or with a woman friend, using mules as transport. In 1901 Boyd Hawes discovered the Minoan site of Gournia, and worked there almost constantly for the next three years. Gournia was the first, and remains the most extensively excavated, site of the Minoan period on Crete.

BROOM, ROBERT (1866-1951)
Scottish physician and paleontologist known for his discoveries of australopithecine (*see* Glossary) fossils from Sterkfontein, Kromdraai, and Swartkrans, in South Africa. Broom began his research on mammal-like reptiles, becoming interested in paleoanthropology after Raymond Dart's discovery of the Taung child, a young australopithecine. In 1934 Broom joined the staff of the Transvaal Museum in Pretoria, South Africa, where he became known for a series of major discoveries of early hominids. In 1937 Broom made his most famous discovery, a robust australopithecine which he named *Paranthropus*.

CARNARVON, GEORGE EDWARD STANHOPE MOLYNEUX HERBERT, 5TH EARL OF (1866-1923)
English amateur Egyptologist, patron and associate of Howard Carter (*see* below). He sponsored the excavations that led to the discovery of the tomb of Tutankhamen in 1922. In 1906 Carnarvon went to Egypt, and the following year hired Carter to supervise excavations in the Valley of the Kings. He died in 1923 from complications of a mosquito bite received when he visited the just-opened tomb of Tutankhamen, sparking a myth that he had been killed by a mummy's curse.

CARTER, HOWARD (1874-1939)
English artist and Egyptologist known for the discovery of the tomb of Tutankhamen in 1922. Carter was born in Norfolk, England, the son of an artist. Under his father he trained in drawing and painting, and at 17 he left for Egypt. Carter gained archaeological experience as an artist on a number of excavations, eventually working for the Egyptian Antiquities Service. In 1908 Carter met the 5th Earl of Carnarvon (*see* above) and became supervisor of the excavations funded by Carnarvon. Carter eventually convinced Carnarvon to fund a search for the tomb of Tutankhamen, an obscure pharaoh who had died very young. In 1922 the discovery was made, quickly becoming known as the "find of the century."

CATON-THOMPSON, GERTRUDE (1888-1985)
English archaeologist known for her work in Egypt and for excavations at Great Zimbabwe, southern Africa. Caton-Thompson's work at Great Zimbabwe showed that the site had been built by a local civilization, establishing the importance of ancient African civilization outside of Egypt.

DUBOIS, MARIE EUGÈNE FRANÇOIS THOMAS
(1858-1940)
Dutch anatomist and paleontologist famous for his discovery of "Java Man," the first known fossil remains of the species now called *Homo erectus.* Dubois' excavations in the 1890s were some of the first to reveal evidence of the process of human evolution. Although the campaign to have his findings recognized by the world as a "missing link" in human evolution was met with considerable skepticism during much of Dubois' lifetime, his discoveries helped to establish the field of paleoanthropology.

EVANS, SIR ARTHUR JOHN *(1851-1941)*
English archaeologist known for his excavations at Knossos on the island of Crete, and for the identification of the Minoan civilization. Evans was born in Nash Mills, England, and after studying archaeology at Oxford University, he became curator of Oxford's Ashmolean Museum. In 1899 Evans began excavating at Knossos, and continued working there until 1931. He associated the labyrinthine palace site and its artifacts with the legendary King Minos, and so labeled the civilization "Minoan."

KIDDER, ALFRED VINCENT *(1885-1963)*
American archaeologist known for his pioneering excavations at Pecos, New Mexico, and for convening the first Pecos Conference, which helped to define the chronological sequence for the various cultures of southwestern United States. In 1914 Kidder, who had studied at Harvard, became the eighth person to receive a Ph.D. in archaeology in the United States. He went on to work in the southwest, as well as in Central America. Kidder helped change the emphasis in American archaeology from the collection of artifacts for museums to the detailed documentation of their context, which allowed far more detailed analysis and interpretation than had been possible in the past.

KOLDEWEY, ROBERT *(1855-1925)*
German architect known for his excavation work in Mesopotamia, especially Babylon. Koldewey participated in numerous archaeological projects in the 1880s and 1890s in the Mediterranean, Turkey, and Iraq before beginning his most notable research at Babylon in 1899. During most of the next 18 years he documented his discoveries there, which included the temple of Marduk, the palace of Nebuchadnezzar, and the Ishtar Gate. He believed that one of his discoveries, an arched structure associated with a well, was the remains of the Hanging Gardens of Babylon.

LEAKEY, LOUIS SEYMORE BAZETT *(1903-72)*
English pioneering paleoanthropologist known for his work in East Africa, especially at Olduvai Gorge, Tanzania. Leakey changed the face of anthropology through his own work, his fund raising, and his sponsorship of other scholars. The son of English missionaries, Leakey grew up in Kenya, where he developed an interest in the ancient artifacts of the region. While studying archaeology at Cambridge University, England, he formulated his then controversial idea that Africa was home to the earliest humans. Leakey spent most of his life going back and forth to Africa, alternating between limited success and virtual obscurity until the discovery in 1959 of the australopithecine *Zinjanthropus* by his second wife Mary (*see* below) established the importance of his work and of his theories. By the 1960s Leakey had established himself as one of the most significant paleoanthropologists, proving that Africa was the "cradle of mankind" and pushing back the dates for early hominids by millions of years. Leakey's legacy lives on in the work of his son Richard and Richard's wife, Maeve, as well as numerous other young scholars inspired by Leakey's work.

LEAKEY. MARY DOUGLAS (NICOL) *(1913-96)*
English archaeologist and paleoanthropologist, second wife of Louis Leakey (*see* above), and discoverer of the australopithecine *Zinjanthropus* in Olduvai Gorge, Tanzania, in 1959. The daughter of a painter, Mary Leakey grew up traveling through England, France, and Italy, becoming fascinated by archaeology after visiting excavations in the Dordogne region

of France at age 11. Leakey attended lectures in archaeology and geology at the University of London, England, but it was her artistic talent that opened the door to a career studying prehistory when Gertrude Caton-Thompson (see page 226) asked her to illustrate a book and then introduced her to Louis Leakey. After working as an archaeologist in England, she married Louis Leakey and went with him to Africa. Mary Leakey's important discoveries while working with Louis Leakey included a skull of the 20 million-year-old fossil ape *Proconsul africanus*, the 1.75 million-year-old *Australopithecus boisei* (named *Zinjanthropus* by Louis Leakey), the less robust *Homo habilis* from the same time period, a million-year-old *Homo erectus* skull, and many more fossil hominids and ancient stone tools. After Louis Leakey's death, Mary Leakey continued her work, making important discoveries at Laetoli, a site south of Olduvai Gorge, which included 3.75 million-year-old fossil hominids and a trail of hominid footprints made some 3.6 million years ago.

MARINATOS, SPYRIDON (1901-74)

Greek archaeologist known for his discovery of an ancient port on the Greek island of Thera, which was destroyed by a volcanic eruption in 1500 BC. Marinatos studied at the University of Athens, Greece, and in Berlin and Halle, Germany. A professor at Athens University, Marinatos later served as inspector general of the archaeological services of Greece. In 1939 he first suggested that Minoan civilization was destroyed by the volcanic eruption on the island of Thera. Other research revealed the site of the Battle of Thermopylae and the cemetery of the Battle of Marathon, both dating to the 5th century BC. Marinatos' later work was the excavation of the buried Bronze Age city of Akrotiri on Thera, which he hoped would reveal evidence that showed how the Minoan civilization collapsed following the eruption on Thera.

PIGGOTT, STUART (1910-94)

British archaeologist known for his work at major Neolithic sites in southern England, as well as his syntheses of Scottish, British, and European prehistory. Piggott began his archaeological work without formal academic training, working as a junior assistant at the Reading Museum, England, before going on to work on a number of excavations. Sent to India during World War II, Piggott documented a number of sites, later publishing two books on his work there. Piggott was appointed a professor of archaeology at the University of Edinburgh, Scotland, in 1946, without having completed a university degree. He eventually gained a degree at Oxford University, England, before continuing his research and prolific writing career.

RUDENKO, SERGEI IVANOVICH (1885-1969)

Russian archaeologist and ethnologist known for his work on the kurgans (burial mounds) of the Altai Mountains, especially for the frozen tombs of Pazyryk in Kazakhstan. Rudenko's early work focused on the living peoples of Siberia and Kazakhstan. Subsequent work combined archaeological and ethnological data, and in the late 1920s Rudenko began his research on frozen sites in the Altai region. He excavated at Pazyryk in 1929 and again in 1947–49. His monograph on this work, published in Russia in 1953, was translated and published in the United States in 1970, greatly increasing the worldwide impact of the research.

SCHLIEMANN, HEINRICH (1822-90)

German archaeologist whose obsession with finding the cities described by Homer in his epic poems led him to pioneer the archaeological study of Mycenaean civilization. Schliemann's father, a clergyman, suffered financial troubles that forced Schliemann to leave school as a young boy. Schliemann eventually became a highly successful businessman, but apparently always dreamed of searching for Homeric cities. Beginning in 1968 he dedicated himself to fulfilling his dreams, excavating at Troy, Mycenae, and Tiryns, among other sites. Schliemann's discoveries were important, and he proved that there was a factual basis for at least some of the places mentioned in Homer's works, but his unscientific methods caused some valuable information to be lost forever. Schliemann's work, however, captured the popular imagination, and helped lead to continued studies of Mycenaean archaeology.

STEIN, SIR MARC AUREL (1862-1943)
Hungarian-born archaeologist known for his explorations of central and western Asia, which included his work at Dunhuang, China. Stein became engaged in archaeological and historical research while studying Sanskrit in India. He became a British subject in 1904, and was later knighted. Between 1892 and 1930, Stein conducted four major expeditions through central Asia, tracing ancient caravan routes. As the superintendent of the Indian Archaeological Survey from 1910 to 1929, Stein discovered and studied numerous important archaeological sites.

UHLE, MAX (1856-1944)
German archaeologist known as the "father of Peruvian archaeology." Uhle was one of the first archaeologists to use artifact style and stratigraphy – the layering of soils and cultural remains within archaeological sites – to develop frameworks of time (chronological sequences) for a clearer understanding of the ancient past. Before the advent of radiocarbon dating this was the most important technique available to help archaeologists construct the sequence of cultures. Uhle's work in South America began in Argentina and Bolivia, under the auspices of a German museum. His work in Chile included the most extensive formal study of Chinchorro mummies. His later work, mostly in Peru, was sponsored by American institutions and some of his most important collections from the Peruvian south coast are housed in United States' museums. Uhle's research and collections from central Peru to northern Chile formed the basis for much Andean archaeology.

WHEELER, SIR ROBERT ERIC MORTIMER (1890-1976)
British archaeologist known for bringing scientific and stratigraphic methods to the archaeology of the Indian subcontinent, and for popularizing archaeo logy through television. Born in Glasgow, Scotland, Wheeler began his archaeological work in England and Wales, excavating mostly at Roman and Iron Age sites. From 1944 to 1947, as director general of archaeology in India, Wheeler introduced modern archaeological techniques to the region and helped to train a number of Indian archaeologists. His work at Harappa, Arikamedu, and Mohenjo Daro raised greater awareness of the archaeology of the entire Indian subcontinent.

WOOLLEY, SIR CHARLES LEONARD (1880-1960)
English archaeologist best known for his excavations at Ur, modern Iraq. Born in London, England, Woolley studied at Oxford University, and after graduating became assistant keeper at Oxford's Ashmolean Museum. After leaving the Ashmolean, Woolley worked on several expeditions, including excavations (1912–14) of the Hittite city of Carchemish, during which he worked with T. E. Lawrence. His most notable work stemmed from the 12 years he worked on the site at Ur. There he discovered fabulous tombs of Mesopotamian royals, the findings of which were published in both technical and popular works. Woolley's work inspired the popular imagination; *Murder in Mesopotamia* by the writer Agatha Christie is said to have been inspired by Woolley's discoveries at Ur.

YADIN, YIGAEL (1917-84)
Israeli archaeologist and military leader who headed major archaeological expeditions in Israel. Born in Jerusalem, the son of an archaeologist, Yadin spent his life in service to what later became the state of Israel. While studying archaeology, Yadin was also a member of the Haganah military organization from 1932 to 1948, becoming chief of the general staff of the Israeli defense forces (1949–52). He later led major archaeological expeditions, including projects at Hazor (1955–58 and 1968), at the Dead Sea Caves (1960–61), and at Masada (1963–65). Yadin became a professor of archaeology at the Hebrew University in 1959, and served as Israel's deputy prime minister (1977–81).

GLOSSARY

ADOBE Clay building material that is molded by hand and then baked hard in the sun. It is still used in some regions of Central America, Asia, and Europe.

ANTHROPOLOGY The study of people and their behavior. Social/cultural anthropologists study human culture in all its aspects; physical/biological anthropologists study the physical characteristics, variability, and evolution of humans in both the past and present.

ARCHAEOLOGY The study of human history and prehistory by means of site exacavation and analysis of physical remains. In the US archaeology is considered a sub-discipline of anthropology.

ARTIFACT A product of human workmanship, rather than a naturally occurring object. Artifacts are the mainstay of archaeology.

AUSTRALOPITHECINE A creature of the genus *Australopithecus*, the ape-like human ancestors that lived in eastern and southern Africa from about 1-4 million years ago.

BARROW Form of earthwork used to cover grave structures. **Long** barrows, common to the Neolithic period, are usually associated with multiple burials. **Round** barrows, more common to the European Bronze Age, covered single burial structures.

BIFACE A hand-held, multipurpose stone tool with a razor-sharp edge used for cutting, butchering, and chopping. Associated primarily with *Homo erectus*, several hundred thousand years ago, biface tools became more sophisticated in time.

CERAMIC TYPOLOGY *See* Pottery sequence

CHRONOLOGY The arrangement of events or artifacts in the order of their occurrence. Archaeologists use the relative chronology of events or finds to help them date a site, artifact, or culture. **Relative dating** refers to a chronology when the sequence is known, but not the actual dates; **absolute dating** refers to a specific time in calendrical terms.

CULTURE HISTORY The basic cultural sequence of an archaeological site, based on details of how long it was inhabited, the lifestyle of the inhabitants, and how the culture changed over time.

CUNEIFORM A wedge-shaped script, or writing system, usually found stamped into clay tablets. Three different forms of cuneiform writing are recognized today: one associated with Mesopotamia, another with the town of Ugarit, and a third unique to the Achaemenid Persians.

DOCUMENTARY EVIDENCE Evidence from any documentary or literary source, including books, inscriptions, sagas, or stories. Archaeologists use documentary evidence alongside physical or archaeological evidence to help them find sites or interpret finds.

EXCAVATION The exploration, by systematic digging into the ground, of an archaeological site.

FIND-SITE The place where an artifact was uncovered.

GRAVE GOODS Artifacts accompanying a burial. These may be rich offerings to the gods or possessions that the deceased is thought to need in the afterlife. Most ancient cultures have accompanied burials with grave goods; this has often led to looting of tombs.

HELLENISTIC A period relating to ancient Greek civilization. It is strictly the period between Alexander the Great's death (323 BC) and the defeat by Rome or the Parthians (30 BC) of the subsequent states that arose after Alexander's death.

HIEROGLYPHIC A script that uses symbols instead of individual letters to represent words, syllables, or sounds. The most famous are those of ancient Egypt, but hieroglyphs have been used by many other cultures, including the Minoan and the Maya.

HOMINID A member of the family Hominidae, which includes modern humans and many of their distant ancestors, such as the australopithecines.

HOMO A genus within the hominid family, of which modern man is a member. The first creatures classified as *Homo* appeared about 2 million years ago and formed a link between australopithecines and modern man.

ICONOGRAPHY The use of drawings and symbols to illustrate a subject. Many societies have used iconography to decorate their temples and other buildings, to tell of their culture, history, and beliefs.

KILL SITE A term used by archaeologists studying the cultures of the American Plains; a place where Native Americans killed and butchered animals for their meat. A kill site can be merely the remains of animal bones, or massive buffalo jumps where whole herds were driven off cliffs to their deaths.

MIDDEN A rubbish dump or refuse heap, usually found on the outskirts of a town. Archaeologists excavate the middens of sites because they often yield many artifacts or other clues to the cultural history of a place.

MODERN MAN Physically modern humans, of the species *Homo sapiens sapiens*, which first appeared about 125,000 years ago.

MUMMIFICATION The process of embalming or preserving a dead body before burial, often by desiccating or eviscerating it before wrapping it in bandages. The process is most closely associated with ancient Egypt where the skill peaked during the 18th, 19th, and 20th Dynasties (1550–1070 BC); it was also used by other cultures.

NEGATIVE EVIDENCE A lack of evidence that in itself provides archaeologists with valuable information. This can simply be due to looking in the wrong place, but it can also be a sign that something was absent in the past, which can be highly significant in itself.

OCCUPATION LAYERS The layers of debris and other relics of human occupation that build up on an inhabited site over time. Their relative sequence acts as a catalog of the changes in society over a given period.

ORGANIC REMAINS Remains of animal or vegetable origin that usually decompose quickly. In unusual circumstances, organic remains can be preserved for many centuries, usually by being in frozen, very dry, or waterlogged conditions.

PALEONTOLOGY The study of life in the distant past, usually through fossils.

PHILOLOGY The science of language.

PORTABLE ART Artifacts or pieces of art that can easily be moved – that is, not wall paintings or buildings, for example.

POTASSIUM-ARGON DATING A method of dating volcanic rocks, and therefore any fossils they might contain. Developed in the 1950s, the method works by measuring the relative levels of argon-40 and potassium-40 present in the rock.

POTSHERD A broken piece of discarded ceramic material found on an archaeological site.

POTTERY SEQUENCE Information used by archaeologists to ascertain the date or chronology of an artifact, building or other archaeological remains. In most civilizations, the techniques used to make and decorate pottery change over time and these diagnostic styles make up a pottery sequence. Because pottery pieces survive well, they are often used by archaeologists to provide a date for a site, since they can be compared with pottery found at sites the dates of which are already known.

PROJECTILE POINT Spearheads and other sharpened points used to hunt animals; the term is closely associated with cultures of the American Plains. The spear point was used until about 7,000 years ago, when it was replaced by the atlatl, a hooked device for throwing a dart or spear. Between 2,000 and 3,000 years ago, the bow and arrow were introduced. The changes in point style over time are used to compile cultural histories for specific regions.

RADIOCARBON DATING A method of dating ancient objects. It provides a relatively accurate date for objects that contain carbon – such as wood, charcoal, bone, and shell – and which are up to 40,000 years old. All living organisms contain small amounts of radioactive carbon-14, which gradually reduces at a known rate after an organism dies until there is none left. Measurement of the amount of carbon-14 in material from an archaeological site can therefore indicate how much time has passed since the death of the organism, and thereby provide a date.

SARCOPHAGUS An outer coffin, usually made of stone and often richly decorated. Sarcophagi are most often associated with ancient Egypt; the name is derived from the Greek word for "flesh-eating."

STELA An upright stone slab or pillar sometimes used as a gravestone. Most stelae have inscriptions or decoration, which can often provide archaeologists with valuable information.

STRATIGRAPHY The relative order of layers of occupation debris, or strata, found at an archaeological site. These strata reflect changes in the cultural history of the site over time.

SURVEY A method of acquiring archaeological information without physical disturbance of the site. It may incorporate aerial or geophysical methods, and offers a relatively fast means of exploring larger areas.

TAPHONOMY The study of the series of events by which archaeological material becomes buried and later fossilized. This term was first coined in 1940 by the Russian paleontologist J. A. Efremov.

THOLOS A dome-shaped tomb, especially of the Mycenean civilization.

TOPOGRAPHY The physical features of an area, both natural and artificial. Archaeologists study the topography of a site in the hope of finding clues to its past uses.

TUMULUS An ancient burial mound of rock or earth.

ZIGGURAT Stepped or tiered pyramid-like tower, built in Mesopotamia to honor the gods.

BIBLIOGRAPHY

GENERAL

Aitken, MJ (1990) *Science-based Dating in Archaeology*. Longman, New York/London.

Bahn, PG (ed.) (1996) *The Cambridge Illustrated History of Archaeology*. Cambridge University Press, New York/Cambridge.

Bahn, PG (ed.) (2000) *The Atlas of World Archaeology*. Checkmark Books, New York; Time Life UK, London.

Fagan, B (1995) *Time Detectives. How Archeologists Use Technology to Recapture the Past*. Touchstone, New York; Simon & Schuster, London.

Renfrew, C & Bahn, PG (2000) *Archaeology: Theories, Methods, and Practice*. Thames and Hudson, New York/London.

Website:
http://www.archaeology.org

STERKFONTEIN

Brain, CK (1981) *The Hunters or the Hunted? An Introduction to African Cave Taphonomy*. University of Chicago Press, Chicago.

Clarke, RJ (1998) First ever discovery of a well-preserved skull and associated skeleton of Australopithecus. *South African Journal of Science* 94:460–3.

— (1999) Discovery of complete arm and hand of the 3.3 million-year-old Australopithecus skeleton from Sterkfontein. *South African Journal of Science* 95:477-80.

Clarke, RJ & Tobias, PV (1995) Sterkfontein Member 2 foot bones of the oldest South African hominid. *Science* 269:521-4.

Johanson, D & Edgar, B (1996) *From Lucy to Language*. Simon and Schuster, New York; Seven Dials, London.

Kuman, K (1994) The archaeology of Sterkfontein: past and present. *Journal of Human Evolution* 27:471–95.

SWARTKRANS

Brain, CK (1981) *The Hunters or the Hunted? An Introduction to African Cave Taphonomy*. University of Chicago Press, Chicago.

Brain, CK (ed.) (1993) Swartkrans: A cave's chronicle of early man. *Transvaal Museum Monograph No. 8*, Transvaal Museum, Pretoria.

Brain, CK & Sillen, A (1988) Evidence from the Swartkrans cave for the earliest use of fire. *Nature* 336:465-6.

Brain, CK & Watson, V (1992) A guide to the Swartkrans early hominid cave site. *Annals of the Transvaal Museum* 35(25):343-65.

OLDUVAI GORGE

Johanson, D & Edgar, B (1996) *From Lucy to Language*. Simon and Schuster, New York; Seven Dials, London.

Leakey, MD (1979) *Olduvai Gorge: My Search for Early Man*. Collins, New York/London.

Leakey, MD (1984) *Disclosing the Past: An Autobiography*. Weidenfeld and Nicolson, New York/London.

Morell, V (1995) *Ancestral Passions: The Leakey Family and the Quest for Humankind's Beginnings*. Touchstone, New York; Simon & Schuster, London.

KLASIES RIVER MOUTH CAVES

Deacon, HJ & Deacon, J (1999) *Human beginnings in South Africa: Uncovering the secrets of the Stone Age*. AltaMira, Lanham MD.

Singer, R & Wymer, J (1982) *The Middle Stone Age at Klasies River Mouth in South Africa*. University of Chicago Press, Chicago/London.

THE AMARNA LETTERS

Moran, WL (1992) *The Amarna Letters*. Johns Hopkins University Press, Baltimore/London.

TUTANKHAMEN

James, TGH (1992) *Howard Carter: the Path to Tutankhamun*. Kegan Paul, New York/London.

Reeves, N (1990) *The Complete Tutankhamun*. Thames and Hudson, New York/London.

GOLDEN MUMMIES

Webster, D (1999) Valley of the Mummies. *National Geographic* 196(4):76–87.

Tyldesley, JA (1999) *The Mummy: Unwrap the Ancient Secrets of the Mummies' Tombs*. Carlton Books, London.

Hawass, Z (2000) *The Valley of the Golden Mummies*. Virgin, London

GREAT ZIMBABWE

Beach, D (1998) Cognitive archaeology and imaginary history at Great Zimbabwe. *Current Anthropology* 39:47-72.

Garlake, P (1973) *Great Zimbabwe*. Thames and Hudson, New York/London.

Huffman, TN (1996) *Snakes and Crocodiles: Power and Symbolism in Ancient Zimbabwe*. Witwatersrand University Press, Johannesburg.

BOXGROVE

Pitts, M & Roberts, M (1997) *Fairweather Eden: Life in Britain Half a Million Years Ago as Revealed by Boxgrove*. Arrow, London.

Roberts, MB & Parfitt, SA (1999) Boxgrove: a Middle Pleistocene Hominid Settlement at Eartham Quarry, Boxgrove, West Sussex. *English Heritage Archaeology Report 17*.

Roebroeks, W & Kolfschoten T. van (eds.) (1995) *The Earliest Occupation of Europe*. David Brown Book Co., Oxbow Books, Oxford.

ALTAMIRA

Bahn, PG & Vertut, J (1997) *Journey Through the Ice Age*. University of California Press, Berkeley; Seven Dials, London.

Beltrán, A (ed.) (1999) *The Cave of Altamira*. Harry N. Abrams, New York.

THE TALHEIM BURIALS

Bogucki, P (1996) The spread of early farming in Europe. *American Scientist* 84(3):242-53.

Keeley, L (1996) *War Before Civilization*. Oxford University Press, New York/Oxford.

Wahl, J & König, HG (1987) Anthropological traumatology study of the human remains of Linear Pottery farmers of Talheim, Kreis Heilbronn. *Fundberichte aus Baden-Württemberg* 12:65-193.

Windl, H (ed.) (1996) *Rätsel um Gewalt und Tod vor 7.000 Jahren*. Museum für Urgeschichte. Asparn a.d. Zaya.

CORTAILLOD

Barker, Graeme (1985) *Prehistoric Farming in Europe.* Cambridge University Press, New York/Cambridge.

Coles, B & Coles, J (1989) *People of the Wetlands.* Thames and Hudson, New York/London.

Whittle, A (1996) *Europe in the Neolithic.* Cambridge University Press, New York/Cambridge.

THE ICEMAN

Bahn, PG (1995) Last days of the Iceman. *Archaeology* 48(3):66-70.

Fowler, B (2000) *Iceman: Uncovering the Life and Times of a Prehistoric Man Found in an Alpine Glacier.* Random House, New York/London.

Roberts, D (1993) The Iceman. *National Geographic* 183(6):36-67.

Spindler, K (1994) *The Man in the Ice: the Discovery of a 5,000-Year-Old Body Reveals the Secrets of the Stone Age.* Bantam Books, New York; Phoenix Press, London.

AKROTIRI

Barber, RLN (1987) *The Cyclades in the Bronze Age.* Duckworth, London.

Doumas, CG (1983) *Thera. Pompeii of the Ancient Aegean.* Thames and Hudson, London.

— (1992) *The Wall-Paintings of Thera.* Thera Foundation, Athens.

MYCENAE

Dickinson, OTPK (1977) The origins of Mycenaean civilization. Studies in Mediterranean *Archaeology* 49: Monograph. Göteborg.

Fitton, JL (1996) *The Discovery of the Greek Bronze Age.* Harvard University Press, Cambridge, Massachusetts; British Museum Press, London.

EGTVED

Cunliffe, B (ed.) (1994) *The Oxford Illustrated Prehistory of Europe.* Oxford University Press, New York, Oxford.

Glob, PV (1974) *The Mound People: Danish Bronze-Age Man Preserved.* Cornell University Press, Ithaca, New York; Faber & Faber, London.

Kristiansen, K (1998) *Europe Before History.* Cambridge University Press, New York/Cambridge.

KNOSSOS

Chadwick, J (1958) *The Decipherment of Linear B.* Cambridge University Press, New York/Cambridge.

HALLSTATT

Cunliffe, B (ed.) (1994) *The Oxford Illustrated Prehistory of Europe.* Oxford University Press, New York/Oxford.

James, S (1993) *The World of the Celts.* Thames and Hudson, New York/London.

Wells, PS (1984) *Farms, Villages, and Cities: Commerce and Urban Origins in Late Prehistoric Europe.* Cornell University Press, Ithaca, New York.

CERVETERI

Bonfante, L (1990) *Etruscan.* University of California Press, Berkley; British Museum Press, London.

Macnamara, E (1990) *The Etruscans.* Harvard University Press, Cambridge, Massachusetts/London.

Rhodes, DE (1973) *Dennis of Etruria: the Life of George Dennis.* Cecil & Amelia Woolf, London.

Spivey, N (1997) *Etruscan Art.* Thames and Hudson, New York/London.

ATHENS

Camp, J (1986) *The Athenian Agora: Excavations in the Heart of Classical Athens.* Thames and Hudson, New York/London.

Lang, M (1960) *The Athenian Citizen: Excavations of the Athenian Agora Picture Book 4.* American School of Classical Studies, Princeton.

Lord, LE (1947) *A History of the American School of Classical Studies at Athens 1882–1942: An Intercollegiate Project.* Harvard University Press, Cambridge, Massachusetts.

Websites:
http://www.attalos.com
http://www.culture.gr

HERCULANEUM

Hibbert, C (1987) *The Grand Tour.* Thames/Methuen, London.

Waldstein, C & Shoobridge, L (1908) *Herculaneum: Past, Present, and Future.* Macmillan, London.

Ward-Perkins, J & Claridge, A (1977) *Pompeii AD 79.* Royal Academy of Arts, London.

Websites:
http://www.humnet.ucla.edu/humnet/classics/Philodemus/philhome.htm
http://volcano.und.nodak.edu/vwdocs/volc_images/img_vesuvius.html
http://acad.depauw.edu/romarch

VINDOLANDA

Birley, R (1992) Vindolanda. *Current Archaeology* 128:344-9.

— (1993) Vindolanda. *Current Archaeology* 132:504-5.

— (1997) The Vindolanda bonfire. *Current Archaeology* 153:348-57.

— (1997) *Vindolanda: A Roman Frontier Post on Hadrian's Wall.* Thames and Hudson, London.

Website:
http://www.vindolanda.com/

SUTTON HOO

Bruce-Mitford, R (1975) *The Sutton Hoo Ship-Burial, Volume 1.* William Sessions Ltd, York.

— (1978) *The Sutton Hoo Ship-Burial, Volume 2.* William Sessions Ltd, York.

— (1983) *The Sutton Hoo Ship-Burial, Volume 3.* William Sessions Ltd, York.

Carver, M (2000) *Sutton Hoo: Burial Ground of Kings?* British Museum Press, London.

Evans, AC (1994) *The Sutton Hoo Ship Burial.* British Museum Press, London.

NOVGOROD

Brown, DM (ed.) (1993) *Vikings: Raiders from the North*. Time-Life Books, Alexandria, Virgina/London.

Dunaev, M & Razumovsky, F (1984) *Novgorod. A Guide*. Raduga Publishers, Moscow.

Kolchin, BA (1989) *Wooden Artifacts from Medieval Novgorod*. B.A.R., Oxford.

Medyntseva, AA (1984) Novgorodskie nakhodki i dokristianskaia pis 'mennost' na Rusi (Novgorod finds and pre-Christian Russian writing). *Sovetskaia arkheologiia* 1984(4):49–61.

Yanin, VI (1990) The Archaeology of Novgorod. *Scientific American* 262(2):84–91.

PEKING MAN

Andersson, JG (1934) *Children of the Yellow Earth*. The MIT Press, Cambridge, Massachusetts.

Chang, KC (1968) *The Archaeology of Ancient China*. Yale University Press, New Haven.

Johanson, D & Edgar, B (1996) *From Lucy to Language*. Simon and Schuster, New York; Seven Dials, London.

Shapiro, HL (1974) *Peking Man*. Allen and Unwin, London.

ÇATAL HÖYÜK

Balter, M (1998) Why settle down? The mystery of communities. *Science* 282(5393):1442-5.

Mazar, A (1992) *Archaeology of the Land of the Bible: 10,000-586 BC*. Doubleday, New York/London.

Mellaart, J (1967) *Catal Huyuk: A Neolithic Town in Anatolia*. Thames and Hudson, New York/London.

Website: http://catal.arch.cam.ac.uk/catal/catal.html

MEHRGARH

Audouze, F & Jarrige, C (1979) A Third Millennium Pottery-Firing Structure at Mehrgarh and its Economic Implications edited by M. Taddei. *South Asian Archaeology 1977 Naples, Istituto Universitario Orientale, Seminario di Studi Asiatici*, Series Minor 6:213-221.

Jarrige, C; Jarrige, JF; Meadow, R & Quivron, G (1995) *Mehrgarh: Field Reports 1974-1985*. Department of Culture and Tourism of Sindh, Pakistan.

Jarrige, JF (1981) *Economy and Society in the Early Chalcolithic/Bronze Age of Baluchistan in South Asian Archaeology 1979* edited by H. Hartel. Dietrich Reimer Verlag, Berlin.

Lechevallier, M & Quivron, G (1985) Results of the Recent Excavations at the Neolithic Site of Mehrgarh in South Asian Archaeology 1983, edited by M Taddei. *Naples, Istituto Universitario Orientale, Dipartimento di Studi Asiatici*, Series Minor 23:69-90.

MOHENJO DARO

Jansen, M (1993) *Mohenjo Daro: City of Wells and Drains*. Bergisch Gladbach, Frontinus Gesellschaft e.V.

Jansen, M & Urban, G (eds.) (1984 and 1987) Interim Reports, Volumes 1 and 2. Aachen, Rome.

Marshall, J (1979) *In Ancient Cities of the Indus* edited by G Possehl. Vikas Publishing House, Delhi.

McIntosh, J (2001) *A Peaceful Realm*. Westview Press, Boulder, Colorado.

CITY OF UR

Moorey, RSP (1967) What do we know about the people buried in the Royal Cemetery? *Expedition* 20(1):24-40.

Woolley, CL & Moorey, RSP (1982) *Ur of the Chaldees, The Final Account*. Herbert Press, London.

Woolley, CL (1934) *Ur Excavations II: The Royal Cemetery*. British Museum Press, London.

EBLA

Roaf, M (1990) *Cultural Atlas of Mesopotamia and the Ancient Near East*. Facts on File, New York.

Weiss, H (ed.) (1985) *Ebla to Damascus: Art and Archaeology of Ancient Syria*. University of Washington Press, Seattle.

TROY

Antonova, I; Tolstikov, V & Treister, M (1996) *The Gold of Troy: Searching for Homer's Fabled City*. Thames and Hudson, London.

Fitton, JL (1996) *The Discovery of the Greek Bronze Age*. Harvard University Press, Cambridge, Massachusetts; British Museum Press, London.

KHOK PHANOM DI

Higham, C & Thosarat, R (1994) *Khok Phanom Di*. Harcourt Brace, Fort Worth, Texas.

— (1998) *Prehistoric Thailand*. Thames and Hudson, New York/London.

ULU BURUN

Bass, GF (1987) Oldest Known Shipwreck Reveals Splendors of the Bronze Age. *National Geographic* 172(6):693–733.

JERICHO

Bloch-Smith, E & Nakhai, BA (1999) A landscape comes to life: the Iron Age I. *Near Eastern Archaeology* 62(2):62-127.

Finkelstein, I (1988) *The Archaeology of the Israelite Settlement*. Israel Exploration Society, Jerusalem.

SOLOMON'S TEMPLE

Isserlin, BSJ (1998) *The Israelites*. Thames and Hudson, New York/London.

BABYLON

Oates, J (1986) *Babylon*. Thames and Hudson, New York/London.

Saggs, HWF (1984) *The Might That Was Assyria*. St. Martin's Press, New York; Sidgwick & Jackson, London.

Dalley, S (1994) *Nineveh, Babylon and the Hanging Gardens: cuneiform and classical sources reconciled*. Iraq 56:45-58.

ALTAI

Polosmak, N (1994) A mummy unearthed from the Pastures of Heaven. *National Geographic* 186(4):80–103.

Rudenko, S (1970) *Frozen Tombs of Siberia: the Pazyryk Burials of Iron Age Horsemen*. University of California Press, Los Angeles; Dent, London.

MAWANGDUI

Hall, AJ (1974) A lady from China's past. *National Geographic*: 660-82.

Qian, H (1981) *Out of China's Earth*. Muller, London.

Rawson, J (1996) *Mysteries of Ancient China*. British Museum Press, London.

MASADA

King, PJ (1983) *American Archaeology in the Mideast: a History of the American Schools of Oriental Research.* The American Schools of Oriental Research, Philadelphia.

Richmond, IA (1962) The Roman siege-works of Masada, Israel. *Journal of Roman Studies* 52:142–55.

Yadin, Y (1997) *Masada: Herod's Fortress and the Zealots' Last Stand.* Random House, New York/London.

Website:

http://www.hum.huji.ac.il/ies/about.htm

DUNHUANG

Giles, L (1944) *Six Centuries at Tunhuang.* The China Society, London.

Stein, A (1964) *On Ancient Central-Asian Tracks.* University of Chicago Press, Chicago.

OLSEN-CHUBBUCK

Frison, G et al (1991) *Prehistoric Hunters of the High Plains.* Harcourt Publishers, San Diego.

Wheat, JB (1967) A Paleoindian bison kill. *Scientific American.*

Fagan, B (1991) *Ancient North America.* Thames and Hudson, New York/London.

CHINCHORRO

Arriaza, BT (1995) *Beyond Death: The Chinchorro Mummies of Ancient Chile.* Smithsonian Institution Press, Washington, DC/London.

Morris, C & Von Hagen, A (1993) *The Inka Empire and its Andean Origins.* Abbeville Press, New York/London.

Moseley, ME (1992) *The Incas and their Ancestors.* Thames and Hudson, New York/London.

SIPÁN

Alva, W & Donnan, CB (1993) *Royal Tombs of Sipán.* University of California, Los Angeles.

Morris, C & Von Hagen, A (1993) *The Inka Empire and its Andean Origins.* Abbeville Press, New York/London.

Moseley, ME (1992) *The Incas and their Ancestors.* Thames and Hudson, New York/London.

CACAXTLA

Diehl, RA & Berlo, JC (eds.) (1989) *Mesoamerica After the Decline of Teotihuacán,* AD 700-900. Dumbarton Oaks Research Library and Collection, Washington, DC.

McCafferty, SD & McCafferty, G (1994) The conquered women of Cacaxtla: gender identity or gender ideology? *Ancient Mesoamerica* 5:159-72.

Robertson, D (1985) The Cacaxtla murals. In *Fourth Palenque Round Table* edited by Elizabeth P Benson. The Pre-Columbian Art Research Institute, San Francisco.

Stuart, GE (1992) Mural masterpieces of ancient Cacaxtla. *National Geographic* 182(3):120-36.

PAKAL'S TOMB

Mathews, P & Schele, L (1974) Lords of Palenque – The Glyphic Evidence. In *Primera Mesa Redonda de Palenque, Part I* edited by Merle Greene Robertson. Robert Louis Stevenson School, Pebble Beach, California.

Ruz Lhuillier, A (1973) *El Templo de las Inscripciones de Palenque.* Coleccion Cientifica, Arqueologia 7, Instituto Nacional de Antropologia e Historia, Mexico.

Schele, L & Mathews, P (1998) *The Code of Kings: The Language of Seven Sacred Maya Temples and Tombs.* Scribner, New York.

COPÁN

Baudez, CF (ed.) (1983) *Introduccíon a la Arqueologia de Copán* (volumes 1–3). Secretaria de Estado en el Despacho de Cultura y Turismo, Tegucigalpa, Honduras.

Fash, WL (1991) *Scribes, Warriors, and Kings: The City of Copán and the Ancient Maya.* Thames and Hudson, New York/London.

Proskouriakoff, T (1963) *An Album of Classic Maya Architecture.* Carnegie Institution of Washington (publication 558), Washington, DC.

Robicsek, F (1972) *Copán: Home of the Mayan Gods.* Museum of the American Indian, New York.

Schele, L & Mathews, P (1998) *The Code of Kings: The Language of Seven Sacred Maya Temples and Tombs.* Scribner, New York.

Webster, D; Freter, A & Gonlin, N (2000) *Copán: the Rise and Fall of an Ancient Maya Kingdom.* Harcourt College Publishers, New York.

PECOS PUEBLO

Cordell, L (1997) *Archaeology of the Southwest,* Academic Press, San Diego.

Kidder, AV (2000) *An Introduction to Southwestern Archaeology.* Yale University Press, New Haven.

L'ANSE AUX MEADOWS

Fitshugh, W (2000) *Vikings: The North Atlantic Saga.* Smithsonian Institution, Wasington DC.

Ingstad, AS (1987) *The Norse Discovery of America.* Scandinavian Press, Oslo.

MACHU PICCHU

Morris, C & Von Hagen, A (1993) *The Inca Empire and its Andean Origins.* Abbeville Press, New York/London.

Moseley, ME (1992) *The Incas and their Ancestors.* Thames and Hudson, New York/London.

Von Hagen, A & Morris, C (1998) *The Cities of the Ancient Andes.* Thames and Hudson, New York/London.

THE *RAPID*

Henderson, G (1980) Indiamen traders of the East. *Archaeology* 33(6):22-7.

— (1981) The American China Trader *Rapid* (1811): an early Western Australian shipwreck site identified. *Great Circle* 3:125-32.

— (1986) *Maritime Archaeology in Australia.* University of Western Australia Press, Nedlands, Western Australia.

INDEX

ACKNOWLEDGEMENTS

PHOTOGRAPHIC CREDITS

ARCHIV FUR KUNST UND GESCHICHTE, LONDON:40,1 32B, 212(National Gallery, Oslo). Erich Lessing/AKG:41L (Cairo National Museum), 82B (Copenhagen National Museum) 85, 90 + 91B (Natural History Museum, Vienna), 138 (National Museum of Aleppo),157 (Israel Museum). Jurgen Sorge/AKG:179. Veintimilla/AKG:197, 199T, 217, 218B.

THE ART ARCHIVE, LONDON:86, 125, 136+180 (British Museum). Dagli Orti/Art Archive:35, 39, 130R.

Paul Bahn:57B.

Dr. Benarndo Ariazza:188–191 all.

THE BRIDGEMAN ART LIBRARY,LONDON:74T (National Archaeological Museum, Athens), 135R, 137(British Museum). Roger Violett/BAL 38t. Heini Schneebeli/BAL:49T

The British Museum:108–111 ALL.

Cameron Collection:78T, 96/97, 160B, 163, 165.

The National Museum:Copenhagen:80–85 ALL.

CORBIS, LONDON:126/127, 132, 141T, 164, 178, 185, 187, 198, 199B, 208, 209, 210, 211, 213, 214. AFP: 44L. Archivo Iconographico:95B, 130T. Asian Art and Architecture Inc.:170, 171, 172T, 173B. Tony Arruza:206T. Betmann:28R, 77B, 121. Jonathan Blair:101R, 102. Pierre Colombel:178. Richard A. Cooke 111:185, 187B, 207T. Gianni Dagli Orti:73, 94B, 98, 139B, 141B. M.Dillon:212/211B. Sergio Dorantes:201 Franz-Marc Frei:93. Mimmo Jodice:103. Annie Griffiths:160T. Robert Holmes:48. Colin Hoskins/Cordaiy Pt Ltd.:48B. Wolfgang Kaehler:74B, 99, 214, 215. David Lees: 134/135. Charles and Josette Lenars: 139T, 154/155, 198, 219, 176.Charles O'Rear:167, 169. Diego Lezama Orezzoli:133.

Craig Lovell:205, 207B. Buddy Mays:208. MIT Coll:47B. David Muench:209, 211. François de Mulder:162. Richard T. Norwitz:155, 159, 175. Bryan Pickering:60/61. Greg Probst:213. Bill Ross:156. Galen Rowell:218T. Ted Spiegel:174. Underwood and Underwood:164R. Ruggero Vanni:37. Patrick Ward:107. Peter Wilson:97. Adam Woolfitt:89L.

WERNER FORMAN ARCHIVE:15+203 (National Museum of Anthropology, Mexico).

SONIA HALLIDAY PHOTOS:122T, 123, 118/119 (Jane Taylor).

ROBERT HARDING PICTURE LIBRARY:194, 195. Bildargentur Schmid:202. Sergio Dorantes:201. Robert Frerck:200. C. Hienz Plenge:192/193, 193, 194, 195.

ENGLISH HERITAGE/Jonathan Bailey:53. Skyscan Balloon Photography:105.

Charles Higham:147, 148, 148L, 148R.

EUROLIOS PARIS/Phillipe Plailly:42, 43, 44T, 45.

Jean-François Jarrige:128.

THE KOBAL COLLECTION:8.

TRANSVAAL MUSEUM/:

Photographer Dr. Gerald Newlands/18, 22. D de Ruiter 25.

NATIONAL GEOGRAPHIC SOCIETY/Bill Curtsinger:150, 151, 152, 153.

NOVOSTI PHOTO LIBRARY:112T, 113, 114T, 115, 115B.

REX FEATURES:55T, 55B.

Pedro Saura:57T.

SCIENCE PHOTO LIBRARY/John Reader/SPL:19, 20T, 21B, 23T, 24, 27 inset, 28L, 29, 120. Volker Steger/Nordstar/SPL:121.

FRANK SPOONER/Grobruck/Contrast/Gamma:70/71. Paul Hanny:69

Hinter Leith/Gamma:70T.

STONE/GETTY ONE:186.

SWISS NATIONAL MUSEUM, ZURICH:64-66 (65B no7563 :66T no3640:66B no7793)

Dr. Anne Thakeray:31T, 33.

The Vindolanda Trust:104T, 107B.

©WESTERN AUSTRALIA MARITIME MUSEUM/photographer Patrick Baker

221 (Peabody Museum of Salem), 221B (noPC/A/662), 222 (no.PC/A/225), 223 (no.PC/3/95).

J.Ziihao: 59B.